THE QUIET WATERS BY

THE QUIET WATERS BY

B

M & M BALDWIN
Cleobury Mortimer, Shropshire
1998

First published 1998

© David Blagrove

Cover designed by David Miller

ISBN 0 947712 35 6

British Library Cataloguing in Publication Data:
A catalogue record is available from the British Library.

Published by M & M Baldwin
24 High Street, Cleobury Mortimer,
Kidderminster DY14 8BY

Printed by MFP Design & Print
Longford Trading Estate, Thomas Street,
Stretford, Manchester M32 0JT

CONTENTS

ILLUSTRATIONS
(between pages 64 and 65)

We are grateful to John Grace for allowing us to use Nos 14 to 19,
to Brian Hicks for No 10,
and to Reading Borough Libraries for Nos 7 & 8.
All other illustrations are from the author's collection.

THE QUIET WATERS BY

"...He maketh me down to lie in pastures green.
He leadeth me the quiet waters by".

Psalm 23, Scottish metrical version. Tune "Crimond"

PROLOGUE

There were two pressers in the queue in front of me. Less than half an hour ago I had not known, nor cared, what a presser was or did. Now I was much better informed, as their London accent, complete with elided or transposed sounds and glottal stops, held a continuous resumé of the state of trade (or, more accurately, 'twade').

Behind me were several building workers, a 'resting' actor and a string of weedy, pallid-faced, hollow-chested no-hopers. The dejected-looking queue shuffled forward a few steps as the desk clerk dispatched his latest client. Now it was the turn of the first presser.

The clerk resignedly took a tatty insurance card from the man, slight, middle-aged, round-shouldered, balding with nicotine-stained fingers, he suppressed a yawn and reached for a form. 'This your correct name and age?' 'Yeah'. The clerk scribbled busily. He was a balding, thin, peaky-faced man of about thirty, who sniffed continually. He peered at his client through steel-rimmed spectacles. 'Occupation?' 'Pwessah'. 'Reason for leaving last occupation?' 'Wedundant'. 'Why aren't you signing on in Hoxton?' 'Be'er chances of findin' summat in Weadin' ain't there?' Grunt, from the clerk, still scribbling. He finished, felt for his date-stamping machine, thumped it onto the form in front of him saying 'Sign here, please'. The first presser did so, stood up and moved a pace or so away from the wicket window. His colleague stepped into his place and the queue shuffled forward again, proffering his insurance card. 'This your correct name and age?'

A friendly voice behind me said 'Takes up his cue perfectly, what timing!' I grinned to myself, as the voice continued 'I really ought to get my agent to do this for me, but these days all they're interested in is the percentage'. This was the actor, an old friend who had been as surprised to see me in the signing-on queue as I was to see him. He was perhaps more philosophical about it than myself.

'The reversals of life!' he had mused 'To such things are we, who aspire to the stars, from time to time reduced by the spin of fortune's wheel'. I found myself smiling in spite of the gloomy ambience of the Labour Exchange and the feeling of shame at standing in this seedy queue of shuffling men. His tall, well-built figure, clad in a carelessly slung overcoat, draping his shoulders like a cloak, and topped by a broad-rimmed hat, made him stand out amid the drab, silent line. Whilst most were desultorily reading the sporting pages of the *Daily Mirror.* Bob was enthusiastically scanning the *Stage.* He dominated the spacious, ink-smelling reception hall with its Government posters on the walls, and chatted easily with a pair of Irish bricklayers and a baker's assistant behind him. I was too taken up with my own problems to care much. I wished that I could be as anonymous as the others and, churlishly, shrank from Bob's cheery attentions.

'Next!' called the clerk as the second presser moved away. I pushed across my insurance card, stamped up to the previous week but one. 'This your correct name and age?' I nodded. 'Why en't it stamped for last week?' 'I've been travelling to get here since then'. Grunt, then, 'Occupation?' 'Canal boatman'. 'Yer what?' 'Canal boatman'. 'That's what I thought you said. Reason, for leaving last employment?'

I was ready for this one. The real reason was that I wanted two week's grace to prepare a tripping boat for the forthcoming summer season. I had been away in the Midlands working canal boats since the end of last summer and had been working for a company, not self-employed. I had left the company on 21st March, it was now 1st April and I was as near broke as I had ever been. I had brought the tripper, a modified working narrow boat, back to Reading from its winter moorings at Braunston in Northamptonshire, but the severe weather of the winter just past had taken its toll. What little money I had would have to be laid out on repairs and refurbishment and Good Friday, the traditional starting date, was just twelve days away. However, leaving employment of one's own accord did not entitle one to unemployment benefit and I had no wish for a hiatus to appear in the rows of insurance stamps on my card. I had thought of this before leaving my Midland employers, so inside my card was a typewritten letter, headed 'Willow Wren Canal Carrying Co' which stated that the above mentioned captain had been discharged as from 21st March, 1963 'there being no current requirement for his services, (signed) L.N. Morton, General Manager'. This document had cost me no less than two double whiskies in The Admiral Nelson at Braunston, plus much mumbling about perjury from the Gaffer, but nevertheless it was my passport to the munificence of the Welfare State.

The clerk looked at me expectantly, I replied 'Redundant'. 'Got any proof?'. I pushed across Morton's letter, he read it quickly, reached for a form and began scribbling. He finished, chunked his stamp, pushed the form towards me and said 'Sign here, please'. I signed, and noticed he was writing and stamping another form. 'You can draw last week's benefit over there' he said pushing the form towards me. Amazed, I walked across to the payment counter to hear an appreciative 'Jammy bugger' from Bob.

The Employment Exchange and National Assistance Office was but a short walk from our wharf and embarkation point at High Bridge, Reading. The small business I was running possessed two narrow boats, one called ENTERPRISE with a certificate to carry 52 passengers on the Kennet & Avon Canal Navigation upstream of Blakes Lock, Reading; the other an unconverted wooden motor boat called BEECH for which we had paid the British Transport Commission the princely sum of £25. The vessel was in trading condition less tarpaulins and engine and was currently under charter to Reading Corporation as a pontoon for bridge repair work. I had spent two days since my return to Reading, with a couple of mates baling and pumping out a winter's worth of rainwater and bilge. Now she was floating beneath Watlington Street Bridge with the Borough Engineer's men setting up their painting stages. While I helped them set matters to rights, Bob's bulky figure appeared on the bridge. It was near lunchtime and he suggested a drink, so we strolled along Kennet side to The Lower Ship, which overlooked High Bridge Wharf.

Over a pint I asked him what his prospects were. He was ever sanguine and told me he had high hopes of a part in a new musical in the West End, based on Oliver Twist. Looking at his 25 stone I opined that he would surely be miscast as Oliver, the Artful Dodger, Fagin or even Bill Sykes, whilst he was surely too young for Mr Brownlow. He snorted derisively and suggested that I reread the book but would say no more. The landlord, a cheerful tubby little man called Ron, drew my attention to the fact that there was someone on the wharf apparently looking for someone aboard ENTERPRISE. Bob peered over the top of the frosted glass bar window and said 'It looks like young Jim'. I went to the door and called across Duke Street. The figure, a thin young man in his early twenties, waved and came over to us. I knew him from my schooldays, he was a few years younger, but he had features which made him memorable even to lordly fifth and sixthformers. He had an angular face with a sallow complexion, topped by a mass of curly hair. Ten years or so later he was still recognisable, but with much more assurance in his manner. I had occasionally seen him about the town in the last year or so, and we had nodded to one another – no more. 'Ahoy there, Jim lad' called Bob in his Robert Newton voice. 'Where away my hearty?' Jim grinned and joined us by the bar. After a few minutes pleasantries, Bob left us and I asked Jim what he wanted. 'I hear you may need a mate' said he. I was somewhat taken aback, I had only been back in town a few days, but news travelled.

The upshot of the next half hour's discussion was that Jim should move aboard ENTERPRISE that very evening and that he would act as unpaid assistant, living rent free, until the weekend after next, following which cash flow would be resumed.

Suddenly life was taking on a more hopeful aspect. I returned home to a pile of bills and correspondence in happier mood than for weeks.

Chapter 1 — A WESSEX RIVER

Reading had been my home town for some 13 years, during the most formative years of my life in fact, and for over half that time my life had increasingly become bound up with the local waterways, in particular the fortunes of the Kennet & Avon Canal.

This last waterway had experienced a long period of decline, largely due to the fact that for 95 years it had been owned and controlled by the Great Western Railway Company, who, not surprisingly, were unwilling to encourage the development of a rival transport medium. The Great Western did, however, play the game according to the rules and when the company's assets were nationalised in 1947 it handed over a waterway running from Reading to Bristol in (just about) navigable condition. For the next 15 years the waterway had been controlled by the Great Western's nationalised successors and for 12 of these years the policy had been of active suppression and discouragement of traffic.

By 1958 the only sections available to normal traffic were from Bath to Bristol, a short length up and downstream of Newbury, and a length of about five miles from Kennet mouth, Reading, to the tail of Burghfield Lock. Of the rest, some long pounds were in water, with reduced levels, and a few isolated locks were workable. But the great flight of 29 locks at Devizes, the potentially popular length east of Bath with its fine bridges and aqueducts, the magnificent steam pumps of Crofton, the Claverton waterwheel, Bradford-on-Avon Dry Dock, the rural wharves of Hungerford, Bedwyn, Honeystreet and Foxhangers lay derelict and crumbling. The Kennet navigation section from Reading to Newbury was one of the oldest small river navigations in England. Its remarkable turf-sided locks and wooden swing bridges, its lengthy canal sections preserved an atmosphere of early Georgian times. Whilst the canal itself, from Newbury to Bath, had a Regency grandeur redolent of beaver hats and empire lines, of brisk stage coaches bearing the Pickwick club, of Jane Austen and Mary Mitford, the Kennet was a quiet byway where one might expect to meet red-faced Squire Westons pinching plump dairy maids; over its creaking swing bridges one expected to see teams of horses dragging swaying Berkshire wains piled high with harvest, it came almost as a surprise to see a Fordson tractor pulling a farm trailer.

Gradually, though, the river navigation was dying. Year by year weeds and sedge choked the canal cuts, lock balance beams broke off, lower gates rotted and fell away from their collars, the iron bearings and turnbuckles of the swing bridges and the ancient pattern paddle gear of the locks corroded and became seized.

However, since 1946, the canal had had friends. Originating as the Newbury Branch of the Inland Waterways Association, an organisation devoted to the complete restoration of the canal had grown up. Until 1962 it had been known as the Kennet & Avon Canal Association, now it was a fully-fledged legal trust. The turning-point in the struggle had come in 1955 when the British Transport Commission's Bill to abandon the Kennet & Avon had been thrown out by Parliament. Gradually and grudgingly the process of dereliction began to be reversed. Parliament stated that no further deterioration should take place pending a decision on the canal's future. Some lengths above Newbury were reopened and the Reading Branch of the Association carried out temporary repairs to the sill of Burghfield Lock in 1958 which enabled craft to go another two locks upstream, to the tail of Sulhamstead Lock.

That same year the Kennet Carrying Company began running ENTERPRISE on a regular service between Reading and Burghfield, the trips being extended to Theale after the Burghfield Lock restoration. I had become very much involved with running these trips and, in 1961, with two friends had taken over the Kennet Carrying Company. This activity had taken me and my partner Bill Fisher to the Midland canal system during the winter of 1961/62 and 62/63 as described elsewhere*. Now I had returned without Bill and was faced with picking up the pieces ready for the forthcoming summer.

ENTERPRISE I have described before. Briefly she was a 72 foot long by 7 foot beam narrow boat, built originally for Fellows Morton & Clayton Ltd. and intended to work over the narrow canals of the Midlands. She had been motorised in the

---

* *Bread Upon the Waters*, volume 3 in the 'Working Waterways' series.

1930s and converted for passenger carrying 1957-58. She had iron side plates with a wooden bottom (a type known as composite), and was powered by a twin cylinder air-cooled Armstrong-Siddeley engine driving through a Parsons gearbox.

During summer 1962 we had also acquired BEECH, another ex-Fellows, Morton boat (or 'Josher'), but all-wood construction with, as has been pointed out, no engine. This craft performed a valuable secondary function, enabling us to undertake waterside contract work and had, during the severe winter just past, provided us with our only cash flow.

The stage upon which most of the company's activities took place was the River Kennet, so in view of the changes which have taken place since, some description of what it was like in 1963 would not be out of place.

The Kennet is a very fast-flowing river with a considerable hydraulic gradient, it flows out of chalk country, rising many miles to the west in the Marlborough Downs near Avebury. This gives it its main characteristic of a fairly narrow valley with few crossing places in its lower part, with a gravelly-based flood plain in the valley bottom. The steepness of the gradient means that there were 22 locks from the Thames to Newbury, one of them, Blakes, being then under the jurisdiction of the Thames Conservancy who had, by complicated descent, inherited it from the Brethren of Reading Abbey. The rest came under the control of the British Waterways Board, successors to the British Transport Commission, successors to the Great Western Railway, who had bought out the Kennet & Avon Canal Company in 1852, who in turn had bought out the Company of Proprietors of the Kennet Navigation whose regime dated back to 1721.

When John Hore supervised the building of the Kennet Navigation in the 1720s the art of inland navigation was in its infancy and the Kennet was the longest and most elaborate work yet undertaken in the South. The nearest work of similar magnitude was the Wey Navigation also connecting with the Thames and this appears to have been used as a blueprint. Money was presumably short, for the navigation was built as cheaply as possible, particular economies being made with locks and bridges which were built almost entirely of wood. Many of the ancient turf-sided locks were still in evidence, the original baulks of timber which had prevented craft from grounding on the sloping sides had been replaced by ex-GWR broad gauge rail, a bridge-section iron girder designed by Brunel and dating from before the broad gauge was abandoned in 1892.

Otherwise these locks had changed little since their original construction. They had an enclosed box-type paddle gear which was worked by a windlass with a long throw and an eye midway between Grand Junction size and narrow canal size. We had our own specially made windlasses, but there were some enormous ex-GWR windlasses about with a S-shaped throw, these were known as 'Dannell Mangle Handles', a euphonious title, 'dannell' being Berkshire dialect for 'river'. According to old photographs the old Thames Commissioner's paddle gear was very similar, the more familiar Thames Conservancy paddle box and wheel seems to date from about the late 1880s. Thames locks mainly date from the 1790s and were probably very similar in design to the Kennet locks of over half a century earlier, one can still detect the turf-sided effect, although now masonry has long superseded the turf, on many Thames locks, where outside the chamber they still have sloping banks.

The section under High Bridge to County Lock, was always exciting and in high water time quite nerve-wracking. There had once I believe been continuous towpath from High Bridge to County Lock but the GWR, it was said, sold much of it to Simonds Brewery in the 1880s. All that was left was a ludicrous length of about 200 yards near Yield Hall, above which was the narrow, twisting 'Brewery Gut' or 'Gullet', which had high concrete walls on each side, narrowing to about 25 or 30 feet under Bridge Street Bridge. Here some girders, which had about four feet six inches headroom, blocked the way. The Corporation had admitted liability for this obstruction and boats with up to six feet six inches headroom could be passed by drawing the paddles at Blakes Weir and dropping the level. However, this put great strain on the ancient gates of County Lock and made navigation almost impossible up Blakes Lock Cut, so it was only done when required. The bridge itself was a rather handsome iron structure with decorative handrails. It vanished with the rebuilding in 1966. After this fearsome piece of water, all was comparatively plain sailing.

County Lock had once occupied the opposite bank, but had been rebuilt in blue brick and repositioned by the GWR about the same time that they filled in the once extensive Reading Basins to build their goods yard. This was a picturesque area with timber sheds, a black-painted toll-house sporting a notice board with cast iron letters, presumably ex-GWR, but now headed 'Docks & Inland Waterways Executive', handsome brick brewery buildings and malthouses, sturdy level crossing gates and rail sidings right down to the wharf. In the lock great care had to be exercised in mitreing the bottom gates, for they met at a very wide angle indeed. I was always worried that one day they would burst outwards, so were the Waterways authorities, for the gates had heavy retaining chains to prevent this happening, but the woodwork of the gates looked so rotten that they might well have pulled right through. The balance beam on the lower weir side gate was very short so as to clear the weir structure and was fitted with massive counterweights. Not so its counterpart at the other end, whose end projected beyond the narrow brick lock island into the weir stream and was thus a ready trap for the unwary.

On the upstream side more Brunel rails were used to make iron guard rails leading into the lockmouth, but the left hand side going upstream was very badly silted, with several trees and bushes growing in what should have been open water, and an 'S' shaped course had to be followed to get in and out. Coming down, one needed all the engine's power to pull the stern end over against the flow, then had to go hard astern to avoid knocking the bottom gates. Fortunately the GWR had built the lock to similar dimensions to Blakes and so one had more length to pull up in than in a normal lock.

Under Berkeley Avenue, which was then the only means of crossing the river between County and Fobney Locks, the river ran beside the back gardens of Elgar Road, then round two sweeping bends beside the 'Jammo' (or, in terms other than Redingensian argot, the Co-operative Wholesale Society's Jam Manufactory), after which the countryside started. Fobney Meadows lay on one side, a sea of buttercups in summer, bordered in the distance by tall elms housing the heronry near Coley Park. On the other bank lay allotments and some municipal tips fringed with willows up until the malodorous entrance to the Foudry Brook. There was a sewage plant here

which has since been greatly enlarged. In those days all
Reading's sewage collected in an underground reservoir near
Blake's Weir, turbine-driven pumps then forced it up to
Manor Farm by the Foudry Brook where it was treated, the
purified effluent then ran into the Kennet, down over County
Weir to Blake's Weir where it drove the turbines which
pumped up more sewage, a sort of perpetual motion some
wags said.

Fobney Lock, which was much deeper than County, had
also been rebuilt by the GWR presumably when Reading
Corporation built their waterworks pumping station on the site
of the original lock. It was, nevertheless, another neat and
attractive place with a red brick bridge over the lock tail,
picked out in blue brick and a brick pump house with a tall
chimney beside the lock entrance. There was an overflow at
right angles to the lock mouth which could be nasty, although
it could be shut off with a board if necessary. The GWR's
engineers had built the lock with battered side walls and no
lower gate recesses; once again though this lock had a very
large chamber, so it did not really matter. More serious was
the lack of landing places below the lock and a very bad shoal
below the pump house.

There then followed a long willow-bordered cut up to
Fobney Hatches (a vertically rising sluice gate is called a
'hatch' on the Kennet). These heavy sluices had to be labori-
ously raised with a handspike and, I have no doubt, were similar, if not identical, to John Hore's originals. The river was
rejoined here and wound its way under the Basingstoke railway line towards Southcote Lock. By now the countryside
had become very pastoral and remote-seeming with little to
suggest the twentieth century, except a concrete footbridge
below the lock and a partly made-up road heading across the
meadows. There was another pumping station here, which
with Fobney, forced purified Kennet water up to a watertower
at Tilehurst. Both these stations had turbine pumps working
off the fall of water, and some fine stand-by single cylinder
diesel engines built by Worthingtons, resembling gigantic
Bolinder engines. The station also generated electricity, of
which some was taken along the towpath by overhead wire to
light a solitary bulb in the nearby lengthsman's cottage. The
lock had been rebuilt by the Kennet & Avon Company before

1852 to the canal pattern. It was similar to Newbury Lock and had lever-operated top ground paddles like those on the Leeds & Liverpool Canal. If one did not shut the paddles down before opening the top gates, the levers fouled the catwalks. Another peculiarity was that the gate paddles were not only opened, like all Kennet locks, by standing on a precarious catwalk, but that the throw was towards the lock chamber. One unwary boater ended up sitting on the sill when his windlass slipped off the paddle – the Kennet was full of little surprises in those days.

Above the lock, on the towpath side was an old brick cottage, dating from the earliest days of the navigation in which the lengthsman dwelt. It was picturesque-looking but inside was a disgrace both to the Waterways (who to their credit, built a very pleasing replacement at Burghfield Bridge some years later) and to Reading Corporation within whose boundaries it stood. There was no sewerage beyond a garden privy, no water save from a well, no electricity other than one bulb as described, no road, no provision for emptying dustbins, and the walls were damp. The lengthsman's family who lived in it were remarkably cheerful in the circumstances and bore their lot stoically.

At Southcote Hatches the river crossed the canal at right angles, the land between canal and river known as Burghfield Island, was then quite desolate and uninhabited. The lengthsman once discovered an old Kennet Navigation milestone on this part of the river, suggesting that the original navigation followed the river channel. Burghfield Bridge was a fine, stone canal-type bridge with a towpath beneath it, the only one on the Kennet between Reading and Newbury to resemble the sort of bridge common on other canals. On the bank at the top end of Burghfield Island was a brick pill-box dating from 1940 guarding the bridge. Just beyond lay our landing stage giving access to the back garden of The Cunning Man, a rural hostelry then kept by a cheery ex-Reading shopkeeper, Reg Wing. The length above Burghfield Bridge, wide, deep and tree-lined, was one of the most pleasing parts of the navigation and marked the terminus of our day-to-day activities. From High Bridge Wharf to the winding hole at the tail of Burghfield Lock Cut and back to the landing stage took just on an hour and a half upstream, the downstream speed record from Burghfield to High Bridge was held by Bill Fisher with a time for the course of 55 minutes, I managed 56 minutes.

If this section seemed difficult to navigate it was an absolute doddle compared with the final section. This, in boating terms, was comparable to the North Face of the Eiger, but we did manage in 1961 to maintain a once-weekly schedule over it. However, in the 1962 season, bad weather and sheer economics forced us to abandon this, although we made several trips with private charters. I also attempted to develop a round coach and boat trip, but the coach proprietors, though keen, were prevented from co-operating because of opposition from the Area Traffic Commissioners who believed we would thus compete with the publicly-owned Thames Valley bus company. Nevertheless, things have changed so much in the Kennet valley, that one feels the picture would not be complete without a short description of this wild and woolly section.

Just below Burghfield Lock, the river had built up a peninsula of silt stretching perhaps a hundred yards downstream; on this trees and bushes had grown to a considerable height, and the lock channel was shallow and silted and narrower even than the Oxford Canal. Immediately below the bottom gates was the sunken remains of a South Wales coal boat brought by the GWR for maintenance purposes, but now with a bush growing through its timbers. The lock had been partially rebuilt in the late forties by the D&IWE, but the contractors had not been permitted to complete the job; although some good work had been done at the top, the bottom gates were distinctly poor, moreover, it was a turf-sided lock. British Waterways had placed a warning notice saying that it was dangerous to use this lock, so for insurance purposes we had to land all passengers below and re-embark them above, doing the same in reverse when coming downstream. The problems this presented with elderly or handicapped people were not alleviated by there being such shallow water above the lock that we could only load or unload passengers by gang plank. The bottom sill of the lock had blown out years before. During 1958, the Reading Branch of what then was the Kennet & Avon Canal Association had carried out temporary repairs with chalk bags and clay, but even so the bottom gates did not mitre together very well, and filling the lock entailed joggling the balance beams until a good mitre was obtained. As the lock filled the gates would make fearsome creaks and groans suggesting that they would collapse outwards, but in spite of everything they held together for years.

Another hazard was the holes made by rats and small animals in the banks if the lock was not used frequently. On several occasions I have seen surprised-looking bunnies come shooting out of the bank on the other side of the towpath slightly in advance of a jet of water. On such occasions one would search for a tell-tale whirlpool in the lock chamber and force in a piece of turf as a plug. Once the boat was through, the top gates had to be closed behind and the lock emptied to preclude any disaster whilst one was upstream. If one had enough crew, this could be done whilst re-embarking the passengers. The lock cut, curving through quiet meadows, was nearly blocked at its top end by reeds and sedge. There was a ten foot wide channel up which we crawled at a snail's pace, stirring up a rich concoction of mud and weeds. The lengthsman would sometimes draw the top paddles when we were clear to try and swill this muck out of the cut, and the navigation certainly got better the more we used it. There followed a river section with some very sharp bends through delightful, lonely meadows to Garston Lock. This had a very bad entrance, there was a very narrow channel and one would frequently stick about a boat's length from the bottom gates. If a crew member could get ashore, the boat could be got moving again by sending down a flush from the lock paddles. The bottom gates were jammed with rubble which some intelligent subcontractors had knocked in when re-bricking behind the gates and had never been completely removed, in spite of heroic efforts by a local sub-aqua club. This lock had been partially rebuilt by the Kennet & Avon Company to canal dimensions, hence the brickwork, but was still mainly turf-sided. A gravel pit had recently been made on the towpath side and a water-skiing club used the nearby pill-box as a store; when this lock was full, water flooded over the sides into this and caused rows, therefore we always drew this one off behind us as well. The next pound had another lock, Sheffield, at its top end, so was what is called on the Kennet a 'dead pound', meaning that it could in theory be drained. In practice the country around was so full of water that I doubt

whether this was possible. After Sheffield Lock with old telegraph poles for balance beams and, immediately beyond,
some large hatches, came the *pièce de resistance* of the
Kennet, Sheffield Swing Bridge. This was used by gravel lorries operating from the nearby pits, so to make things as convenient as possible for road users and as diabolically inconve-
nient as possible for river users, the bridge was jacked up
solid when not in use for boats. The jack handle was kept in
the garden of a nearby cottage where lived a sweet old couple
who spoke the ancient, rich, almost incomprehensible
Berkshire dialect, full of near-German words and phrases. I
remember the old lady one day telling a passenger about to
step into the narrow road in front of a car to 'Boide whur tha
bist' i.e. stay where you are.

Once obtained, the jack handle needed about 120 turns to
lower the bridge onto its pivot. Then, once the bridge operating handle, a long tubular steel piece, had been inserted into
holes on the upstream side, the pushing and heaving started.
One could assist by gently nuzzling the boat's fender into the
bridge girders and shove with the engine. One contribution to
this scene was my own, this was the drop barrier on the side
away from the pivot, which was suggested by me in a report
made to the Inland Waterways Redevelopment Committee in
1960. Although it has probably aided road safety in the main
it has, I am told, claimed its share of motor cyclists who have
not noticed it, swept round the bend to the bridge and been
consequently dismounted, their steeds sometimes going in the
bridge hole. The operation of opening the bridge would soon
result in a queue of impatient motorists, many of whom would
sound horns angrily but who, when it was suggested that they
gave a push if they were in such a hurry, would remain scowl-
ing in their sacred driving seats. Once through, the bridge had
to be closed and jacked up again before proceeding up the
last, attractive reach to the tail of broken-down Sulhamstead
Lock. There was just enough room to wind by tucking the
stern into the lock cut and letting the current from the weir
stream swing the fore-end round. With good luck the time for
this section was one and a half hours from Burghfield Bridge,
one could get back to High Bridge in two and a half hours
with good organisation, but we generally reckoned the round
trip as taking seven hours.

Once round, we normally returned to Sheffield Bridge where unjacking and rejacking had to take place, and made a stop there for passengers to stretch their legs. If we had a good lockwheeler, he would be sent on foot to Burghfield when we left Sheffield Lock and in this fashion we were able to maintain some sort of scheduled timing. It was the numerous crew necessary which made the public trips uneconomic, nonetheless there was always a sense of pioneering adventure in a run to Sulhamstead.

We found, and this lesson nearly all cruise operators learn, that private charter provides the bread and butter whilst public cruises supply the jam. In this respect the shortcomings of the narrow boat were very obvious and, being wise after the event, we should have done much better with a wide boat. In later years Bill Fisher was to prove this point with an extremely successful business venture based on Newbury. Leslie Morton, in reflective mood, had once said 'There's money in fornication', by which he meant not running a floating bordello but more providing a means to an end. Having seen *les bateaux mouches* on the Seine and the well-appointed Danube steamers in Austria, I could see what he meant about providing a romantic ambience, and to the time of writing I don't believe it has been done with complete success on the British inland waterways. On the Thames, where conditions ought to be right, the best that operators seem to come up with is the pseudo-American 'Riverboat Shuffle' or even more appalling, the 'Disco Boat'. What we would like to have done would have been to run a boat with a small dance floor, a select bar, covered accommodation when required, tables for serving light meals and perhaps a small musical group. Unfortunately England is perhaps not ready for such a venture, and I doubt whether many parts of the canal system are suitable, though rivers like the Thames might be. Today suitable hulls may be obtained fairly simply but in the 1960s it was Hobson's Choice. A Josher hull can carry 52 souls in serried ranks, but there is little room to move, dancing is next to impossible, a bar is a squeeze and means that those sitting near it get served quickly but get drinks slopped over them from their comrades returning past them. Lavatory accommodation is limited and the addition of live music results in a jam of bodies, the nearest being deafened as well as crushed.

Of course we still had to discover these limitations and went ahead attempting to make private evening cruises go with a swing. We tried running special evening trips with a resident musician and arranging parties aboard. These had their drawbacks, among them being the fact that the passengers would be at the height of their merriment when coming back into town and, in spite of earnest requests for quiet, would occasionally carouse to the annoyance of nearby residents. Still, we never had a party as offensive as a modern football coach party when the drink takes them.

On one of these early parties I made the acquaintance of a clean-featured, bright-faced, young man of about 20 who came armed with a huge Grimshaw guitar. He played it with great verve and had the ability to draw forth music above the average guitar plucker. He came on several trips and we soon developed a good repertoire of rural-style ditties for the amusement of the passengers. His name was John Grace and years later, when we both had turned respectable and were living at Stoke Bruerne, he came to make a record of some of the songs of the canals I had collected over the years. We were destined to make some eventful canal journeys together.

We had our share of problems unconnected with the state of the navigation, one of the worst being that perennial hazard of urban boating, the bankside attacker. The sprawling estates of Reading extended up the Kennet valley parallel with the cut as far as Burghfield, the remoteness of whose meadows was thus an illusion, and meant that at weekends and holiday times bored youths, often armed with airguns, would lurk on bridges or towpaths ready to shoot or throw things, or merely abuse the passengers with vile language. They were usually full of fight and viciousness when separated from the boat by a strip of water and when there were several of them. We wearily tolerated them since there was little else we could do. ENTERPRISE'S career on the Kennet had been dogged by this sort of nuisance since tripping began in 1958, and it showed little sign of abating. Eventually, one afternoon in the summer of 1962 matters came to such a head that we were forced to take matters into our own hands.

Bill Fisher and I were heading downstream with a chartered party of women and handicapped children when, at Burghfield Bridge, we beheld a gang of some 12 youths, of an age which should have known better, on the bridge. Some spat on the passengers, some threw hurtful insults and jeered at the children and several bricks were dropped, fortunately hitting the awning, not the passengers. Bill ran forward, his face white with anger, to get off the fore end, I went hard astern and the stern slewed into the offside bank just below the bridge by the old pillbox. There was a five-bar gate leading onto the main road so jumping off, I ran up the bank to this gate. Our friends were still on the bridge, so I told them what I thought of them. Their answer, seeing I was alone, was a volley of oaths and a rush in my direction. Now I am certain that before that time I would have either fled or faced the foe with raised fists in best Queensberry Rules style, neither of which measures would have been effective.

A few weeks on the cut with boaters had, however, taught me a thing or two in looking after myself, and I had prudently kept my windlass in my belt. Drawing it out, I informed them that the first across the gate would get it on the side of the ear. They evidently did not believe me, so I showed one of them that I meant what I said. He lay quite still for a while. I dealt with two more, by which time a sort of berserker rage had descended on me, and I had a fourth by what boaters call a 'Brummagen Kiss'; this being to seize the lapels, butt the head into the opponent's face and knee him in the groin all in one movement; when the remainder got me on the ground and began kicking my head. At this moment when all seemed lost, I heard a dull ringing sound as Bill, who had had to run all the way from the towpath bank, arrived windlass in hand and began smiting the foe from the rear. Within seconds this second assault caused our attackers to break and run, taking their wounded with them. Bill helped me to my feet and we both helped the stragglers on their way back across the gate with well-aimed kicks in the pants. They straggled down the road with bleeding noses and cauliflower ears mouthing threats of terrifying revenge as we returned to the boat. I was still mad with rage and steered down to Southcote in a blind fury. At the lock I went into the pumphouse to telephone the police and report what had happened, I replaced the receiver, went out into the whirring of turbines and smell of warm oil and remembered no more until I woke on the bed in ENTERPRISE'S cabin, tied up at High Bridge Wharf, with the ample bosom of

Sally, our catering assistant wobbling uncertainly before my eyes as she brought me a cup of tea. Apparently I had suffered delayed concussion, but was otherwise none the worse. Whether or not word got round about our stand at Burghfield Bridge I don't know, but significantly there was never again any trouble, in fact for the remaining years I was to spend on the Kennet, I enjoyed the best of relations with fishermen and other frequenters of the towpath.

Another, less unpleasant, but potentially dangerous situation eventually ended in comedy when one night we arrived late at High Bridge and Bill who was steering, elected to tie up facing downstream instead of winding and tying up facing upstream. We were entertaining in the cabin our actor friend Bob who, weighed 25 stone. The cabin doors were open and he, full of bonhomie, bade us good night and stepped out onto what he thought was the wharf and was in fact the river. Bill felt the stern rise and the propeller blades race as Bob's mighty bulk sent a depth-charge like wave underneath. Fortunately he could swim and I grabbed his hand before he was swept away downstream. John Grace and myself heaved, Bob's head appeared over the gunwale but he was far too heavy to pull in, besides only one could get in the doors at once to pull effectively. In the end I had a brainwave, further downstream the bank shelved and there were shallows. Taking the long shaft, I got Bob to float on his back, hooked the end in his waistcoat and poled him down river to the shallows like a harpooned whale. Alas the place he chose to land was the roosting place of swans, he crawled ashore plastered in swan muck and feathers amid hostile hissing. We got him into the cabin and dried him off but there was no change of clothing which could possibly fit him. Bill remembered an old tarpaulin in the fore-end, so Bob eventually went home, like a Roman Emperor, with the grave dignity of the acting profession, wrapped in a top cloth lettered 'Severn & Canal Carrying Company'.

Our relationships with the three main authorities in our life proved to be one of love and hate. With British Waterways we had perhaps the best relations of all. The Inspector at Newbury, Cyril Rogers, under whose jurisdiction we came, was very much committed to the cause of saving and re-opening the Kennet & Avon. In consequence whenever British

Waterways could help us they would do so. Eddie Chappell their local lengthsman was in any case an old friend and, in contrast to the attitude sometimes found elsewhere, the local Waterways staff were always helpful and did not do obstructive things. I am sure they realised that we were all on the same side, that their future jobs and prospects depended on restoration and development. It was only with the higher echelons that the few difficulties we had with BW occurred and these were more of a political rather than a bureaucratic nature.

Our landlords and most immediate authority was Reading Corporation, and here we normally had good relations with its many departments, however, the Bridge Street Bridge girders were a bone of contention with the Town Clerk's Department, as were sundry obstructions such as the scaffolding we had unexpectedly encountered the previous year under Forbury Road Bridge. As a democratic organisation they could, however, be dealt with by enlisting the aid of friendly councillors when necessary.

The Thames Conservancy controlled the Kennet by ancient right from a point downstream of our wharf; their Chief Navigation Inspector, a man of severe rectitude, was not at all sure that our activities were praiseworthy. By strict right we should have had a pleasure craft licence by virtue of the fact that part of our operations took place over the TC's water, but since the Board of Trade debarred us from carrying passengers beyond Blakes Lock and we did not use their lock save as a tug, nor did we ask them to dredge or otherwise spend money on the river we felt it was unreasonable for them to demand such a licence. At that time the fees demanded at locks for pleasure craft of 70 feet in length were exorbitant, being seven shillings and six pence as against eight pence for a tug, whilst commercial vessels when loaded paid 5/8 of a penny per ton per mile. These toll charges caused more argument than anything else, and relationships sometimes were strained.

Chapter 2 – THE CONSERVATORS' SERVICE

The weather at Easter was pretty average that year. In other words it was cold and overcast, with flurries of sleet from time to time. Jim had made a couple of trips to Burghfield and back with me, learning the road. Much cleaning, polishing and tidying-up had taken place, including the replacing of some ten tons of ballast, the refitting of seats for 52 passengers, the re-rigging of awnings and side sheets. In all this I had been greatly helped by our Company Secretary, Edwina, who was in firm control of the catering side of the business, and by Peter, a stalwart who lived nearby and who had attached himself to us the previous year. Both these last had full-time jobs, but at least, with a mate full-time I was able to meet the Good Friday deadline.

We restocked the bar and catering servery and opened for business, having placed newspaper advertisements and displayed printed handbills. A few hardy souls turned up, we ran trips each day, but returns were meagre and there were no party charters in the immediate future.

It was becoming abundantly obvious that the business could not support more than one full-time employee. I was loath to turn my back on a life style which was so rewarding in non-financial terms, but one had to live. It had to be Jim or me, and this decision weighed heavily with me in the weeks following Easter.

I still had the faithful and massive old bike that had accompanied me for miles round the Midlands, with which one rode ahead to get locks ready ('lock wheeling'), or went shopping, or rode off to find a telephone; so on the following Sunday I left Jim and Peter to work the afternoon trip and in the manner later advocated by Norman Tebbitt, set off for a bike ride with the intention of seeing what job opportunities might present themselves.

At last spring had come. It was a bright, mild afternoon with young leaves breaking out and blossom decking the gardens of Caversham. I rode round to the mill, where we had some hopes of water traffic, then wheeled the bike over the long weir footbridge, known as 'the Clappers', to Caversham

Lock. A few cruisers were about and the lock was being operated by Eric Schofield, the lock keeper from Blakes. Of the usual lock keeper, Dick Knightley, there was no sign. I asked Eric where he was. 'Day off' was the reply. 'I'm on two days here, 'cos the relief keeper's packing it in and taking some leave'. I rested the bike against a fence, walked down the far side of the lock and pulled the bottom gate closed. 'Thanks, Dave' said Eric across the lock, then, 'Why don't you put in for it?' 'Put in for what?' 'The relief's job, of course. Be just up your street'. 'Well, I must say I had been thinking of trying the Conservancy'. 'There you are then', said Eric, winding down the bottom paddles. 'Go and see Peter Harvey tomorrow'.

We walked up towards the top gates. Eric ran his eyes over the boats in the lock and went into the hut to fill in the log. When he came out he said 'It ain't a bad little number you know'. I asked what the job was. 'Goring to here, two days each at three locks and one at one, then you get your days off. Worst thing is the hours in summer, 9 am till sunset, but winter's OK, you get 10 guineas a week and a travel allowance and uniform'.

I began to prick up my ears at this. It could be the ideal answer to my problems, on the other hand, my relationship with the Thames Conservancy had not always been exactly cordial over the years that I had run ENTERPRISE. However, I mused as I rode home, it could be worth a try. I could not face another week of queueing at the Labour Exchange, even Bob had moved on now and was actively rehearsing.

So it was, that at 9.30 next morning I presented myself at the red brick neo-Georgian offices of the Reading District Navigation Inspector by Reading Bridge. I approached the reception desk somewhat nervously, the secretary-receptionist looked up and smiled: 'Hello, David, what can I do for you?' I started. I had played opposite her in amateur dramatics some years ago. 'Oh, hello Sylvia. I've come about a job'. 'What for? The upstream Relief?' I affirmed this was so. She giggled 'Oh, we are honoured. Well go in and see them, they've finished the water levels now'. 'What, no appointment?' I asked. 'Of course not, not here' she said, 'Go on in'. Across the corridor was a door marked 'P. Harvey, District Navigation Inspector'. It was slightly ajar, from within came the sound of laughter and whiffs of tobacco smoke. I knocked on the door, somewhat diffidently. 'Come in!' roared a voice. I walked in to a wall of blue smoke. The same voice said loudly 'Bloody hell Dave! what do you want at this hour?'

Leaning back in a swivel chair, puffing at a pipe sat the District Inspector, Peter Harvey, a lean jovial-looking man in his early forties. He was in the naval-officer style uniform of the Conservancy, the jacket of which had two gold rings on its sleeve and was draped over his chair back. On another chair was the Assistant Inspector, a man of my own age, who I recognised as Chris Groves, a fellow canal enthusiast - in fact I had first met him years ago up the Kennet, where he was navigating a motorised punt. He had one gold ring on his sleeve, but since both inspectors were in their shirt sleeves, their badges of rank were on their shoulders, in the form of stripes. They both looked expectantly at me. I said 'I've come about the Relief's vacancy'. 'You must be bloody mad' said Peter Harvey. 'Has ENTERPRISE sunk?' asked Chris Groves solicitously. I assured them both that I meant serious business. Peter Harvey looked solemn. 'I'm not sure that you've got the right qualifications for the job' said he. My heart sank, I had not realised that the job required special qualifications. Harvey continued: 'Can you swim?' I nodded 'Can you read and write?' I replied that I could manage this 'Do you know how a lock works?' 'Yes' 'Then you're in. Welcome to the Conservators' Service' he shook my hand, and a grinning Chris Groves followed suit.

In retrospect it seems a very casual way to start a new career, but in fairness I must point out that, although my applying for the job was a complete surprise to both of them, I was by no means a stranger and, toll arguments apart, the Kennet Carrying Company had done several carrying and towing jobs for the Conservancy to their satisfaction.

Harvey said 'You'll never be able to afford to run Rolls-Royces and yachts, but it's not a bad living. You'll work seven days on and two off, and once a month you'll only have one day off - just the same as the regular lock keepers. We'll get you fixed up for a uniform next week, you can start on Saturday and in the meantime go out to the locks and make yourself known to the lockies, they'll give you all the low down. Anything you want to know from us? I asked him about pay and conditions. He confirmed what Eric Schofield had said and concluded 'Don't be late for duty, don't fiddle the toll money, don't fornicate on duty, use your noddle. That's about it'.

And so I entered the services of the Conservators of the River Thames. In many respects I was to find the Conservancy to have much in common with such organisations as the Great Western Railway, in others it had more than a whiff of old-fashioned local government, but above all it had style and panache. Behind the easy-going, calm facade there was a solid, competent, professionalism along with an absolute respect for the *status quo*. The navigation staff, to which I now belonged, demonstrated this to a high degree. Every lock keeper was not only a person of standing and consequence in his local community, but without exception all the ones I worked with were men of character and integrity.

I discovered this later that day when I biked out to Goring. It was another sunny, spring day, and traffic was reasonably light on the main road. I turned right at Streatley crossroads coasting down the hill to the long bridge which crossed a miniature archipelago below the main weir and lock. The bridge was of concrete construction but made to look as if it were timber built, near the far end it crossed the main weir stream and lock approach. Here I halted for a while, leaning my bike against the bridge parapet and took stock.

Looking upstream, from left to right, was an open overfall weir, then a weir with vertically rising gates, or bucks. One buck was half open releasing a roaring torrent of greeny-yellowish water into the pool below. The force of the fall sent racing humps of water down the weir pool towards the bridge, where it calmed down, though still running strongly and bearing flecks of creamy foam on its surface as it swiftly curled away beneath the bridge. At the right hand end of the weir was the lock island, crowned by a red-brick, angular Victorian lock house. A grey painted lock office with a black stovepipe above its roofline stood half way down the lock side flanked by neat flowerbeds and gravel paths. The top gates stood open with a uniformed figure leaning on the balance beams, a hire cruiser was slowly manoeuvring itself into the chamber. To the right, lawns and chestnut trees flanked the lockside, beyond this ran another backstream with boathouses.

By the time I had remounted and pedalled round the end of the bridge where it dipped into Goring High Street beyond the Post Office, performed a U-turn to the right, headed back between the bridge and Goring Mill, crossed the wooden Mill Weir bridge, parked my bike and walked up to the lock, the lock keeper had closed his gates and was going into his office to book the cruiser. I stepped over the chain which blocked the bottom gate walk way and crossed over the gates. The lock keeper came out of the office walking towards me. He was a shortish, wiry little man with an upright, military bearing. His leathery face looked stern. 'Can I help you?' he inquired cold-ly. 'I've been sent to see you by Mr Harvey. I'm the new Relief' said I. His face cracked into a wide, gummy smile and he held out his hand. 'Harry, Harry Coley' he said as we shook hands 'Follow me around and I'll show you how it all works OK?' so saying he marched down to the bottom gate, mounted the walkway and began addressing himself to the paddles. The Thames Conservancy had its own individual style of gate pad-dle gear, which comprised two ratchets with a cog between them. One ratchet was attached to the paddle, the other to a counterweight. The whole was contained inside a neat-iron casing and operated by means of a spoked iron wheel. The upper ends of the paddle and counterweight rods protruded up through the casing and were tipped with red or white paint respectively. It was thus possible to tell at a glance whether the paddles were up or down. A run-back was prevented quite simply by short pieces of thin rope, spliced at each end, one end going over one of paddle rods, the other over a spoke on the operating wheel. There were two methods of getting the paddles up. One was, as Harry now proceeded to demonstrate, to stand at right angles to the wheel and slowly pull the spokes toward one; the other used by steamer or canal boat crews, young summer assistants and similar desperadoes, was to rest one hand on the wooden hand rail of the walkway, the other on the inside rim of the wheel and then whirl this arm around swiftly, shooting the paddle upwards. There were two sets of paddles per gate at Goring, which made for extra work, the normal ration was one. I crossed to the other gate, faced Harry and began pulling the spokes. Harry paused when the red-tipped rod was the same height as the white-tipped one.

Water welled up in the deep chasm below the gates, then

rose bubbling and surging above the surface. The boat in the lock began to sink down. 'Always keep an eye on 'em' said Harry 'they often tie up tight, then can't loose off as it empties. Some of 'em catches the 'ulls on the copings'. He gave a wheezy chuckle 'tips em over summat smartish'. He leaned his hands on the handrail, gazing up the lock. 'Ah, they'll be all right now. We'll give 'em full paddle' so saying he wound the paddles to their fullest extent. I did likewise. The water heaved noisily below the gates then gradually fell quiet, subsiding into small whirls and eddies before lying still. Harry walked to the end of his gate's balance beam and leaned against it. I did likewise with the other gate. The balance beam was painted glossy grey, its top curved to shed the rain, it looked very neat and trim compared with the gates of canal or river Kennet locks — until I tried to shift it. Bottom gates are always heavier than top gates because they are taller and have a lesser proportion of their weight in water, but this one was the very devil to move. I glanced over my shoulder. Harry's gate was already moving. Suddenly I felt the beam start to move and, very slowly, I walked backwards in a wide arc pushing the gate.

Between Regent's Canal Dock at Limehouse and Tyseley Wharf, Birmingham, the Grand Union Canal has 151 locks, each one being worked by boat crews. I made a mental note not to grumble again about the heaviness of Grand Union gates. I learned later that Goring was notorious for having the heaviest gates on the Thames.

The hire cruiser spluttered its way out of the lock, a few were waiting below, tied to the piles on Harry's side. He waved them in then walked along the lockside taking mooring lines and dropping them over bollards for the crews. I walked up the other side doing the same. One privately-owned cruiser shunned my assistance, the woman in blue slacks standing on the stern hurled a crumpled ball of rope at a mooring stump as she passed. The rope fell in the water and her husband in the wheel house went frantically astern. Blue exhaust smoke rose as the woman desperately pulled the line in, then began winding it between the palm of her hand and her elbow, as if it were knitting yarn. Husband rushed across the wheelhouse and grabbed a hanging chain, then realised he was still in astern gear. 'Let me take the line' I called, and gratefully the woman threw the reconstituted ball of rope at me. I just managed to grab it and take a turn on a stump before the cruiser's stern swung broadside into the hire cruiser on the other side of the lock. Goring had a set of intermediate gates which were supposed to be used in periods of drought to save water from the short reach above, but this day there was no need for them so they remained open. Once the boats were safely in, we closed the gates, wound the paddles down and set off towards the top. I was instructed to draw two half paddles, then come to the office where Harry would show me the Launch Log Book.

The office had Harry's name in white letters on a black board above the door. It was possibly ten feet square with a cast iron range at the back facing the door. Down the side nearest the house was a sloping desk beneath a window. On the desk was the Launch Book. Every vessel passing up or down had to be entered, its name and licence particulars; whether powered or unpowered, tug, barge empty or carrying merchandise, houseboat or fishing craft had to be entered in the correct column. On a shelf above the desk were books of toll tickets and permits. At the back of the hut, on a shelf, were some ominous-looking iron hooks attached to a thin rope. 'Body drags' said Harry laconically, catching my glance.

Harry scribbled away in the Launch Book then marched out into the sunlight. The lock was nearly full, so we wound the top paddles fully. Soon the lock was full and we could open the gates. I pushed the offside one and Harry grinned 'saves using the hitcher'. He nodded from across the lock at a long aluminium pole with a hook on the end which lay along the catwalk. The rules said that both gates were to be opened for craft, so the thought of shoving one gate with a hitcher when working alone was a sobering one.

The boats started up in a blue haze of smoke and, one by one, burbled out of the lock past us. As they swung up the short upstream reach towards Cleeve, Harry peered after them. 'Nuffink comin' down, close up, and I'll show you the weir'. We pushed the gates to. I walked across the catwalk and joined him outside the lock house. A path led behind the house to the weir. 'This 'un's what we call a 'buck weir'' Harry called, climbing the concrete steps leading to the weir bridge. Two massive, vertically rising sluices operated by hand cranks stood side by side, one of them nearest the house, was half open. The water roared and tossed in the channel beneath, a rivery smell hung in the spray. 'This un's the 'house buck weir', that un's 'Number Two'' called Harry above the din. I leaned on the upstream handrail and watched the deep, greeny water as it funneled itself into the vortex above the gate. Glossy-smooth it slid towards the buck, then dipped into the roaring green void. I shuddered involuntarily at the thought of that terrible strength which lay beneath the river's peaceful surface. I began to realise that this river was not just a geographical feature, nor a pretty plaything, nor yet a highway, but all these things and more. It was a living, thundering, limpid, clear, dark, tyrannous monster that allowed itself to be tamed by man yet, like a wild beast, could at a trice snatch and destroy the puny little lives who dared control it. No wonder the ancients worshipped river gods, no wonder he was called 'Old Father Thames'. There he lay, a placid silver ribbon across the meadows of Streatley, girded with fresh green willows, bordered by the velvety lawns of Goring, as peaceful as a romantic picture. Yet here he was, a few yards away beneath my feet, thundering and roaring in all the power of his hidden deeps. I began to realise, with excitement, that the shepherding and conservancy of this giant was a not unworthy task and that I should have to learn and respect the lore of the river. Hitherto I had moved across the river's surface, albeit with respect and circumspection, but now I was to be a humble human conductor of his irresistible flow.

I parted from Harry after a cup of tea brought to us by Enid, his wife, then pedalled back the way I had come, up Streatley High Street turning left at The Bull, past the flint walls and ochre tiles of that idyllic village onto the main road. At Basildon I turned off onto a side road which led to an iron bridge over the railway. Here I paused for a few moments to watch the trains take water at speed from the water troughs, which were then a feature of this part of the valley. From the bridge one could see the distant signals guarding the approaches to Goring and Streatley and, in the other direction, those of an intermediate section of line. Beneath ran four tracks, hedged by many-barred telephone poles and their drooping wires. Down towards Gatehampton Viaduct, which took the railway across the river, rose the bulky iron tower of the water-softening plant (for steam locomotives furred-up like giant kettles on untreated chalk stream water), the troughs between the rails extended in a quadruple curve nearly as far as the viaduct. The gentle spring breeze ruffled their surface slightly and hummed in the telephone wires, in the far distance the yellow painted arm of the Goring down main distant dropped to 'clear'. Glancing up the line I saw white steam rising above the trees at the end of Basildon cutting, then, leaning very slightly into the curve came the noble sight of a steam-hauled express in full cry. The bridge beneath my feet began to tremble very slightly as the locomotive powered itself along the gleaming track towards me. I could see that it was an ex-Great Western 'Castle', its green paint well-polished, the brasswork of its safety valve bonnet and beading flashing in the sunlight, the copper cap of its chimney sending an orange glint back beneath its rapidly beating smoke plume. Coupling rods whirling it bore down onto the troughs, white steam suddenly erupted from in front of the cab as the driver tugged his whistle cord in warning. The brown and cream and maroon coaches roared and rocked behind, vanishing suddenly in a great spray of water as the tender scoop bit into the troughs. I crossed over the bridge to see her ride through, the fireman, grasping the scoop handle ready to whirl it back when his gauge showed 'full', raised his hand in greeting. Water spurted back, dowsing the bogies of the leading coach. As the train faded into the distance I could see the fireman's blue-overalled figure rapidly turning the handle. His driver stood, left hand on polished steel regulator, right arm leaning on the sliding cab window, gazing forward through the spectacle glass. The bridge shook as the rattling 'duddlety-dun, duddlety-dun' of the coaches echoed off the brick abutments, then the last coach was through, her red tail lamp rocking slightly, and the noise receding sharply as a turned-down radio set. Rapidly the rear end of the train diminished in size as it swung round the curve towards Goring. A whiff of South Welsh coal smoke hung momentarily in the air, then was gone. Behind me a fast goods, headed by a dingy green 2800 class, came rolling and clanking along the down relief line. I ducked down behind the parapet as a column of water rose skywards from the open manhole on the tender, the fireman wrestling to raise his scoop having overfilled his tank.

Such a scene, steam trains with their wild music and cries, the panoply of Edwardian technology of the Late Steam Age set against the swelling greens of Gatehampton hill, Hartslock Wood and Basildon meadows seemed as immutable as the Thames itself. Only now do I realise that never again was I to see this scene. Something I had known all my life and which was always so satisfying to see, I fully expected to last for ever. I am glad that on that day I still had time to stop and stare, for within a terrifyingly short space of time it was swept away into the same limbo as Brunel and his broad gauge. No Inter City 125 can ever, for me, replace those majestic sights.

It was tea time when I biked into the carpark of The Swan at Pangbourne and rested the machine against the grey-painted fence in which a gate opened onto a long, twisty, weir bridge. The gate was unlocked, so I pushed it open, mounted a short flight of steps and set off across the bridge. A wide, noble reach, on the right fringed with tall willows and poplars on the left with handsome low buildings and boathouses swept down for nearly half a mile to the weir bridge. This weir was very different from the one at Goring. For a start it was not so high, merely half Goring's fall, it seemed, but secondly the moveable tackle was completely non-mechanised. It comprised poles and posts, painted grey and nothing else - no cranks, ratchets, paddles, sliding gates or means of lifting them. I passed across the first main weir puzzling over this phenomenon and traversing an overfall across which a thin skein of water was trickling. The bridge path twisted to the left leading me to a second weir, which had its tackle partly drawn. Leaning against the rail were some long posts with horizontal boards nailed to them, and some square posts of similar length, the water ran unchecked through a gap perhaps 15 feet wide, then a row of square posts broke its flow for the next few feet. The swift, glossy water swept silently down into the weir pool where it broke surface in three consecutive roaring billows. Another overfall brought me to a third weir beyond which stood the lock and its white, Gothic-windowed, lock house. A tall, thin, man of about 40, with a tanned, cheerful face came towards me from the lock office. He was smartly dressed in Conservancy navy blue uniform trousers and jacket and had the bearing of one who had spent time pacing heaving decks. He walked round the end of the top gate

beam and called: 'What's your lay, my covey?' I grinned,
foolishly, thinking I had perhaps misheard 'Sorry?' 'Your lay,
old coz. D'you want me?' 'Oh, I see' said I lamely 'I'm supposed to be coming as your Relief.' The lock keeper threw
back his head and laughed. 'I thought that's what you were. I
heard you were about today. I'm Fred'. We shook hands and I
told him my name. Together we walked down the lock side.

If I had thought Goring attractive, this was an idyll. I was
to become familiar with the place in every sort of weather, but
the loveliness of it never failed. Just sometimes it was lovelier
than others. Today, with spring sun shining on the blue and
silver ripples in the reach above it was in one of its best
moods.

Facing downstream the lock was bordered on the left by a
rustic fence against which roses were trained and a neat
flower bed laid. Behind the fence were more gardens and
trees through which peeped mellow brick gables and the shingled spire of the parish church of Whitchurch. A beautifully
manicured lawn lay parallel to the lock chamber, separated
from it by a gravelled path, below the bottom gates, great
trees rose on both sides of the lock cut. The house, a pretty
survivor of the days of the Thames Commissioners, sat amid
more lawns and flower beds with its front door facing the
weir pool and bridge. A fence ran from the house to the lock
office, separating the ornamental garden from the vegetable
garden. The lock office was similar to Goring's bearing the
legend 'F.H.N. Maggs, Lock keeper'. A gravel path ran along
the right hand lock wall, in front of the office, to the bottom
gate. A neat Gents and Conservancy notice board with hinged
iron leaves completed the lockside arrangements, but by the
bottom gates a large sign indicated 'Sanitary Station'. This
far, the scene remained constant through rain or sun, snow or
heat, fog or gale, what made it so memorable was the ever
changing colour. On this day there were the fresh and
swelling greens of the surrounding trees, the blaze of tulips
and flash of narcissi in the beds of dark earth, the purply-blue
of tumbling aubretia, the pinks and whites of blossom. It was
a deeply satisfying picture and yet another powerful image of
a memorable day. 'Like gardening, do you?' asked Fred. 'Not
really,' I replied truthfully 'but I think I could get to like it'.
'Hm!' said he looking hard at me 'Are you hoping to make a

career of the Conservancy?' 'I'm not sure at the moment. It seems a good job, but my real interest is with canals and canal boats.

Fred's face brightened 'Ah yes! I've got you now. You were through here a few weeks back on ENTERPRISE and flogged me some coal for the office. Good stuff that was, I've pinched some for the living room fire'. 'That's the boatsman's trick for getting down river from Oxford for nothing' I said 'you bag up what's left over from the last load and sell it for cash plus a toll ticket'.

Fred chuckled and rolled off towards the bottom gate. A cruiser was nosing into the lock cut from downstream, so I went over to the outside gate. The red rod was up and the gate twitched immediately I touched it. Fred called 'Half a mo!' and removed an iron pin from the mitre post. Immediately the gate began to swing. By comparison with Goring this was child's play. I remarked as such to Fred. 'Well, for a start the fall here is a lot less, the lock chamber is smaller, and we've only got one set of paddle gear per gate. Makes quite a difference'.

After making the lock and releasing the cruiser upstream, some downstream traffic arrived, one of them being the hire cruiser I had helped through Goring a couple of hours earlier. When they had gone and we were closing the gates, the telephone rang. Fred marched majestically to the office to answer it. As I came into the office he was saying: 'Quarter buck closed in, right. What's Cleeve doing?' pause 'all rymers in, OK I'll close in a bit', pause 'Yes, he's with me now. Been helping with the lock' pause 'OK Harry cheerio!' He put the receiver down. 'That was Harry. He's shutting in a bit, so I'm going to do the same. Come on. I'll show you the mysteries of paddles and rymers'. He took a large coil of thin hemp rope and marched forth.

I had noticed on the top gates at both locks were large warning notices to the effect that a strong stream was running and that craft should stay well away from weirs. Although it was nearly the end of April, we were still experiencing the aftermath of the fearful winter of early 1963. The frost had broken in early March, but weeks of snow and frost were still running out of the Cotswolds, Chilterns and Berkshire Downs. I had ridden the flood down from Oxford a month previously and had met no traffic whatsoever. By now the river was beginning to see the stirrings of holiday traffic, yet the weirs still disgorged the long-pent waters from the chalk and lime-stone hills. It was, however, beginning to slow down, and here was proof.

We went to the Middle Weir, from which we had a clear view upstream. 'Never come out on your own without a weir line' said Fred. 'There's a few been lost pitching rymers'. So saying he seized one of the square posts, tied a clove hitch about the top end, through which a short round dowel passed at right angles, and, resting it dowel uppermost over his shoulder, gave me the rest of the weir line ('Hang on to that like Billy-o'), then placing his right foot on a beam above the open weir and the left foot on a beam, which he called the 'shying beam' and which was perhaps two feet away from the first, he shot the square post butt-end into the water. Instantly the water took it and sucked it in an upright position hard back against the weir beam. The weir beam had notches cut in it to receive the rymer post, so Fred bent over, seized the dowel handle, twisted it sharply and with a 'clunk' the rymer sat snugly in its recess. 'There's a wooden sill on the bed of the weir with corresponding notches' he explained, 'the bottom of the rymer sits in that'.

He pitched several more then invited me to try. Somewhat nervously I positioned myself and shot the rymer downwards. Immediately it went sideways, shot through the weir and was retrieved by means of the weir line by a wooden-faced Fred. He gave it to me for a second attempt in which I all but fol-lowed the rymer down the weir. The third time there was a satisfying 'clu-clunk' as the rymer caught the sill and slammed into the weir beam. I twisted it and it went into its slot, slightly awry. Fred urged me to twist it slightly the oppo-site way, and it clunked home firmly.

The noise of the weir changed as the line of posts advanced across the gap, the river still surged and roared, but at a higher pitch, while the billows in the weir pool decreased in height. 'We'll put a few bottoms in' said Fred, and took one of the poles with transverse boards fixed to it. Some I noticed had poles in the centre, others had the poles offset, the one Fred had had a central pole. Going to one end of the weir, he placed the boards on the upstream side of the rymers, pole facing downstream, and with a swift movement, shot it to the bed of the weir. The pressure of water forced the boards tight against the rymers. He let me do the same with the next two paddles, and continued the row until half the weir was closed in. Once again the note of the water changed, this time becoming softer. Fred stood looking upstream. 'This was the old flash lock, before the pound lock was cut' he said. 'The old 'uns say there used to be a winch in those willows to pull boats up through. The old lock had a swinging weir beam, not this fixed bridge, but otherwise it can't have changed much'.

Suddenly I realised I was involved in something that was of real antiquity. The railway technology was early 20th century, the Thames locks were of the 19th century, the Kennet locks smacked of the 18th, but here was a simple mechanical device for raising and lowering water which did not employ rotary movement. It was the technology of the Middle Ages and maybe of Classical times. Very likely the Romans had navigated the Thames to Dorchester, quite possibly the Vikings brought their longships upstream, certainly the monks of Abingdon navigated the river before the Norman Conquest and the weir was probably ancient when Domesday was compiled. In the 1960s we were just beginning to understand the worth of ancient technology, but how many preservers of defunct windmills, waterwheels, locomotives, steam engines and so forth would have given a thought to the humble paddle and rymer weir still performing its original function on its original site after at least a millennium?

Back at the office, Fred took down the weir log and water level record and wrote 'closed in six rymers and six bottoms, Middle Weir'. He picked up the telephone giving the number for Mapledurham Lock. Pangbourne exchange was still manual and the operator evidently knew the Thames Conservancy staff, for she said that the keeper's wife was working the lock while he was cutting the grass. Eventually the lock keeper came on the line. 'Hullo Len, Fred here' pause 'Yes, I'm just shutting in a bit. Six rymers and six bottoms' pause, 'while the instrument squawked quietly in his ear 'yes, the new Relief's here. You know, David, got ENTERPRISE. A cackling laugh came out of the earpiece, 'What? Poachers make the best gatekeepers? Ha! Ha!' crackle, crackle from the instrument. 'OK I'll tell him. Much on the way up?' pause 'No, not much

coming down, a couple of cruisers that's all. OK old son,
cheerio!' with which he put the receiver on its rest. He turned
to me 'Len says he's going out this evening, and Kath's running the lock while he does a bit of garden work, so you'd
probably best go there another day'.

So I never went to Mapledurham that day as a learner. I had
that pleasure to come. Fred's wife, Hazel, came walking
across the weir bridge, back from her job in Reading, so fortified with tea and cake I pedalled home in happy and satisfied
mood.

Next day I presented myself at Reading Bridge House for
instructions and uniform. Sylvia gave me a typed sheet with
my duty rota until Christmas marked on it, and Peter Harvey
and Chris Groves measured me for my uniform. Some of it
could be had off the peg, but other items had to come by special order once I had served a month's probation.

Nothing demonstrated the paternal attitude of the
Conservancy to its staff more than did the issue of uniform.
Evidently the view of the Victorian gentlemen who formed
the Conservancy Board back in 1857 was that of wealthy and
enlightened landowners. The lesser orders who accepted the
position of servants were accorded the status of liveried
retainers. It was assumed that such a retainer arrived naked
and homeless and thus required complete accoutrements. The
issued kit list included a serge uniform, trousers, jacket and
waistcoat complete with the Conservator's brass buttons, a
best uniform in barathea, cap, great coat, navy sweater, gum
boots, woollen stockings, black socks, overalls and sou-wester
oilskins. I received the serge uniform and cap, but the other
good things were to follow. The cap had a brass badge and a
white cover, which was due to be put on next week, for the
Navigation Staff wore white cap covers from May to October.

Having received and signed for the equipment, which I
placed in a holdall, I felt that perhaps I should visit
Caversham Lock and acquaint myself with it. I knew the sur-
roundings well enough, but the weir was different again from
the others I had seen, and besides, I felt some trepidation
about the lock keeper for the following reason.

One evening last summer, Bill Fisher and myself had
brought ENTERPRISE round from High Bridge Wharf to
Caversham with the intention of sounding out the backwater

above the weir, which led to Caversham Mill. We had hopes of carrying bales of cork upstream from London to the firm which processed the stuff at the mill. We had a battered old army bugle aboard which Bill had learned to blow with magnificent effect, so as we swept up towards Caversham Lock, we beheld the bottom gates closed. Bill then committed what I later found out to be a cardinal sin. He blew to attract the lock keeper. What made matters worse was that Dick Knightley, the keeper, was at that moment on the towpath indulging in his passion for tinkering with motor cars. Bill's tremendous rasp caught him head down beneath a raised bonnet. Dick jumped, knocked away the bonnet prop as he did so, causing the bonnet to close on him like a crocodile's jaw. We were still tittering, when he strode red-faced and angry to the lockside. 'Twenty bloody years I was in the Navy' he roared 'fifteen on the river. I know all the bloody sound signals and there's no such thing as 'ta-tatty-ta-tatty-ta-ta-ta'.'

This was too much for us, and we both exploded in mirth and continued snickering as the lock filled. Dick inspected every inch of the boat minutely to see whether we infringed bye-laws and let us out, muttering darkly. When we came back, we sneaked through after closing and thereafter kept a low profile.

Now, the incident did not seem quite so funny as last year. I began to think that perhaps I might have made an enemy, so I approached Caversham Lock, set amid the chestnut trees, with caution.

There was no sign of a lock keeper as I crossed the gates, but the paddles were up and the lock filling, with several boats in the chamber. Dick Knightley emerged from the lock office and caught sight of me, his face broke into a wide grin. 'Well I never! It's about time you blooming old bargemen learned how the other half lives! Glad to have you with us'.

So the ice was broken. We became good friends thereafter, and Dick even come close to admitting, after several months, that to persons of weak intellect and with a basic sense of humour, the sight of him being engulfed by a car bonnet might conceivably have a remotely funny aspect.

Over the inevitable cup of tea Dick explained some of the details of Caversham. Unlike all the other locks, it was in the heart of the Conservancy's empire. Adjoining it was the main engineering store for the Reading District, which occupied most of the lock island. Here were tied the two District tugs CHURN and CHERWELL, and numerous barges used by the engineers, also the District Inspectors' launch, the Chief Inspector's launch and the Conservators' magnificent steam inspection launch DONOLA. All these latter craft were maintained and crewed by a staff of boatmen, based at 'the Yard'. Only just out of sight, but visible from the weir, was the main Engineer's workshop, and the offices of the Chief Engineer, Land Drainage Department and the Chief Navigation Officer, not to mention the Reading District Inspector. Therefore, as Dick pointed out, one had to tread very warily indeed. Because of its prime location, Caversham Lock possessed a rain gauge which had to be read each morning, and its reading recorded. The Chiefs would go into a huddle in times of heavy rain and issue orders for drawing weir tackle.

Caversham Weir itself had been rebuilt in the 1950s. It comprised several modern radial gates, raised or lowered electrically, and some small radials controlling an overfall. The electricity was switched on in a shed behind the lockhouse, to which Dick conducted me, flourishing a key taken down from a hook in the office. The weir had two half gates running and all its small radials open. When the current was switched on, we walked out to the nearest radial gate. 'You always shut in away from the lock island and draw towards it' said Dick. 'The last one to be drawn is always the one nearest the island, 'cos otherwise you put too much water under the Engineer's barges'. He nodded upstream. A gaggle of grey-painted barges and lighters lay out in the weir stream, tugging at their moorings as the current surged past them. The weirs were still being closed in, so Dick showed me where the control buttons were placed and bade me close in a quarter gate. I pressed the green start button, and watched as the black, greasy, cables slowly unwound, as the heavy gate sank into its slot. 'That'll do' called Dick. I pressed the red stop button and the gate obediently stopped. He glanced towards the moored barges, the water creaming round their upstream ends had slackened appreciably. 'You'll be shutting in again at Goring tomorrow' said he.

We strolled back to the lock, several cruisers were waiting below, so we let them in. The lock chamber was very much smaller than Goring, and comparable to Whitchurch in size, so it was necessary to pack boats in fairly tightly. I assisted with this, then we filled up. The lock cut above curved away under trees, so I quickly learned that, at Caversham, it was very much a case of he who hesitates is lost. As the upstream boats passed them, Dick waved. One who was not too quick in loosing off from the piles was shut out and formed the first in the queue for the next. 'They soon learn a bit of smart boat work' chuckled Dick.

I spent the rest of the morning working the lock and yarning in between. I decided that the Conservators' service was going to be an interesting one, and looked forward to starting on the morrow. When lunch time came, I left the lock and returned to High Bridge Wharf to make final arrangements with Jim, who was now comfortably ensconced aboard ENTERPRISE. Looking over those years of my life I am struck by the number of times that the direction of it changed, almost on a whim of fate. Inside three days my prospects and expectations had changed completely. Had I been given the power of foresight, I would have seen an even more radical change coming but, mercifully, that power is withheld from most of us and in any case, I would not have missed what was to come for anything.

CHAPTER 3 — CONSERVANCY TRADITION

My father always rose just after seven on a weekday so, as I was living at home, he gave me a call at quarter past. It was the last week of April and the spring-like weather was holding. The morning sun struck through the leaves of the chestnuts opposite and gave contrast to their white candle blooms against the spreading green fingers of the leaves. Already the groundsman was setting forth with his mower along the cricket pitches over the road, leaving broad stripes across the dewy grass and sending whiffs of petrol smoke behind him as the ancient Atco puttered back and forth. The scent of new mown grass drifted through the bedroom windows as I went to breakfast.

My mother, evidently fearing starvation in the wilds of Goring, had prepared a large breakfast of porridge, sausage, bacon, fried bread and strong tea, and insisted that I pack my duffle bag with a large pack of sandwiches and cake. I sat, picking at the food, and proudly displaying my new navy blue uniform with its brass buttons. I finished eventually and went outside for my bicycle, tucking the trousers into my black socks. On with the cap, and a quick check in the glass that the apparition therein was sufficiently dapper, and I was away, pedal down, leg swinging over crossbar.

The Conservancy hours were 9 a.m. until sunset, so by leaving at 8.00 I had a good hour for the ten-mile pedal to Goring. Off across the Green, past the parade of shops, and there was my one-time boss waiting at the bus stop. Although he was one of the most successful professional men in the town, he never used a car to go to work. As I drew alongside him he lowered his *Times* and looked solemnly at me. I nodded 'good morning' to him, he gave an ironic smile and said 'Well, at least you get up in the morning nowadays'.

However, I was determined not to let his sarcasm spoil the morning, so waving adieu, I treadled off, under the fresh green and blossoms, down the long hill into town, then set off along the dreary Oxford Road towards Streatley. Beyond Purley the road gave a glimpse of the green hills enclosing the Thames, with the shingled spire of Whitchurch nestling at their foot. In Pangbourne queues stood at bus stops awaiting the bus to Reading and the shop or office, including Hazel, Fred's wife, who waved as I passed. But I was heading out into the country to work. I was bound for one of the prettiest places in the Thames valley, not for a noisy shop or dusty office. So, I was in high spirits as I rode down the village street of Streatley, its blossoms and its gardens scenting the fresh morning air, and wobbled round and across the mill bridge to Goring Lock.

The Post Office clock said 8.57 as I creaked past, by the time I had rested the bike against the old brick office on the island it was exactly 9 a.m. I crossed the top gates, noting the headwater reading on the nearby pile as I did so, lifted up the bootscraper outside the office door to extract the key, and opened the office. My first task was to check the head and tail-water levels, enter them into the register and total the craft entries for yesterday. Harry had left out all the documents that I might need — dinghy and launch tickets. Return Journey Pass forms, weir fishing tickets, mooring tickets and notices to be served to unregistered craft. I took out my Oxo tin of sand-wiches and placing it in a safe place on the shelf above the window, settled down to the book work for a few minutes. The telephone rang after five minutes. It was Reading wanting my head and tailwater figures. No sooner had I put the receiver down, then I saw a boat pulling in towards the downstream layby, so off I went to open up for him.

As I let him out of the top gates, Harry appeared with two mugs of tea, and wandered into the office. I filled up with downhill customers, went to the bottom, drew off and returned to the office. Harry stood watching from the door-way, a near-smile on his face. It was gone half past nine already. We sipped the tea, sugared from a cavernous tin of caked granulated, and Harry asked me how I was liking it. 'A lot on 'em can't stick the uniform and discipline' he said 'Course it ain't like the army though, you 'as to think for yourself in this game. I 'ad this assistant once, says to me 'there's too much bullshit about the TC! I turns round and I says to 'im 'You don't know what bullshit is, mate!' Ha! Ha! some o'them young 'uns ud not last five minutes in the regulars'. 'Were you a regular soldier then, Harry?' I asked. 'Not 'arf mate' he said, squaring his shoulders. 'First battalion,

Surrey Regiment. Before the war and all through it. Went to France in '39 an' that were bloody it'. 'I suppose you were at Dunkirk' said I. 'Don't talk about bloody Dunkirk' he said with feeling. 'What a bloody shambles! Tell you what mate. I gets off aboard a destroyer, 'as to wade out for the boats to pick us up, bloody Jerries dive-bombs us, but we gets back to Blighty; into a train. I goes straight to sleep. When I wakes up we're in bloody Wales!'

He walked with me to the bottom gates and helped push them open. The boats in the lock spat and spluttered, ropes were cast off, one by one they filed out, some of the crews nodding or waving as they passed. Another file of craft had assembled below and came in when I signalled. As we walked back up the lock I asked Harry how long he'd been on the river. 'Most of me life mate, 'cept for the army. Used to be down at Shepperton. You'd 'a liked that. Plenty of barges — big 'uns, not like your monkey barges. A lot used to come up to the River Wey from London, we used ter see 'em loosin' off from the tug below the weir pool. Then we used to get coal barges for Staines gasworks, timber up to Windsor and Reading, grain for Sonning Mill an' all that'. 'Did you ever get any narrow boats?' I asked. 'Monkey barges you mean' he chuckled 'Bloody 'winkle pickers', that's what we used to call 'em. No, not a lot. 'Fore the war we sometimes saw 'Fellows Mortons or them blue 'uns'. 'Grand Unions?' I ventured. 'That's it. They used to go up to Oxford if they couldn't go to Birmingham up the canal. Summat about a tunnel up that way giving trouble I remember, but I never saw 'em after the war. 'Course there were some other ones — a bloke called Knill, toff 'e were, but a real gentleman with it, he came through a few times, and old John Gould of Newbury. He fetched a few load o' turf for Chaplins down at Hampton, that'd be more'n ten years back now'.

'Yes, I know John Gould very well, and I remember John Krill's boats on the Kennet'. 'Ah, well, we didn't 'ave much to do with monkey barges, but I knew plenty of the old river bargemen and them off the tugs'.

Harry eventually broke off his reminiscing to point out that I hadn't checked the Gents. A thoughtful Conservancy had provided a urinal at each lock for gentlemen *in extremis*, but, oddly, no such facilities for ladies. Perhaps this was a throwback to Victorian attitudes which assumed that the female sex did not perform bodily functions of this nature, or perhaps a canny calculation that the provision of such necessaries for ladies would require more elaborate plumbing. Nevertheless, lock keepers were instructed to check the installations regularly, to prevent the appearance of pencilled ruderies (it was before the days of felt pens or aerosols) and to ensure that no unseemly behaviour was taking place. There was a convenient break in the traffic, so, emptying the lock, I turned to the matter of the Gents. The custom of emptying a full lock when no downstream traffic was imminent had always puzzled me. On the Grand Union and its associated canals, locks were always left full, with the gates open, for the benefit of oncoming traffic. Traffic following always had someone out on a bike 'lock wheeling' to turn the lock round. Harry enlightened me. It was to discourage the growth of algae and weed on the lock sides, which were always kept spotlessly clean. 'And by the way' he went on 'when you've finished the Gents you'd better scrub off the lock steps. They got to be done every day'.

I took a long handled stiff broom and a can of disinfectant from the lock office and set forth for the necessary office. A few buckets out of the lock, a few drops of disinfectant and some scrubbing and all was sweet. I then set about the steps which reached down to water level on both sides of the chamber.

'That's it' said Harry, passing by. 'You leave 'em slimy, an' some bugger'll slip on it, then turn round and sue the TC. You can drop yourself right in it'.

I finished one side, then boats appeared below, so off I went and poled the outside gate open before pushing the inside one. The chamber filled with boats, mainly hire cruisers, then I had the tedious task of hooking an eyebolt on the mitre part of the opposite gate, and pulling it to with the hitcher. The gate closed oh, so slowly and although I was very fit, with muscles tempered by months of tiller-pushing, windlass-winding and coal-shovelling, I still found it heavy work. As I walked up towards the office, the telephone rang. I lifted the receiver. 'Goring Lock'. 'Cleeve here' came a voice. 'You the new Relief?'

I affirmed this was so. Cleeve Lock was less than half a mile upstream, but just out of sight, concealed by willows.

The reach from Goring to Cleeve is the shortest on the river, followed by the longest, nearly nine miles up to Benson. 'I've got all the bottoms in, I've just shut in all the tops on the middle weir'. I wondered what I ought to do and wished Harry were here to ask but he had disappeared in the direction of the village. Cleeve continued 'I should think you need to close in a quarter gate'. Relief swept through me. 'O.K.' said I 'I'll do that in a minute. I've got five boats in here at the moment'. 'Well, there's nothing coming down for a while. Don't leave it too long or you'll run your head water off. Don't forget to let Fred know at Whitchurch. Good luck, cheerio'. The line went dead.

I let the boats out, walked round to the weir and wound one sluice gate down until it seated on the bed of the weir. The roaring of the water gradually subsided until all that remained was a series of trickles. The next-door buck was still half open and making a thunderous racket, but the din was nowhere near what it had been two days before. The long pent waters of the Downs and Wolds were at last dying down after the recent hard winter. I did some quick calculations in my head. It was seven weeks to the day since the frost had broken sufficiently to allow boats to move on the Grand Union Canal. Before that there had been ten weeks of frost and snow which had halted all traffic. Old hands reckoned that the run-off period took as many weeks as the frost, so discounting heavy rains and flash floods, we should be closing in for another three weeks yet.

I rang Fred and passed on the weir information. 'Good on you coz', he said 'I was about to ring you. Chris Groves is on his way up to you'. The telephone evidently had other uses. The position and whereabouts of Inspectors was always carefully plotted. I later learned that they usually patrolled at weekends (today was a Saturday) and visited every lock on a Monday morning to check the books. The Inspector had recently taken delivery of a new type of launch, rather smaller than their predecessors. Chris Groves arrived about half an hour later steering TILLINGBOURNE alone, with his head poking above the small shelter cabin, reminiscent of the giraffes aboard the circus train in 'Dumbo'. I had the lock ready and in he swept. I took his lines from him, then he came ashore looking critically at my recently scrubbed steps. After a brief word or two he went straight to the Gents to check up on the naughty inscriptions, found that no new ones had appeared, and congratulated me on keeping things in the Conservancy way. I had taken the opportunity of informing Cleeve before he arrived at Goring, for I reasoned that by the time I had closed my top gates and got to the phone, he would be almost in sight of Cleeve Lock. This precaution stood me in good stead with the Cleeve lock keeper thereafter.

Without my realising it, the morning had gone. Glancing at my watch I saw that it was nearly 12.30 p.m., and soon after I saw Harry's figure coming from under the Goring end of the bridge heading home for lunch. 'You wants to put the lunch boards out, cock" he called as he went in the office, so I did as bid at the next lull in traffic. The lunch boards were placards which were hung from top and bottom gates informing the world that the services of the lock keeper would not be available for half-an-hour. I fetched these out, placed them in position, then went to get my Oxo tin of sandwiches. I reached contentedly for them, from the top shelf above the desk, placed the Oxo tin on the desk and opened them up. A set of pink and white false teeth grinned up at me from within and I started back amazed. At the same instant Harry emerged red-faced from his front door and advanced menacingly on the office, bearing another red Oxo tin in his hands. 'Where's my bloody teef?' he hissed gummily. 'Are these them?' I asked. 'Course they're my teef! Oo's else d'ye fink they'd be, the Archbishop o' Canterbury's?' 'Well, where's my sandwiches then?' 'Are these yourn then?' I resisted the temptation to ask him if the same prelate had lost his sandwiches, and told him 'Yes'.

He seized the teeth, blew on them and popped them in. Instantly his face changed, his jawline filled out, and he looked 20 years younger. 'You had me worried for a minute or two. I can't eat Enid's dinner wivvout these buggers' said he. 'Not half as much as you worried me' I countered 'I thought my sandwiches were gonners'. Harry chortled loud and left for his lunch. However, later that afternoon the Oxo tin reappeared, but I did not dare look within to check its contents.

I settled down to my sandwiches, leafing through an old notebook off one of the shelves as I did so. It was written in several hand writing styles and comprised memos to lock

keepers dating back to the 1890s. Each entry was signed by
the then District Inspector, the last memo was entered about
1913, presumably by that time the Conservancy had acquired
a typewriter. In this book were cautionary tales of misde-
meanours and actions taken. Peculating lock keepers were
'dismissed the Conservators' Service'; vessels were not to be
allowed to carry gas tar or other liquids in an undecked hold
following a capsize at Oxford in the 'nineties; the lock keepers at Hurley and Temple were both dismissed the service for
fighting, and on an August Bank Holiday too; weir tackle was
being misused by millers; and so it went on, a fascinating
glimpse of the real river of Jerome K. Jerome's time. He it
was who wrote: 'the Conservancy of late seems to have constituted itself into a society for the employment of idiots. A
good many of the new lock keepers are excitable, nervous old
men, quite unfitted for their posts'.

With such thoughts did I occupy my lunch break, then it
was back to work to clear the build-up of cruisers which had
occurred during that time. For some reason Thames boaters
tended to leave locks to the lock keepers, although there was
nothing to stop them working the locks themselves when the
lock keepers were off duty. Unlike canal locks, which were,
and still are, of a do-it-yourself variety, Thames locks were
never closed or locked save for repairs and the right of navigation was taken very seriously.

One thing which had changed greatly since Jerome's day,
and even since my own youth, was the numbers of non-
mechanically propelled boats. The lock charge for a skiff,
punt, randan, gig or dinghy, if not mechanically driven was at
that time 3d for a single journey, whereas the smallest launch
paid two shillings, the biggest ones paid eight shillings and
six pence, and a houseboat paid an exorbitant half guinea per
lock passage. By 1963 most boats, hired or private, had a lock
pass paid for in advance, but occasionally one had to issue
tickets and take tolls. However, nearly all non-mechanical
craft still paid their tiny fee, yet in spite of this, the Thames
oarsman was a dying breed, save in competitive rowing which
continued to flourish. I was pleased therefore to see, in the
late afternoon, the unmistakable outline of a camping skiff
plugging its way slowly upstream towards the road bridge.
The occupants were a young man and a large black retriever.

He came in, shipped his oars as he came in the bottom gates and glided towards the stone steps in the chamber. I walked down and took his line while he scrambled ashore. He told me that he had come up from Richmond, on the tideway, and was making for Oxford, intending to lie overnight on the Cherwell by Magdalen Bridge on the last night of the month, so as to hear the choristers of Magdalen welcome in May morning. Apart from kayaks, he had only seen one other hand-propelled craft the whole way up river. Like steam on the rail and the cargo-carrying narrowboat on the canal, the rowing boat or punt was fast disappearing as an everyday sight. I watched him pull away towards Cleeve, with a feeling of regret.

As yet, few privately-owned craft were about, and since Saturday was change-over day for hire craft, the afternoon was fairly quiet, but one little incident stood out. About tea time, a smart blue-hulled cruiser appeared below and was let in the lock. Its owner and skipper was an antipodean so I shall call the vessel EMU. EMU was every bit of 25 feet long, with a central wheelhouse, but she was a Walter Mitty's dream. Above her bows rose a pulpit of chromed rails, a mast with many burgees rose atop the fore cabin. Then came the wheelhouse with a radio loop on its roof and a radar aerial, within was a teak wheel, a chart table with dividers and sextant handy, a chronometer and lockers for signal flags. At the stern a minute pram dinghy depended from davits. The skipper and his wife both wore yachting caps and blue trousers and jerseys, the latter with the boat's name in white. The skipper came in and tied up somewhat fussily, insisting that he have no other craft either abreast of him, or within ten feet astern. He was close to the top gates and I was sorely tempted to whip the paddles up full. However, I repressed this desire, and made polite conversation instead. While I did so, Harry came out of the house bearing two mugs of tea, there being a break in the afternoon's TV coverage of racing. He noted the chart table, the dividers, sextant and parallel rulers lying in negligent fashion on the chart of the Thames. Absolutely dead pan he addressed the skipper in a solicitous tone: 'Sure you can find yer way up to bloody Cleeve, mate?' I felt it necessary to go and shove the top gates open before I had an attack of suppressed hysterics.

Inexorably the shadows were lengthening, shade was gradually creeping up the green bulk of Streatley Hill although chimneys and rooftops and the new green of treetops were still bathed in light. Boats began to tie up on the concrete wall below the bridge. Traffic, already light, diminished to a trickle after six. Still I plodded up and down, turning the lock round once every 15 minutes according to the log, then, with an hour to go before sunset, Harry came out once more. 'Ain't much about mate. I'll keep an eye open for the next hour. You get on yer bike an' bugger orf home'.

And indeed I was ready. Suddenly I realised that I was faced with a ten mile ride home after a full day's work. Bidding Harry adieu, I went to collect the bike. 'Bus gets in at quarter past tomorrow morning' said Harry 'I'll look after things till then'. Gratefully I nodded acknowledgement and set off homewards. It seemed a very slow journey home, and I was glad of a break in Reading where Jim gave me a full account of the day's work with ENTERPRISE. It seemed he was coping well so, after a quick pint with him I went home and collapsed wearily in bed.

Reading Corporation did not run buses until late on a Sunday morning, so my father ran me down to Reading bus station which, in those days occupied a section of road in between the Great Western and Southern railway stations. The red Thames Valley single decker groaned its way out along the Oxford Road, but traffic being light, we made good time out through Tilehurst and Pangbourne to Streatley, where I was dropped outside The Bull. By 9.20 I was on the lockside, to be greeted by Harry in his shirt sleeves weeding the flower beds.

Sunday on the river, even in early spring, was not a day of rest. It was the last week of the Easter holidays, so hire cruisers were plentiful. To start with there were those from Caversham Bridge or Benson, then came the first ones up from Wargrave and Henley about midday. In the afternoon came the cruisers which had left Oxford or Cookham on Saturday. On top of these were the private launches and cruisers, though these were as yet few in numbers.

At lunch time came another surprise, Harry came marching down the lockside with a plate of roast beef, Yorkshire pudding, roast potatoes and greens. 'Enid's sent this' he announced. 'Keep yer sandwiches for tea!' Fortified by this, which was followed by apple pie and custard, I set about the afternoon's work, which was brisk to say the least. By tea time the evensong bells began to ring out from the two rival towers of Goring and Streatley, I was beginning to feel weary. Sunset was at 8.20 p.m. that evening, so I had time for a swift pint in The Bull before catching the 8.35 bus home.

I rode out to Whitchurch next day, because the distance was only half that of Goring. In fact, I gave up cycling to Goring thereafter, for the distance, combined with the heaviness of the work meant that the journey home was dolorous. However, whenever the weather was fine I continued to ride out to Whitchurch. This Monday morning was once more fine and spring-like, the river flowed quietly up to the long weir bridge, sunlight striking off the wavelets. Once more I gave thanks for my good fortune at being in gainful employment in such a beautiful part of England.

I noticed that Fred still had some rymer posts out on the middle weir, glanced at the head water gauge, propped the bike against the office and opened up for business. I hung up my bag and coat, walked down to read the tail water, and was met by Fred bearing two cups of coffee. 'I never showed you the Sanitary Station' he observed. 'Today's dustbin day, they come to The Swan this morning'. The import of this news was soon made plain, for on entering the fenced-off compound, I was greeted by a long line of full dust bins. Fred told me that they all had to go across the weir bridge to the pub. My heart sank. By the bins stood a circular tank with a manhole and a horizontal iron wheel. This contraption was for the reception of waste from chemical closets, whose formaldehyde laden contents were supposed to break down organically and ultimately allow the liquid to leak away. There were no public health services on Whitchurch Island, the bath, basins and WC fed into a septic tank and drinking water was pumped up from a well. It seemed to me that this was a decidedly odd place to put a sanitary station, there was a landing stage below, but potential customers had to wobble precariously up steps to empty their horrendous buckets. Inevitably, Fred said, fearsome disasters occurred with carrying handles coming adrift, or people slipping on the steps. He warned me not to allow customers to lift their buckets out while boats were in the lock. 'That way' said he 'lies much tribulation'. I felt unable to press him further on the subject.

The projecting iron wheel had to be given several turns each day. I think this was supposed to aerate the tank's contents, but the task gave rise to caustic comments from other lock keepers about Whitchurch being the ideal place for stirrers of such a substance.

An iron incinerator completed the equipment. In this the river users were encouraged to place combustible items and these, Fred, with a manic glint in his eye, proceeded to fire up with the aid of some paraffin. While the incinerator roared and crackled, he produced a small two-wheeled trolley with a single steel handle, a semi-circular frame of steel tube, and a hook halfway up the handle. The hook engaged in the carrying handle of a dustbin, the handle was tilted back and lo! the bin settled comfortably in its frame, ready for pushing on wheels. I was impressed with this natty device and made several journeys across the weir with the bins.

Fred meanwhile mowed his grass and weeded. By the time I had finished with the bins the first boats of the morning were about. As I plodded up and down, he watched me carefully and, by about 11 o'clock had evidently come to the conclusion that I was not too dangerous to be let loose. He had seemed rather brusque and formal at first, but was thawing rapidly. I learned that my surmise as to his previous career was correct. He had been in the Royal Navy during the Second World War and had been a petty officer. He still retained more than a little of naval style. He had begun lock keeping after the war at Sunbury as an assistant, then taken his first lock at Rushey, above Oxford 'Up west" as he put it. Fred's knowledge of and interest in the river was deep and extensive. He was a keen fisherman and gardener and also collected books. He knew his Thacker, that doyen of river historians, and his Isaac Walton. He collected, and was something of an expert on, muzzle-loading guns. Later that morning he introduced me to another timeless fact of Thames life.

During a lull in traffic I had been reading through the information and regulations which a lock keeper was supposed to digest, and discovered yet another class of vessel for which a special toll was payable. This was a 'licensed fishing boat'; in order to claim this dispensation, the craft had to be specially registered and the index number with its port of registry reference displayed on the bows. In other words, just as one might see a trawler or drifter at sea marked LT99 or PZ99 denoting that it hailed from Lowestoft or Penzance, so one was presumably liable to come across craft from such fishing havens as Marlow or Henley. Shortly after I had mastered this information, a figure appeared at the office door. It was a little, old man with scrubby moustache and a stubbly chin, rheumy eyes behind steel rimmed spectacles, cloth cap, nondescript jacket and trousers, muffler and wellingtons. 'Where's bloody Maggs?' said the figure. 'Day off' I replied 'What's up?' 'I bloody wants to come through the bloody lock''. 'Hang on, I'm coming'. I went with the customer to the lock tail where, lying by the Sanitary Station piles, I saw a decrepit old punt with an outboard. 'I only wants one bloody gate' said the old man, so I let him in on the one gate and closed up behind him. 'Day ticket or have you a pass?' I called. 'Yer what?'' came up from the punt. 'Two shillings for a day ticket' I replied. I was quite unprepared for the torrent of abuse which then ensued. The regulations mentioned the bye law offence of 'profane, abusive or indecent language on or about the Conservators' property' and here it was in full cry, rising like fog from the depths. 'Well please yourself old chap' I replied 'but everyone who comes through has to pay or have a pass'. The flow increased to a flood and I retired baffled. Fred came out of the house, hearing the din, and came to the lockside. 'Hullo, Jack, what's up?' The old chap paused in mid-oration 'I'm trying to tell this bloody jumped-up little whippersnapper he can't charge me two bloody bob'. Fred looked at me and grinned from ear to ear. 'Allow me to introduce Jack Webb, professional fisherman' he said. Only then did I notice that the punt carried the initials RG for Reading, followed by a number, on its bows. So Reading was a fishing port after all!

In fact J.L. Webb was the very last of the old-time Thames professional fishermen, whose trade went back far into the ancestry of England. Anglo-Saxon abbots and bishops employed such men to supply tables on Fridays and in Lent, the records of the mediaeval river are filled with the activities of fishermen. In modern times river fishing had become a serious sport, but here, before my eyes, was someone who earned his daily bread from the catching of fish, in the manner of the ancients. Jack owned a fishing tackle shop in Reading, along with a maggot farm (a particularly disagreeable form of cottage industry which was not popular with neighbours), and went out after live bait and coarse fish with his motorised punt.

The matter of the toll having been amicably settled, Jack puttered off upstream and the lock settled back into its ordered routine until, after lunch, I spotted a stranger coming across the weir bridge. Fred had enjoined me to keep a strict eye on unauthorised visitors for, by using the weir, lock and a footpath by Whitchurch Mill, it was possible to avoid paying toll to the nearby toll bridge, and this caused ructions between the Trustees thereof and the Conservators. Accordingly I started forward to interrupt the intruder, but Fred, who was gardening outside the house saw him at the same time. 'Ah, my little old coz' he said 'here's my new assistant'. The newcomer was, perhaps, a year or so younger than I. He had dark, aquiline features, a slim body and humorous eyes. I had joined the Conservancy at an opportune time, for May 1st was two days away. On this date two things happened. The navigation staff donned white cap covers and summer assistants were taken on. This young man was, Fred explained, going to start on Wednesday as his amanuensis.

'He's called Peter, but answers to the name 'Sam" said Fred by way of introduction, and we shook hands, Sam grinning cheerfully. He had a way of speaking that was both staccato and droll; we hit it off from the start and have remained close friends from that day to this. Not the least that we had in common was that he too had returned home lately from a roving career, but his had been of a more spectacular nature than mine, for he had spent some time as a steward with the P&O company aboard their cruise liners. On top of that, he came from an old river family which were once narrow boat owners and coal merchants. His father and older brothers still ran the coal business, but based at Goring & Streatley railway station rather than on the waterside.

I learned all this, and much more, as the afternoon passed. Sam was at a loose end following the closing of The Swan at 2.30, so he helped me work the lock all afternoon, fortifying himself with cups of Fred's tea and copious draughts of snuff, a custom I found curious in one so young. Indeed, there was much about Sam which did not conform to the stereotype image of his generation.

After Hazel, Fred's wife, and his two sons returned home from work and school respectively, Fred came and sat in the office. The traffic slackened to a mere trickle by 6 o'clock as the evening shadows lengthened. Tales were exchanged and Fred impressed upon us his rules for maintaining a seemly lock. 'No running on the lockside' he said 'Oh, my goodness me, no. Anyone can fall over a stump or a rope. No radios or carrying on alarmingly in the lock. Unfortunately we no longer have the power of arresting an offender and carrying him before a magistrate — we used to in the good old days — but you can take names and addresses, and it's an offence not to give it'.

Twice in days to come was I to see Fred in action against those who threatened the peace of his beloved lock. On the first occasion, his request to a holidaymaker not to tread on the flowerbeds was received with a derisive laugh. Fred's jaw stiffened and he told the man 'show some respect for my lock'. The reply was 'It ain't your lock, mate, its the public's'. Fred assumed his petty officer's stance. 'This is MY lock" he thundered 'I've signed for it'. Silence ensued.

On the second occasion a cruiser full of drunk rowdies caused havoc with the peace. Fred stood on the top gate catwalk his arms folded and boomed down into the chamber. 'This is a ROYAL river, and you will kindly comport yourselves with due decorum'.

He told us how the river entered one's being. Some men could not bear the thought of parting from it at retirement. There was one, he said, due to retire who finished at sunset on his last day. 'Never came home all night. Next morning, up came a tug and barge, the crew couldn't get the bottom gates open. They fished around with a hitcher, up comes Jack's shoe and a trouser leg. He'd tied the garden roller round his neck and gone off the lockside. Never drew his pension'.

There was the legendary lock keeper of Sonning who turned the lock into a veritable flowering paradise and year after year won the prize for the best lock garden. 'People came for miles to see it. You remember the pictures in Great Western carriages? Nearly every compartment had a picture of Sonning lock. When old Ted retired the villagers had a whip round. Set him and his missus up in a nice little bunga-

low and a post office on the South Coast. I think they gave
him the deeds of the house at a farewell do in the village hall'.
'Do you run a shop, or anything?' I asked. 'Hazel sells a few
ice creams in summer, and I do a bit of tackle dealing, but this
lock's no gold mine. Sonning now, he's got a general shop
and café there. 'Course he's got room on the island.
Teddington — that's shift work, like Molesey, because of the
tides, head lock keeper there's on a thousand a year.
Sandford's got a nice little business I hear, well so have quite
a few, but the only one on your beat is Len at Mapledurham.
Kath runs a shop evenings and week ends, sells sweets, ices,
cigarettes, that sort of thing, out of the front door, and Dick at
Caversham sells ices, but he's too near headquarters to do
much'.

The evening drew on, a chill came with it and I closed the
office at 8.20 feeling the need for a Conservancy overcoat.

Although Mapledurham village is in Oxfordshire, the lock
of that name sits on the Berkshire bank and is inaccessible on
foot from the village. I had never been there by road before,
so following directions from Fred and Sam, I came out by bus
next morning. Ken Clark, my ex-boss, was waiting at the
Corporation bus stop, his head buried in *The Times*. He was
much amused at my latest career and proceeded to quiz me in
his best forensic manner. I was astonished at how much I had
learned in three days.

The Thames Valley Traction Company dropped me in
Purley village at the top of a steep lane leading down from the
main road. The lane crossed the railway and flattened out just
beyond. A five-barred locked gate stood on a right-angled
bend at the foot of the hill. The lane, now a potholed track,
went round to the right through a ramshackle collection of
shanties, old railway carriages, bungalows and caravans
which was officially called 'Purley Park' and unofficially
'Dodge City'. Today this is a very respectable, even up-mar-
ket area, but then it was still largely a pre-Planning Act lais-
sez-faire development with no sewage and well-water for
drinking. Some of its inhabitants were none too choice.

Climbing the gate, I set off along a rutted track trough hay
meadows spotted with buttercups. The red lock house, a twin
of the one at Caversham, guided me towards the lock, which
was virtually invisible, although the weir could be heard mur-

muring a quarter mile or so distant.

Eventually, crossing a concrete bridge over a dry ditch, I came upon the lock. It was unlike any of the others in several ways. First it was much larger, second it was in a much more open setting and third it was mechanically operated. There were no balance beams or paddle wheels, which gave it a utilitarian air.

I had been told to look under the shoe scraper and there, sure enough was the key. I unlocked the office door and went into a very different atmosphere from the other three locks. This was a spacious, airy room with windows on three sides, a desk in the front centre and control panels at each end. I gawped at the sight, wrote down the tailwater figure, and was about to turn and go out for the head water figure when a voice behind me said 'Mornin''. I turned to see a fresh-faced tall man of about Fred's age smiling at me with his hand out. He had a large golden retriever with him. We shook hand firmly 'I'm Len' he said 'This is Rusty', introducing his dog. 'I've seen you through here on ENTERPRISE. 'That's right' I said 'you issued me a merchandise toll ticket last year'. 'Cor yes! I remember. What a hoo hah there was over that. Still you were in the right'.

Len's reference was to yet another dispute over tolls. One afternoon last year a man had introduced himself to Bill Fisher and myself at High Bridge Wharf. He owned an ex-Thomas Clayton (Oldbury) Ltd. 'gas boat' called DON. This craft he intended bringing to Reading from the Oxford Canal, he being in between jobs. He had built a short extension cabin forward of the engine room but the boat was otherwise in trading condition. The Thames toll for such a craft, classified as a "merchandise-carrying tug' was 8d per lock. As such he came down from Oxford to Cleeve, but was spotted by the Chief Inspector below Goring Lock, where he had spent the night and the Chief telephoned Fred at Whitchurch ordering him to charge 7s 6d launch toll and report him as an unregistered launch. This was a most heinous crime as far as the Conservancy was concerned. DON thereafter pulled into the bank below and her skipper, faced with a bill of 22s 6d plus back payments of the balance from Oxford, plus £10 registration fee faced financial ruin, he having merely a few pounds saved until his next job. Could we, he asked, suggest a way round this impasse.

My solution was, to invoice all his cabin furnishings to Kennet Carrying Co. Ltd. as cargo; to declare the same as weighing two tonnes and come down on a merchandise ticket at 5/8d per ton per mile. This worked out at about a shilling.

Next day Bill and myself went to Pangbourne, armed with this invoice, and helped navigate DON downstream. Mapledurham was our first lock and here Len issued the toll ticket. It was the first one to be issued in the book, which dated from 1920 or thereabouts, and Peter Harvey spotted it next week when he came to check the toll money. 'That' said Len, soberly 'was when the shit hit the fan'. We were, strictly speaking, in the right, but the Conservancy did not like being outsmarted, and the Chief was highly peeved. (He got even a few weeks later, but that is another story).

I felt somewhat embarrassed that I should have caused Len trouble, but he laughed the matter off, saying that a little bit of stirring did no harm at all. 'Any way, you'd better come and find out how this thing works' he said. 'It's quite simple, but I like to have the window open so's to see what's going on. Also, you can't see the boats down this side when the lock's empty, so I usually step outside to make sure they're OK before flooding up'. He pulled down a master switch at the back, immediately lights came on in the control room. 'Now then, here's the bottom gate console. These buttons control the paddles. That's it, one for open, one for close. These control the gates, open, close just the same like. Now, what you've got to watch is not straining the motors. See, the bottom gates have got direct drive. They were the first powered gates on the river see, and they were still finding things out. If you start the gates going before the water's made a level you'll burn out the motors. Otherwise it's all straight forward. The top ones now' he moved across to the other control panel 'they've got a fluid flywheel, so you can start them before the lock's full. You can stop both gates and paddles with the stop button. Here you are, there's a boat coming down. Let's see you fill her up'. I did as bid. The bottom gates and paddles were already closed, so I pressed the 'raise' button. A click came from the steel switch box behind me, followed by an audible humming. A black 'H' shape began to rise on each gate with a concertina between its legs, and in the lock water started to boil and bubble. Very quickly the chamber filled, I pressed the open button and was thus ready to entertain my first client. Rusty observed me, his nose resting on his paws.

After the boat had been dispatched downstream, Len suggested we looked at the weir. He left the bottom gates open, for there was an awkward eddy below which made tying to the layby piles difficult, so it was better if boats came straight into the lock.

We crossed the top gates onto a grassy island, set with a few blossoming fruit trees, onto the concrete weir bridge, Rusty running about, nose to ground, investigating smells. The first part of the weir comprised large modern radial gates, similar to Caversham, but manually wound, then came an overfall with smaller radials controlling the top flow, then a paddle and rymer weir which was, Len said, on the site of the old flash lock, then a long overfall weir with no bridge, but a series of vertical posts fitted with iron grooves at intervals set across the brow of the weir. 'We put lasher boards in there when the water's low' said Len. 'Where's the old mill?' I asked. Like Sonning Lock, Mapledurham Mill was a favoured subject of the Great Western's publicity department and often featured in railway carriages.

Len pointed to a backwater slipping away behind a willow clad island. I turned and looked upstream. A magnificent broad reach set with distant eyots stretched for over a mile. Straining my eyes I could just make out the white paintwork of Whitchurch toll bridge at the top end of the reach. To my left were broad, lush level pastures, dotted with willows and grazing cows, leading to the low hills of Purley and Sulham. To the right noble chalk hills, their green grass set with beechwoods rolled almost to the river's edge. Below my feet the river sang over the weir sending up that most haunting, dank, rivery smell that hangs about Thames weirs. Once more I felt exultation surge through me at being in gainful employment in such paradisiacal places.

Back in the control room, Len put the electric kettle on, I filled the lock for a few hire cruisers, and he told me something of himself. His father was a lock keeper, still working at Temple, just above Marlow, so the Thames tradition was ingrained in him. He had served in the Parachute Regiment in the Second World War, had seen action and been taken prisoner at Arnhem, then had come back to the river. Like Fred his first lock was 'up west', at Godstow in fact, and we knew several canal boatmen in common, for Clayton's gas boats were still running in those days from Oxford Gas Works with tar and sometimes worked via Godstow and the Duke's Cut en route for the Oxford Canal. He also knew another acquaintance of mine, Pat Saunders, who had distinguished himself by running a horse-drawn wide boat as a hostel venture upstream of Oxford. Some years before, Pat had made national headlines when he horse-hauled FIREBRAND from the tideway to Oxford, a feat never since repeated.

Len reached up to a shelf above the window and fetched down a cardboard box. He opened it and took out a piece of flat glass. Blowing dust off it he said 'Hold this up to the light'. I did so and saw that it was a glass plate negative. A quaint old cottage, embowered in fruit trees, stood by the leaky wooden gates of a turf-sided lock. The cottage windows had pointed tops to them, just like Whitchurch. In the garden was a Victorian family, a man in old fashioned peaked cap and whiskers, boys in reach-me-downs, a woman and girls in white pinafores. 'That's the old lock and cottage' he said 'it used to be on the island till my house was built in the 'thirties. I reckon the TC was only a year or two old when that was took'.

Mapledurham Lock had, like Whitchurch, Caversham and Goring, been built in the 1790s by the Thames Commissioners, replacing the awkward and dangerous flash weirs. Obviously the house was contemporary judging by its vernacular style. The Commissioners relinquished their control of the river above Staines to the Thames Conservancy in 1864, and this picture evidently dated from about that time. I noticed that the paddle gear was identical to that on the Kennet. 'Things have changed a bit' said I. 'Yes, I suppose so, but things die hard. What did you pay for ENTERPRISE as a tug?' '8d per lock'. 'What about from Penton Hook down?' '1s 6d per lock and 3s for Teddington'. Len grinned 'There you are then. Penton Hook to Teddington's the City Locks. Next time you're through look on the houses. You'll see the City of London crest'.

Way back in mediaeval times, the City of London claimed navigation jurisdiction over the whole river. By the 18th century this practically extended to London Stone at Staines, where the Colne enters the Thames, and where at one time apprentices were wont to bump the Lord Mayor on the stone. Penton Hook was the first lock downstream of the stone. So much I knew from the history books, but suddenly the significance of the City of London crest on our brass buttons and badges dawned on me. And even now the old boundary was reflected in the otherwise inexplicable toll charge differences. Thames tradition ran deep.

Len eventually left, with the dog, to go shopping with Kath, his wife. I was alone for the rest of the day, which passed quickly and uneventfully. Evening came, Len returned and, about 6.30 he came into the office. 'Not much about. You bugger off home'. 'Are you sure? I'm quite happy to stay'. 'No, that's O.K.. I'll see you tomorrow'. So I packed up and made my way across the fields towards Dodge City. The evening was still and clear, every colour in the countryside stood out in pristine condition.

An old chap clipping his hedge near the gate paused as I went to clamber over. 'Evenin''. 'Evening' I replied 'It's been a grand day'. 'It 'ave that' he said, sniffing deeply 'That'll rain like 'ell afore mornin''. 'You reckon so?' 'Oh ar! Them old lavatories are makin' a fair ole stink'. Faintly, on the air, I noticed the tang of raw sewage, and was glad to add yet another piece of local lore to my growing store.

The ancient was quite correct. I arrived next day, May morning, in drizzling rain. Puddles lay in the ruts and the meadow grass was sodden. I thought of the young man I had met at Goring the other day and hoped that he would not have been disappointed.

Len was out all day, so I settled down into the routine of the lock. The weather made no difference to the traffic, which remained brisk all day, mainly downstream hire boats for Maidenhead upwards and upstream hire boats for Oxford down. The Chertsey and Sunbury ones had long gone.

Little by little the river was taking me over. Already I was familiar with many hire fleets and their foibles, I was learning four different weirs and locks, I was learning every day more of the lore and legend. I was beginning to understand the importance of tradition in the morale of the staff who shepherded the great living waters with such loving care.

CHAPTER 4 — THE RIVER IN SPRING

Circumstances of employment, coupled with chill penury had, for months past, meant that I had not had a haircut. It was before long hair became fashionable, and I was beginning to weary of looking like a mid-Victorian poet, so, my first day off being a Saturday, I invested a small part of my first pay cheque in a haircut. I forget now at which tonsorial emporium the operation was performed, but I knew that I was determined to present a new, clean-cut image to the world. My smart new uniform needed an equally smart coiffure I thought, so I instructed the barber to cut it close and brush it forward in the manner of an up-and-coming group known as 'The Beatles'. The result was dramatic, friends and colleagues alike were stunned. John Grace dubbed it 'Norman style', and in truth, Bishop Odo of Bayeux had a hairstyle very similar. Peter Harvey was even less complimentary, when the following Monday he beheld me, hatless, in the office at Goring, where he was checking the week's toll money. 'What the hell have you been doing to your hair old son?' he exclaimed. Somewhat sheepishly I explained that I hoped it would last me for some time. 'Some time!' he laughed 'I should bloody well think so. That's going to last till you draw your pension!'

But persiflage bounced off me. The haircut reflected my spirits, which were rapidly recovering themselves. Jim was coping ably with ENTERPRISE, assisted by Peter and Edwina, I took the boat out on the Sunday afternoon trip, giving him a rest and at the same time glad to feel the pulsating throb of the footboard beneath me, and the firm, positive thrust of the tiller. We swung cheerily round the bends of the Kennet to Burghfield and back, such a contrasting environment to the majestic Thames. I was, for once, really looking forward to going back to work next day.

I suppose there must have been some wet and cold days that May, but in retrospect I don't remember any. That month, and the next, seem to be bathed in golden sunlight and glorious evenings, when swallows hawked low over the still reach above Goring, when the chestnut blossom was perfectly mirrored in Pangbourne Reach, when low shadows crept up the hills above Mapledurham and cricket bats thudded on leather in Kings Meadow hard by Caversham Lock. The beginning of May brought the summer assistants, these posts were temporary and were filled as and when labour became available, some lock keepers used their wives — a favourite arrangement 'up west' where jobs outside were few and locks remote, some had no road access to this date. On the other hand, some lock keepers preferred their wives to pursue their own careers and so the assistant was recruited, usually by the lock keeper himself, sometimes by the District Inspector. Universities and colleges provided some, others were literally casuals recruited from the labour exchange or elsewhere, a few were looking for a career on the river and using this as the first step on the ladder.

Harry had one assistant called Steve who was of the student category. A pleasant young man, he was 'not currently studying', a euphemism for having dropped out. The hippy fashion was still in the future, but Steve was a gentle, good-natured lad whose hair and straggly beard were the harbingers of the future. He lived, it was generally believed, in a tent near Gatehampton. The National Health Service being largely unchanged then from Aneurin Bevan's day provided free prescriptions, so Steve and his pals would obtain linctus on a prescription and bomb their brains into fragments at linctus and codeine parties. It was, I suppose, marginally better than glue or gas sniffing. In fairness, Steve never let me down by non-appearances.

Sam, at Whitchurch, soon became a fixed part of the scene. A day at Fred's was hardly work at all, for Sam had quickly weighed up the job and the lock was a light one to work. We developed various ploys to brighten up the day, not least being lock-packing, the object of which was to see how many craft could be put through at one locking. The presence of another keen river man gave more time for chat with boat users, for already traffic was showing signs of building up. One such chat gave rise to a long and valued friendship.

Among the private cruisers I had noticed a very smart wide-beam one bearing the Inland Waterways Association and Kennet & Avon Trust burgees. I was a member of both these organisations so, one lovely May Sunday morning when Sam was doing the booking, I paused to talk to the middle-aged

couple aboard. The boat's name had puzzled me, for it was
WAGON MOUND. I asked them the reason for this curious name
and the lady smiled and said 'Well, you'll really have to ask
my son, he'll tell you'. She indicated a tall, dark young man
of about my age, sitting beside the wheel house. He said 'It's
the name of a ship, which was involved in a law case relating
to limitation of damages caused by the negligence of a third
party' he paused 'sorry if it's a bit technical, but I'm a
lawyer'. I pricked up my ears at this and said 'Oh. Does that
replace the previous rule *in re Polemis*?' The trio's eyes
widened in amazement. The young man laughed 'Do you
have to know maritime law to work for the TC?' I said 'Not
really, but I used to study law'. 'Well I never' said the mother
'I've seen you before somewhere'. 'K&A Branch meetings or
rallies perhaps?' 'Ah yes, ENTERPRISE. We went on one of
your trips'.

The conversation developed until Sam coughed pointedly
from the lockside. He had opened his gate and was leaning on
the beam grinning. WAGON MOUND spluttered into life and
nosed out. The family's name was Segal and years later Chick
and Iris, the mother and father, became near neighbours of
mine at Stoke Bruerne.

In the running of the lock we were greatly assisted by
Fred's dog, Mick. Mick was a unique breed, known in the
Reading district as a 'Labradach', for he had the upperworks
of a black Labrador mounted on the undercarriage of a
Dachshund. Railway enthusiasts likened him to a 4700 class
goods engine, which had an express boiler mounted on small
wheels. Nevertheless, Mick was a stalwart hound, who loyally
enforced his master's prohibition on lockside running. Any
one who proceeded at other than a smart walk was issued a
warning bark, followed by a cannon-ball-type assault on the
legs. This caused a sad confrontation with the Chief
Navigation Officer, known as 'Old Joe'.

One fine morning the Chief's launch WINDRUSH appeared
below the lock, heralded by an advance telephone call from
Len at Mapledurham. The Chief, a dignified figure with much
gold braid on his arms and scrambled eggs on his cap, greeted
Fred gravely as his launch came into the lock in stately fashion. His boatman made fast by the steps on the office side,
Fred marched to the top gates and ceremoniously drew the top

paddles. He was just drawing the outside top one when the telephone rang. Fred unhurriedly put the beckets on the paddle wheel and began to make his way majestically towards the office. The Chief was impatient. Telephones should be answered. 'Buck up, Maggs!' he called, rushing up the steps to answer it himself. Alas, Mick saw the movement, and being no respecter of persons hurled himself at the Chief, collecting a mouthful of Old Joe's trousers en route. 'Tch! Tch!' said Fred afterwards 'The Chief carried on alarmingly about it'. The tale went the rounds, for a while Mick became quite a folk hero.

An advantage, or disadvantage depending on one's viewpoint, of Whitchurch Lock was that it was almost equidistant from three pubs. Two of these were snug little hostelries in Whitchurch village, approached by means of footpaths at the back of the mill and church; the other was The Swan, which was at the end of the weir bridge and in sight of the lock. It was quite near enough for a tray to be brought and it lay en route to my bus stop and Sam's house.

By one of those curious anomalies of the Thames, The Swan, although sited on the Berkshire bank, was in Oxfordshire. Only recently had changes in licensing hours stopped a curious Pangbourne custom. Until the year before Berkshire pubs had closed at 10.00 p.m., Oxfordshire at 10.30. This meant that the dedicated drinkers of Pangbourne would clear the pubs at closing time and stagger off down the road to continue for another half-hour. Another, more important, change had been made by Charles Spackman, the landlord, in that the cosy old Public Bar had been incorporated into a restaurant. The dispossessed drinkers had been mollified by Charles' instruction to the staff of the lounge bar, which faced onto a riverside terrace, to serve the old Public Bar regulars at Public Bar prices. Sam and his father counted as such and I was quickly accepted likewise.

Although it gave a distinctly 'up market' impression from the outside, The Swan was in fact very much a local pub. It sold excellent snacks at lunch time, and Sam and myself arranged matters so that we each had an hour, instead of the 'lunch board' time of 30 minutes.

One of the regulars was a dapper little man, who was the village bookie. He had a mordant sense of humour, coupled with an amazing fund of racing anecdotes. He always addressed Fred as 'Mr. Chubb, the lockmaster'. Sam, knowing his *Compleat Angler* recalled Walton's nomenclature 'The Chavender, or Chubb', thus Fred acquired the name 'Chavender', which mystified many.

With the onset of the flat season, the Sports Editor of one of the national papers had a bet with one of the big bookies, to the effect that it would possible to win one million pounds on a twelve-horse accumulator bet, starting with a £1 initial stake. This system he called 'the Roll Up'. Sam and myself discussed it eagerly. The prospect of riches galore was most alluring, so we decided to invest 10 shillings each in a joint Roll Up. Old Jack, the bookie, was much amused. 'My goodness, gracious. Upon my soul. Are you both determined to impoverish me? Even though I say so who shouldn't?' In spite of his protestations we laid the bet and it fell down first time. The Sports Editor was contrite. Accidents could happen, his public must have patience, next time it would go the full course. The look on Jack's face when I dropped into his office next lunchtime told me that, whilst he believed that a fool and his money were soon parted, far would it be from him to try and prevent such a divorce.

I nearly fell off the seat of the bus next morning, on my way to Mapledurham, when the Sports Press revealed that the horse had won. Sam came on the telephone first thing agog with the news, then things lay doggo until two days later, at Caversham, I read of our second success. Two days off and it came up again at Goring, and by the time I was back at Whitchurch we had clocked up four successive winners. The notional winnings now amounted to about £25 which, whilst not a million, was substantially more than a week's wages apiece. Jack looked inscrutably over his *Sporting Times* in The Swan and said nothing. Our fifth winner came in at long odds, raising the total to over £100 and the sixth took it to over £500. A week later Jack was muttering about 'laying things off' and becoming distinctly uneasy in our presence. Even Fred, who was phlegmatic about easy money began to show interest. We promised him a secure post as gamekeeper on the large landed estate we were going to buy, then, about the seventh horse the inevitable end came to our run of luck. Jack once more walked with a springy step and surveyed the

world with a confident eye. Sam and myself ruefully contem-
plated a shattered fortune and doubtless bookies all over
Britain said 'Phew!' From that day onwards betting on horses
has failed to turn me on.

Since Mapledurham was mechanised the Conservators felt
that it did not require an assistant. Certainly the work was
lighter, but as spring advanced and boat traffic began to build
up, there was little time for idleness. And it was here, in the
beautiful jewel-like setting of the rolling hills and woods that
I was abruptly jerked out of complacency and confronted by
the fact that Old Father Thames was still at heart a savage and
cruel beast who would not be trifled with.

It was about three weeks to a month after I had begun the
job. The weather was sunny but with a hint of chill in it still.
All the radials were now closed in and all the rymers and paddles were in at Whitchurch, so the deep, dragging currents of
the winter river were stilled. A small two-berthed hire cruiser
from Wargrave came upstream with a young couple aboard,
very much wrapped-up in one another's company. In the lock
they gazed lovingly at one another and seemed oblivious of
the world. They headed upstream out of the lock cut, the
young man steering, the girl sitting behind him, gazing at him
still.

The next afternoon I had put the lunch boards out and was
eating my sandwiches peacefully, when I saw the girl running
towards me along the towpath. I thought idly that perhaps she
wanted the telephone, then, suddenly, she burst into the office,
her face distraught and white, soaking wet. 'Quick! quick! my
boyfriend's in the river!' she panted. I leaped to my feet and
grasped Len's emergency weir line. 'Can he swim?' she
shook her head dumbly. 'Use the 'phone and get the ambulance!' I ordered and dashed out, seizing the hitcher as I ran.
About two hundred yards above the lock the little cruiser was
lying nose-on to the bank, I dashed towards it, looking wildly
at the water for signs and loosening my jacket and tie ready to
dive in. I saw a few yards downstream, and about ten feet out,
a coat or jacket nearly waterlogged. 'It must be his' I thought
and hurled my cap and the hitcher down on the bank as markers. I reasoned that he had fallen in off the stern of the boat,
and looked desperately for any signs. The engine was still
running and in gear so I switched it off. Silence fell. No

sound, save the distant murmuring of the weir overfall and the rustle of willow leaves; no sign on the surface of the water, which was slightly rippled by the breeze. I slowly walked back to where I had dropped the cap and hitcher. The floating coat had disappeared. I prodded the depths with the hitcher, but the water was so deep against the bank that I could only bottom it for a few feet out. Despondently I turned back to the boat and, remembering my forensic training, merely secured her fore and aft with her ryepecks. The police would certainly want to know her exact position. I found a branch which I drove into the bank where my markers had been, and returned to the lock.

Len was out for the day, I was completely alone, save for a distressed, soaked and sobbing girl. I made her tea, made her take off her wet things — at which I chivalrously went outside, turned on the electric fire and sat her down in a chair with a blanket and overcoat round her. She could hardly speak, but had managed to telephone for an ambulance. In this, the girl on the manual Pangbourne exchange had been most helpful. I told her that I would have to call the Police and, the incident being on the Berkshire bank, rang Pangbourne Police Station.

Fortunately no boats came downstream, I opened the bottom gates and let a few upstream boats in but refrained from letting them any further, lest their wash, or the draw from the paddles disturbed anything. Agonisingly slowly the minutes crept past, then the ambulance arrived, followed by a police car with a sergeant and a constable.

The girl was taken away by the ambulance men, I made a statement and then rang Fred asking him to stop downstream traffic until the frogmen had been. The policemen busied themselves about the boat with notebooks and tape measures. They came back to the office. 'Reckon 'e's a goner all right' said the sergeant matter-of-factly. The constable regarded the girl's lacy underwear, still drying by the electric fire. 'If you ask me, they was out for summat more than fishing. Them little ole' drawers ain't the sort as my missus 'ud wear when she comes fishin' wi me'. 'You're a dirty ole man' said the sergeant, 'but you could be right'.

Later on that afternoon the frogmen came. The policemen had gone to the hospital to take a statement from the girl, they came back just as the frogmen retrieved a sodden, bulky bundle from the river. I was standing by the top gate and they signalled thumbs-up sign that traffic could restart.

There were a few, shocked holidaymakers on cruisers waiting in the lock. Suddenly the fun had gone out of the Thames. I filled the lock quickly and rang Fred, telling him all was clear.

A little later the policemen came back and told me the whole story, which they had pieced together. It was a London couple who had stolen a few days together, hoping to marry later that year. He was a non-swimmer and had no life-jacket. As they came down the reach to Mapledurham, she had tried to fold up the cockpit canopy because the weather had turned sunny. He had come to help, missed his footing and plunged straight out of sight. In desperation she took the wheel, never having steered before, turned towards the bank and leaped for the bank, missing her footing as she did so. It seemed he had fallen in some yards upstream of where the boat came to rest, but he had drifted downstream. 'You know where you put that stake, mate?' asked one of the frogmen cheerily. I nodded. 'You were dead right. That's where we found him. Only took us a minute or two. Ten foot out, in fifteen feet of water'. Suddenly the adrenalin, which had been keeping me going all afternoon, failed. The awful realisation of what I had not done swept over me, I sank my head in my hands and groaned.

The policemen and frogmen were more than kind. They told me that I had nothing with which to reproach myself, that nobody could have done more. But, to this day, that floating bundle haunts me. Perhaps, had I jumped in and pulled it ashore, he might have lived. It was the second tragedy that had struck near me on the water inside six months. The other concerned a boatman's wife on the Grand Union Canal. It was not the last but since those days I have always set my face against trifling with the water. I firmly believe that it is fine to boat on or be beside, but if people must get in water then let it be on a bathing beach or a swimming pool. Rivers and canals are not easily mocked.

I was somewhat cheered, a few days later, when something occurred which, firstly, took my mind off this tragedy and, secondly, was the cause of a very profound change in my life.

I received a telephone call one evening from Denys

Hutchings, the Secretary of the Kennet & Avon Canal Trust.
Hutch was an old friend and fellow campaigner and he was as
nearly excited over the telephone as it was possible for his
unflappable nature to be. He told me that Lionel Munk, the
Trust's chairman, who ran a large fleet of hire cruisers based
on the canals and Thames, had donated the Trust a spoon-
dredger. This was an antique device now rendered obsolete by
virtue of British Waterways Board's purchase of hydraulic
dredgers. However, the River Kennet had not been dredged
for many years, nor was it likely to be in the foreseeable
future; but if the Reading Branch cared to use the spoon-
dredger, a small amount could be done. So far, so good, I
thought, but where do I come in? Hutch was coming to that.
The dredger presently lay at Thrupp, on the Oxford Canal.
Would we send ENTERPRISE up to fetch it? Captain Munk
would pay the bill if it were not too unreasonable. I swiftly
gave him a price and next day he telephoned acceptance. I
was delighted at this unexpected job, but Jim was even more
so. He was used to the Kennet by now and his soul craved for
more adventure. So we laid our plans. At the end of the first
week in June I had two days off on a Sunday and Monday.
These were usually ENTERPRISE'S quietest days, indeed we
normally regarded Monday as a 'dead day'. Jim, with Pete's
assistance, would take ENTERPRISE off after the Saturday public trip and bring her round to the Thames. I would see her
through Caversham Lock and join them later that evening
above Whitchurch. Fred would arrange an overnight mooring
for us. Next day we would run upstream and go up the canal
to Thrupp, wind round and on the Monday come back with
the dredger, at least as far as Goring, for I had to be on duty
there on Tuesday morning.

Thus the plan. I was elated at the thought of once again
doing some 'real' boating, especially involving the Thames,
so I was even more delighted, when at about 6 o'clock on a
golden June evening I saw ENTERPRISE'S brass-rimmed chimney and exhaust stack slipping along the meadows below
Caversham with, a few feet behind them, the heads and shoulders of Jim and Pete. A few minutes later she swung round
the bend into full view, her Armstrong-Siddeley Merganser
throbbing cheerfully. Dick Knightley came over from his ministrations to a motor car on the lock side. 'She looks tiddley,

Dave' he commented, a compliment indeed from an ex-Chief Petty Officer. 'It'd be a shame for you to have to go up to Fred's by bus tonight'. 'Well, the job is the job' I said 'but I envy them this evening'. He grinned sympathetically. 'I know you do you young bugger. Go on, I'm not going to be going anywhere till sunset and I've got my assistant to help look after things — there's not much about'.

I thanked him but he cut me short. 'Come off it. One day I'll want you to do me a favour'. So, I paid myself a tug toll, issued myself a ticket and we set off through a perfect late spring evening. The wide reach by the Conservancy yard was well-populated with boats, people sat in camp chairs on the Islands above, tennis plunked in the grass courts, the steamer crews waved to us from Salters' moorings below Caversham bridge. All along the Thames Promenade on one side and the Warren on the other, the people of Reading enjoyed their greatest natural asset. Yet it was surprising how little this amenity was used, or appreciated. True, there were perhaps several hundred people about, but Reading, even then, had a population in excess of a hundred and twenty thousand. The beautifully kept parks of Kings Meadow, Caversham Meadow, Caversham Court and Thames Promenade were seemingly deserted, for they could have comfortably accommodated many times the number or users.

Just opposite the imposing residence of the Chairman of Reading Football Club, a wealthy business man who was a great river lover, the immaculately groomed Thames Promenade ended and abruptly the towpath reverted to rushes and reeds. Here swans were raising cygnets, and fleets of yellow mallard chicks twittered behind their stately, quacking, mothers. Scours Lane and Norcot Deeps, where local legend claimed the river was bottomless, passed by, with the railway high above us on a brick-faced retaining wall. Already the Oxfordshire bank was becoming rural, on the Berkshire side were the estates and trolley buses of suburban Tilehurst, until, beyond the old Roebuck ferry house, the towpath changed sides for a short way and the river swung away from the railway, past the bungalows of Dodge City towards the mellow ochre gables and twisted brick chimney stacks of Mapledurham House.

Through the islands, we bore round across the weir outfall

towards Mapledurham Lock, to be greeted by a cheerful Len. Kath, his wife, was working the controls while Len gardened. Already roses were beginning to bloom in the lock garden, the evening was heavy with their scent mixed with mown grass, hawthorn and phlox. It seemed impossible that only days ago such a grim tragedy had overlain this lovely spot.

Then it was away again, up the majestic reach to Pangbourne. Placid cows and courting couples watched us pass impassively, under the white iron toll bridge we slipped, getting waved straight into Whitchurch Lock by Fred and Sam. Above the lock we slipped quietly to a mooring outside The Swan. The weir was quite shut in and fly fishers were casting from a boat below in the weir pool. We slid across a glassy surface and tied snugly to the terrace of the pub. It had been a perfect evening's run marred only by a leaking exhaust manifold, which blew back smoke into the steerer's face. Later, Fred and Sam joined us in the bar, whose French windows were wide open, allowing the customers to spill onto the terrace. There was a party of girls at one end, very nattily dressed. Sam knew one of them, who told him that they had been to a wedding that afternoon. A tall, slim auburn-haired girl with hazel eyes was in the party, being squired by another friend of Sam's. Inevitably we joined the party, which proved to be a merry one. Closing time came and we suggested coffee on the boat, this idea being taken up enthusiastically by Fred and the girls as well as half the patrons of the bar.

Once aboard ENTERPRISE someone produced a bottle or two, then someone else suggested a cruise. Fortunately ENTERPRISE possessed navigation lights, so off we set up the reach. There was a full moon in a clear spring sky, a slight mist rose off the water, the tall trees along Pangbourne Reach stood silent and motionless as we passed. Just below Hartslock Island we ran into a bank of fog so, edging towards the Oxfordshire bank on tick-over, I swung the tiller over and turned to the left. A white wall of vapour rose in front and then cleared to show the green paintwork of a moored Maid Line cruiser dead ahead. The thought flashed through my mind that Lionel Munk would be exceedingly displeased were I to ram one of his cruisers amidships at midnight when en route to perform a service for him, and with a boat load of Conservancy personnel at that. Fortunately the current was swinging the fore end, and holding the tiller over the opposite way and going full astern, ENTERPRISE obediently swung away from danger. Low whistles arose from various parts of the boat.

I decided that my turn had come to chat up the girls. I handed the tiller over to Jim and went below. Alas, they seemed to be unimpressed by a dashing boatman and were more interested in other male members of the party. Abashed I returned to the cabin where grave damage was being done to the contents of bottles.

At length we returned to The Swan mooring whence the girls and Pete departed by taxi for Reading, the slim auburn-haired girl still being escorted, to my chagrin, by the same friend of Sam's. Before they left Fred invited them all to a party in three weeks' time. Jim and myself barely had the strength to tidy the boat up before collapsing in bed.

In spite of everything we were up by eight next morning finding, to our amazement, a Sunday paper, courtesy of The Swan's management stuck in the cabin slide. We set off into the still sunlight, already the sun felt warm and the few mist patches were being boiled away. The water was glassy smooth reflecting the trees and hills, the broad herring-bone vee of our wake sent glittering reflections behind us. A scent of coffee and frying bacon came from the cabin where Jim was ministering to the galley cooker. Up to Hartslock Island we forged, the Maid Line cruiser still laid, curtained, against the bank. As we passed, a bleary-eyed pyjama-clad figure flung back the wheelhouse canvasses and waved, blissfully unaware of how close to disaster he had been during the night.

Gatehampton viaduct's twin arches were perfectly reflected in the still morning, the white stucco of the Grotto had its twin on the river surface, nestling amid the green woodlands on the Berkshire bank. Harry was just coming on duty as we nosed up to Goring Lock. We filled the lock for him and I once more issued my own blue tug ticket, then we were away, out of my home waters, up the short willow-fringed reach to Cleeve. Cyril French, the lock keeper, had been tipped off by Harry that we were about, so there was little delay.

So it went on all morning. Wallingford lay in deceptive-looking somnolence, its many-arched bridge and classical spire looking down on us as we forged upstream. By Benson Lock we began to meet a few holiday boats, but little delayed us up through Days, Clifton, Culham and Abingdon.

The lock keeper at Abingdon saw us through and hung out his lunch boards behind us, so I was not surprised, as we beat up the long straight below Sandford Lock to see the buff coloured board dangling from the bottom gate.

Sandford Lock was a beastly place to have to wait below in those days. The weir outfall came in from the left, while to the right was an overfall from the Mill. The lay-by was marked by a line of tall white posts with no means of getting ashore to work the lock. Accordingly I slowly nudged up to the vee of the gates, observing meanwhile that the red paddle rod was up, indicating an empty lock. Jim went up to the fore end with a view to climbing up the framework, a technique used at Fobney and Southcote when the gates were closed against upstream boats, but unusual on the Thames to say the least. Now Jim, excellent company and keen boatman that he was, was not the most beautiful of nature's creations. He had swarthy, angular features, crowned with an unruly mop of curly hair, and his affable and gentle nature was well concealed by the appearance of a desperado such as might have robbed a galleon on the Spanish Main. I watched him swing, ape-like, up the gate, clutched in and gently drove the gates open, canal-style.

There came a fearful yell from the depths of the chamber (and Sandford is the deepest lock on the Thames) as ENTER-PRISE thrust herself in. I hastily went into neutral and ran forward to see Ron, the lock keeper, and his assistant shinning up the side chains from a dinghy. They had been scrubbing down the lock walls with caustic soda in the gate recess when the huge bottom gate had burst in on them and they had been confronted by a fearsome face which needed but a parrot and an eye patch, which suddenly appeared at catwalk level.

Ron had once been lock keeper at Blakes on the Kennet, and as such was an old friend, but he was also rather excitable. It took all my powers of diplomacy to calm him down, though his assistant saw the comical side of things.

Apart from this slight misfortune, nothing else marred our journey upstream. The lock keeper at Osney was having his day off and the lock was manned by another ex-canal boatman, Stephen Woolford, who had until recently operated a horse-drawn trip boat on the Oxford Canal. Stephen was delighted to see something painted in the cheerful colours of the canal, rather than the everlasting white, mahogany, blue or green of the river.

Above Kings Lock we made a sharp turn right, into the weir stream, soon followed by a sharp left turn into Wolvercote Mill Stream. Jim's eyes opened as we sped down this narrow, twisting, but deep channel to the spot where Duke's Cut branched off to the left. Almost immediately our speed dropped as we entered the shallow backwater which connects the Oxford Canal to the Upper Thames. There is another connection lower down in the City of Oxford, I had come that way three months back, when the River was high, but for single boats the Duke's Cut was quicker in those days, especially since there was a railway swing bridge over the lower connection, and this bridge sometimes took a long time to negotiate. I have always liked the section through Medley and Godstow, across Port Meadows because the character of the Thames changes above Oxford. This part is the first section of 'up West', when the river becomes wilder, lonelier and less sophisticated.

The Duke's Cut is so called because it was built privately, by the Duke of Marlborough, whose seat is at nearby Blenheim Palace. It was intended to shorten the distance for traffic going to and from 'up West' and the Oxford Canal and to act as an alternative route for downstream traffic avoiding the old flash locks at Kings and Medley. It has one lock, a shallow regulating one under a railway bridge, and it was Jim's first narrow lock. His eyes, already wide, nearly started forth from his head at the sight of this tiny construction into which ENTERPRISE just fitted.

A drop of a few inches in Duke's Cut Lock led to the junction with the main canal and an immediate rise in Duke's Lock just beyond. Inside the space of a quarter mile the atmosphere had changed completely. Beside the lock was a neat cottage, far more redolent of the Midlands than of the Thames valley in its vernacular style: the lock with its neat, utilitarian paddlegear, black and white gates, mossy brick sides and chipped concrete coping was not only a different size, but from a different world. The willow-fringed levels and ever-present hills of the Thames countryside were gone. Ahead the canal lay through fields and hedges like a country lane which had been flooded.

At the same time our speed dropped appreciably. It was foolish to go ranting along on full throttle for the stern would soon settle on the canal bed, a breaking wave would develop along the banks and fuel would be burned needlessly. All that was required was about half throttle, and we gently plodded beneath the Woodstock Road, up to Kidlington Green Lock where the Oxfordshire meadows were invaded by new bungalows, outliers of what the inhabitants proudly referred to as 'England's biggest village'. Above the lock houses came closer although the canal itself lay quietly under branching trees just as I remembered it from early boyhood, when a beloved aunt with whom I sometimes stayed nearby, used to take me for walks beside it, little dreaming of the seeds she was sowing and nuturing.

Since the canal builders had had to contend with occasional outcrops of limestone locally, several of the bridges were built of this greyish rock. One such, Sandy Lane Bridge, carrying a quiet road to Yarnton, had slumped somewhat with the years. The arch was slightly distorted and at a queer angle.

Beyond Roundham Lock, the last one in our journey, we encountered our quarry, an ancient iron spoon dredger, tied up on the outside bank. The fore end of this craft had a stempost almost semi-circular in elevation, the hold was partially filled with hoggin, the cabin was locked and displayed little sign of expecting our arrival. Presumably the tiller was in the cabin, for none was visible on the weatherbeaten ramshead and rudder which swung, creaking, as we passed. Half way along the hold was mounted a stout wooden king post, to which was attached a long-handled scoop, capable of holding two or three hundredweight (100-150 kg) of muck, a winch forrard and a working platform astern completed this latest piece of Georgian technology. Of officials or other British Waterways employees there was no sign.

However, we had to go on another mile or so, to Thrupp before we would be able to wind the boat round ready for our return, so on we plodded. By now it was tea time, people were coming home from their Sunday afternoon's activities, amongst them a Company's man (British Waterways employee) whom I recognised as Jack Skinner, a one-time boatman, who was leaning on his garden gate at Langford Lane, as we drew near. I slowed down to talk to him and he told me that the gang were expecting me tomorrow morning. I wondered why we needed a gang just to hand over an ancient dredger, and he enlightened me. 'You'll never get the jib through Sandy Lane Bridge, so we've got to take it down for you'.

I was glad to hear this, for the problem of the low arch had been exercising my mind ever since seeing the dredger. Also there were the even lower girders of Bridge Street, Reading, to consider, though here we could drop the water level if necessary. I told him that we would be down after breakfast and motored on. As we approached the bridge by The Britannia (now The Jolly Boatman) I beheld a bulky figure, clad in white overalls and donkey jacket, lurking in the bridgehole. 'Ullo coz' said Peter, stepping aboard as we passed through 'What's been keeping you?'. Considering that we had parted early that morning some forty miles or so away, I resisted the temptation to crown him with a windlass. In point of fact I was very glad to see him, because we had only done the easy part until then. The hard slog, with a novice crew, was yet to come.

Thrupp hamlet, a row of stone cottages facing the canal across a country lane, appeared. We had to pass by, go under the drawbridge at the end of the straight and turn round in the wide hole just beyond. Jim hoisted the drawbridge and we nosed through, ready to turn on the right angled bend which lay by the side of the canal maintenance yard. At the noise of our engine a cheery, red-faced countryman came out of the yard. He was Aubrey Jones the section inspector who had known the canal all his life. Although it was a Sunday evening, Aubrey, typically was pottering about in the yard, so most fortuitously I was able to confirm the arrangements already made with Jack Skinner.

After winding, we slipped back through the drawbridge and found a good, deep mooring right outside The Boat. Here the differences between the canal and river worlds were again apparent. The talk and the gossip was of the canal and canal people, as one with a foot in both camps, I realised with a pang that I still missed the canal life, and hankered after it.

By eight o'clock next morning we were off, and down to Roundham Lock in time to surprise the Waterways gang. A knot of men, including Aubrey Jones and Jack Skinner and a cheerful little shop-steward called Rex, were waiting. We locked ENTERPRISE through, then came back to help.

The dredger was bow-hauled into the lock and brought down tight onto the single bottom gate. Two stout wooden baulks were laid across the gunwales of the boat, projecting above the locksides and resting either side of the king post. Once all was positioned to the satisfaction of Aubrey, Jack and Rex, a paddle was carefully drawn, and the dredger began to sink down. Soon the baulks were resting on the copings and the king post, caught between them, began to be lifted up from its mounting. When the lock was about two thirds empty, Aubrey called 'Whoa up!' The paddles were closed in and the dredger pulled gently back from under the hanging king post until her stern rested against the top sill, where Jack secured it with a boatman's hitch round the top mitre post. Then, very gently, the lock was refilled and the dredger rose again with the king post now a couple of feet ahead of its mounting. As the heavy post rose of course it came off the baulks, but a steadying rope had been attached to it. As two men took out the supporting baulks, the rest of us, four each side of the lock, took the strain. Once the baulks were removed, we gently lowered the post until it rested against a cross beam.

The rope was detached, the lock emptied once more. Aubrey gave me the cabin key. I extracted the tiller, and we were ready to go. It was only just after 9 a.m., the Thames would only now be waking up!

Perhaps this operation might seem pedestrian and commonplace, but to me it was beautiful in its simplicity, in its application of scientific principles by ordinary working men, in the sheer competence with which they set about a task which might well have baffled people with far more impressive technical qualifications. In their confident use of natural forces in handling a heavy weight they were the true heirs of those unknown masters who have left their mark on the English landscape ever since Stonehenge was raised.

We bade the gang farewell and set off for home. To start with I put the dredger on a short line, rather than pull her close-hauled on cross straps, for she had possibly ten tons of ballast in her, and so would have been a heavy drag. We gingerly passed under Sandy Lane Bridge. Pete steering the dredger, and, apart from the slow-going, had little trouble back to Duke's Cut, although the three locks had, of course, to be worked twice over.

By noon we were heading back up the Wolvercote Mill stream, then it was out into the weir stream, catch the two boats abreast heading upstream, then swing hard left into the lock cut.

The two boats just fitted into Kings Lock, I decided to remain abreast and chance the hairpin bends from there to Godstow. Fortunately we met no upstream boats although Jim was stationed at the fore-end with our ex-army bugle to warn any oncomers. We swept round the turns in fine style and shot the downstream arch of Godstow Bridge with room to spare.

Godstow Lock had once been kept by Len from Mapledurham. The lock keeper had taken over from him, and was an old friend of his, so goodwill messages were taken aboard. Like all the Thames locks, Godstow was looking its best, for the lock garden inspection was not far off. Wallflowers, snapdragons, phlox, and aubretia flowered in profusion, making a bright splash against the mellow old walls of the bridge and nearby priory. Across Port Meadow the towers and spires of Oxford rose in welcome, sunlight glinting off green copper and leaden plates. I made a mental roll call as we swept down the magnificent wide reach towards Medley. The Radcliffe Observatory, St. Mary's, Magdalen Tower, All Souls, the Radcliffe Camera, the Sheldonian, Tom Tower, there they all were, in stately huddle against a sky of white, woolly cumulus.

As the day wore on, the fine weather of the last few days was replaced by overcast, until just above Abingdon Lock a drizzle began. We pulled on oilskins, but the contrast with the previous pleasant conditions had us all shivering and feeling glum. It was alright for the steerer, because the warmth of the air-cooled engine wafted up about one's knees. By shutting the back doors and the skylight, one could keep pleasantly warm, if not dry, but for the others there was nothing else for it but to take refuge in the motor boat's cabin, which was cold and cheerless without a fire. All our coal had long since been burned and the gas cylinder supplying the galley stove obliged us by running out. Thus we faced a gloomy prospect of no hot drinks or warmth until at least Benson, where we could replenish our gas.

With these thoughts in mind we came into Culham Cut, to be met with a sight that all canal boatmen recognised as a gift of the Gods. There, about 200 yards above the lock lay a Conservancy steam dredger, her fires banked and her crew just knocking off for the night, a great pile of coal lying in a barge nearby. As luck would have it, several boats were waiting ahead of us in the lock layby, so for once I did not claim commercial priority, but held back alongside the dredger while a rummage crew, armed with buckets boarded her. Less than two minutes sufficed to replace stocks, and before the lock had refilled I had chopped up some kindling and applied a match to an oily rag in the stove. Smoke poured out of the chimney and Peter was bidden to break up some lumps, He reported, with a frown, 'They ain't half some big lumps coz, and bloomin' hard too'. The coal was indeed in massive, grainy lumps, very unlike the Coventry nuts used by British Waterways steam dredgers. A blow with the lump hammer sent splinters everywhere, but eventually some small lumps were obtained and fed onto the stove.

The lock keeper had evidently observed our activities from afar and was of a mind to report us, until he recalled that I was a fellow servant of the Conservators at which he chuckled long and loud and suggested that we go back and help ourselves further.

Down the long reach by Appleford I wrestled with the draught, poked and cursed, but the coal was curiously unwilling to catch. A further anointing of raw diesel dripped down the chimney, caused a spectacular eruption which blew the stove lid across the cabin and misted up Peter's spectacles, but gradually a steady crackling from within told me that it was beginning to catch.

Below Clifton Hamden the drizzle eased and we went topsides to straighten ropes and clean up generally, closing the cabin doors and slide. It was not until we had passed Days that I thought that I had better undo the gas bottle ready for a quick change and went inside for the gas spanner. The stove was pulsating and glowing cherry red in places, the heat blasted out of the doors at me and with it a steamy vapour from damp clothes which had been hung up. The coal was of course, best Welsh steam coal — no half measures for the Thames Conservancy and was capable of steaming not only a humble dredger but a Dreadnought at Jutland or the Cheltenham Flyer. Fortunately the stove was mounted on a fireproof base and the panels were well-insulated, but I was able to boil a kettle in about two minutes on the hob plate.

Although the rain had stopped, it was an overcast evening and traffic was light, most hire cruisers were already tying up for the night. Still we forged on downstream on the light summer current. Sunset was about 9.15 p.m. that day, so after Benson Lock I knew we would have lock keepers on duty for another three hours, and lock keepers that I knew at that. In spite of the heavy dredger abreast of us, ENTERPRISE was shoving downstream at over four miles per hour. Nearly 8 o'clock at Goring, 'in 13 hours time', I thought, 'I shall be on duty here', and Harry had the lock ready for us. Fred's white cap showed on Pangbourne Weir as we ran down the reach from Hartslock and Jim opened the bottom gates while Fred telephoned Len to leave the power on and a window open. Sunset came as we ran down the long reach past Hardwick. The tower of Mapledurham Church with the clustering chimneys of the great Elizabethan house were just visible among the trees and Len, pottering in the lock garden in the afterglow, let us through into the long reach down to Caversham. I put the lights on as we left Mapledurham Lock, we picked our way through the islands in the twilight before night finally fell down Norcot Scours. We were all familiar with the waters from here on, keeping going with frequent hot drinks, and taking turns to steer. Nobody wanted to go below as we approached the myriad lights of Reading.

In the darkness of Caversham Lock Cut, I ran the fore ends up to the catwalk of the top gates. Dick could not have left them open for us because a public footpath crossed them. Under the trees, by the steps below, I could see several cruisers tied for the night. When we opened the bottom gates my headlight shone forth illuminating them. Of course we had to close in behind us, so I lay in the lock tail while the crew closed the gates and wound down the paddles. The engine echoed deafeningly off the concrete walls, I swung the boats away from the moored boats, from the cabin of which white, startled faces peered, then we were clear, into the weir stream and racing down for Kennet Mouth. A wide swing under Horseshoe Bridge then speed dropped as ENTERPRISE began to stem the Kennet current. Up through Blakes, past sleeping houses we went, finally tying at High Bridge Wharf just before midnight. Peter was due at work at 7.30 a.m., Jim had a booked trip at 2.30 p.m., and I had to be at Goring by 9 a.m. Wearily I threw my bike ashore and pedalled home.

I was not in the most merry condition when I greeted Harry next morning. He was astounded to see me, and so my stock rose high with him. About midday a hire cruiser came upstream. As he rose in the lock I got chatting to the skipper. I asked if he was enjoying his holiday. 'We were' he said 'but we had a most disturbed night. Some mad hooligans came out of Caversham Lock at midnight with two great barges and nearly rammed us'.

I solemnly agreed that such behaviour should be reported to the Conservators.

Chapter 5 — STEAMERS

Ever since Whitsun (we kept religious holidays then, not the secular 'Late Spring Bank Holiday'), steamers had been a feature of the Thames scene. To be precise most were now diesel-powered, but there were two real steamers left in regular service.

Steam on the Upper Thames antedated the coming of steam railways to the Thames valley by a comfortable margin. The first reference I have come across is of a 'steam barge' passing through the Kennet & Avon Canal en route from London to Bristol in 1816. Presumably this was either a stern wheeler or one with a paddle wheel operating within the hull, for side-wheelers are not really suitable for the confines of canals. By the 1840s an attempt had been made to establish regular commercial navigation between London and Oxford using steam tugs fitted with electric lamps 'on the Staite and Petrie principle' for night work. In the 1870s and 80s steam engines began to be installed in pleasure launches and on the river of *Three Men in a Boat* the steam launch was a common spectacle.

Salter Brothers of Oxford began a service from Oxford to Kingston in the late 19th century, with the boats taking two days for the voyage, including an overnight stop at Henley. This service was given a boost by the Second World War when it provided a rare opportunity for Londoners and others to escape the bombing and other toils of wartime for a day or two. The then Great Western Railway encouraged this by offering combined rail and steamer tickets. GW stations in my early youth all had timetables prominently displayed which were headed 'Salters Steamers Every Day' and which carried a photograph of a steamer under the majestic shadow of Cliveden Woods. It was always a sign of summer when these began to go up in booking offices and on prominent places in riverside towns. Even at the time of which I am writing, Reading General Station had, in the subway a typical ex-GW cast iron notice board, complete with pointing finger, which said 'To the River and Salters Steamers'.

Unhappily, changing times since the 1940s were beginning to have their effect on the steamer service. The most obvious of these changes was in the propulsion. In my childhood during and after the Second World War, petrol rationing swept the private and hire cruiser off the water and gave steam a new lease of life. The steamers were the largest and most prestigious craft on the whole river upstream of Kingston-upon-Thames. They varied in length from about 70 feet up to 100 or so, this being the shortest length of lock chamber below Oxford (they never penetrated upstream because of the low headroom at Osney Bridge). The hulls were painted glossy black with green boot-topping at waterline, the name in bold white capitals stood out on either side of the bow and was painted again under the long overhang of the counter along with the magic word 'London' as Port of Registry. The name was almost impossible for anyone to read unless they were either in the water or crouched on a lockside, but nevertheless it imparted an air of the great wide oceans beyond. I was terribly disappointed to learn that they did not operate on salt water because of the deleterious effect of that liquid on their boilers.

At the stern was a small open deck sometimes covered by a green awning, above the counter, then came a mahogany varnished cabin extending to nearly amidships. This contained the saloon where stolid ladies dispensed tea from steaming urns; unkind people said that they boiled up river water or else drew it off the boat's boiler. The saloon was lined with stodgy, shiny bench seats, presumably stuffed with horsehair and at the foreward end were Gentlemen's and Ladies' lavatories containing, wonder of wonders, flushing WCs. These were a source of awed speculations among my boyhood friends, who all wanted to know where 'it' all went. ('Did it really go in the river?' 'Yeugh! I'm not swimming there again,' and so forth.) In fact, the method was quite advanced, they used cess tanks, which were sucked out from time to time, a malodorous operation if one inadvertently got down wind of the machine.

A flight of steps led upwards to the deck from the front of the cabin, while the cabin roof, railed round, contained rows of slatted wooden seats. The aspect was not unlike the upstairs of an open-topped tramcar, though wider. Some of the seats were even reversible, as on a tramcar, so as to accommodate parties, and something akin to 'modesty screens' along the rails prevented naughty males from glimpsing the nether regions of ladies. This was not always effective, for a lasting war-time memory is of a young woman ascending the steps and being caught in an updraught. It was not so much the sight of RAF blue bloomers which aroused the interest of the several boys down below, but the fact that she had painted her legs tan, with a pencil line down the back (for stockings were of the greatest rarity at that time) and the artwork ended some distance short of the knicker line, leaving a white gap. My grandmother, who was present, sternly bade me avert my eyes from this unseemly spectacle.

Along the upper deck rails were numbers of life rings, lettered 'Salter Bros. Oxford', a painted board stating that passengers could join or alight at locks, and the end of a heavy manilla rope, which drooped from there to a large brass cleat amidships on each side. Outboard of the cabin windows, along the top of the hull, was a narrow catwalk. Immediately in front of the cabin was the engine room skylight, not unlike a giant cucumber frame. Below this lay the engine, a multi-cylindered affair, frequently bearing the name of 'Sissons, Gloucester'. This seemed to me as a child to be a most onomatopoeic name for a steamer's engine. The engines were always spotlessly kept, most engine-rooms in those days made an operating theatre seem grubby by comparison. Brasswork and copper pipes gleamed, steel plates and rods glistened, the steam pipes, lagged in red or white set off the green paint and mahogany lagging of the cylinders. Above the engineer's head was the telegraph with its indicator showing such instructions as 'Full Ahead', 'Half Ahead', 'Slow Ahead' and 'Finished with Engine'. It was operated by the captain, and made thrilling bell sounds when it worked. At the forrard end of the engine room was the boiler and fire doors, with bunkers either side, served by circular iron manholes in the decks. The water level gauges either side, the pressure gauge in the centre, the clanging black fire door and white lagging were all spotless, and from this ensemble rose the most delightful smell of warm oil, steam coal smoke and Thames steam. This latter was quite different from railway steam, it had a tang not unlike boiling rice.

Next came the funnel, the most distinctive feature of a highly distinctive craft. This was always painted white and,

although there were other firms which operated steamers on
the Thames besides Salter Brothers, this was a universal practice. However, a distinction could be made in the topping rim.
On some it was plain white, some black, some green and on
some it was polished brass, the latter gracing SONNING when
captained by Jock Izzard. In winter the boats were all laid up
below Folly Bridge, Oxford and their funnels removed until
spring. I remember seeing them from the top deck of the
Abingdon bus. standing on their ends and leaning against the
wall of the Folly Bridge yard looking like gigantic cigarettes.

These funnels were hinged with a counterweight. A rope
was attached to an eye towards the top, which enabled the
crew to pull it down so as to pass under low bridges. When
this happened, the exhaust steam would condense and form a
steamy cloud which wafted back over the upper deck and lin-
gered behind after the boat had gone through. The exhaust
steam passed through a feedwater heater before reaching the
atmosphere, this, combined with the fact that many engines
were compounds, with up to three cylinders on the biggest
boats, meant that there was no explosive chuff! chuff! such as
one heard from steam rollers or traction engines, or most
noticeably, from railway locomotives. Indeed river steamers
were very quiet and well behaved compared with steam
power ashore. Roaring safety valves and gunshot exhausts
might well accompany a train journey, but the loudest sound
made was a mellow 'hoo-ooot' uttered by the big brass steam
whistle at the base of the funnel and controlled by the captain.

This worthy was mounted on a dais just ahead of the funnel,
to one side being the whistle chain, to the other the pedestal of
the engine-room telegraph, and in front the great mahogany
and brass wheel. In my youth the captain frequently wore a
reefer jacket and naval cap and was a grand personage indeed.
Jock Izzard always wore a white collar and navy tie with a
gold pin and was a man much respected in Abingdon and
Oxford, his wife was the manageress of Salters' café by
Abingdon Bridge and used to favour me with the odd straw-
berry ice in a thick glass dish when I made youthful excursions
on the boats.

The captain was separated from the public by a green canvas dodger which enclosed three sides of the steering position.
In front of him lay the forrard deck, with more wooden-slatted

seats beneath a green canvas awning, supported on an iron frame and held out by battens. A central hatch led to the crew's quarters, and in the very bows was a small triangular deck with another brass cleat to which was attached the heavy manilla fore-line, always cheesed down in a Flemish coil.

In later years I realised that the general arrangement of these steamers was in direct descent from the stately oared barges of mediaeval London; pictures by Canaletto and preserved craft show a very similar arrangement, less the machinery.

By the 1950s, steam was becoming *passé* for such craft. The soaring price of coal, labour and boiler inspections were inexorably forcing the operators to change over to the less labour-intensive and more economically run diesel engine. This was at the expense of quiet and smell, for the noise of the multi-cylinder diesels and the stench of their exhausts was a decided minus point. At the same time the wages paid could no longer attract the skippers and crew of the old sort, for Salters were in direct competition on the labour market with the car factories at Cowley and Abingdon as well as the burgeoning light industries of the lower part of the valley. A few older men stuck with the jobs, but increasingly the crews were recruited from labour exchange casuals and redundant merchant navy men. A few of these had a deeper understanding of the river and its ways, but far too often they were of the 'cowboy' persuasion whose navigation was hit or miss. Lock gates, other craft, landing stages, even bridge piers were frequently on the receiving end of steamers, while complaints of excessive wash increased.

Some time in the mid-fifties, Salters took over Cawstons of Reading, who had several steamers, all wooden, notably QUEEN OF THE THAMES and MAJESTIC. The QUEEN was notable for being strengthened by a longitudinal girder, which ran right through the saloon. This was, apparently, part of the Great Western's Appleford Bridge, replaced in the 1920s. Jack James, who became the first caretaker of the British Waterways Museum at Stoke Bruerne, carried this from Appleford to Caversham by horse-drawn narrow boat. These craft carried a different livery of white hulls with red lettering and boot-topping, which was gradually applied to the rest of the fleet from then onwards.

The Oxford-Kingston service began to suffer as river traffic
increased and relations with the navigation staff soured. In my
youth there were two scheduled runs each day in either direction. The morning steamers worked to Henley, stopping for
lunch at Wallingford or Windsor, the afternoon ones went as
far as the lunch time stop and stayed there overnight, whilst
other steamers worked Between Wallingford and Windsor,
taking a whole day. Thus it was that as a boy I could catch a
downstream steamer from Abingdon Bridge at 4.00 p.m. and
alight at Culham Lock in time to catch the upstream boat from
Henley, which got me back to Abingdon about 5.00 p.m. The
two steamers used to meet in the reach between Culham and
Appleford. If Jock Izzard was on with SONNING, I was allowed
to pull the funnel down for Abingdon Bridge and the two
wooden bridges in Culham Cut (there were two in those days,
there's only one now). It was rumoured by lock keepers in the
sixties, but I cannot vouch for the truth of this, that Salters
used to contribute handsomely to the lock keepers' annual
dinner, which assisted their punctuality. However, as river
traffic began to increase in the 1950s, the prospect of congestion at locks grew and schedules began to go by the board.
Also the public were perhaps becoming more sophisticated in
their amusements, more people had cars, less people were
using the buses and trains with which the steamers connected.
Timekeeping became worse as the Conservancy ceased to
give the steamers priority at locks. The lock keeper at
Abingdon in the forties was called George Newin. He had
somewhat poorly fitting teeth, which produced a whistling
noise on pronouncing sibilant sounds, and to hear him say
'Salters' Steamers' was an experience we boys relished, it
was a great mental exercise to try and bring the conversation
round to the subject so as to hear the whistle. However, he
could always be relied upon to do this at least four times a day
when, consulting his watch, he would set the lock for the
'scheduled service steamer'. The steamers would always
announce their arrival, when the lock approach was blind,
with a long blast on the steam whistle and these lengthy
'bloo-oops' are an abiding memory of childhood summers,
echoing up through the town and startling the birds in the
riverside trees.

The impossibility of running to schedule over long distance

wrought havoc with the timetable; by 1963 the services had been altered so as to run once per day at weekends only, save in July and August when it was every day. The runs were also changed, being Oxford-Wallingford-Caversham Bridge (Reading); Caversham-Marlow-Windsor and Windsor-Staines-Kingston, so it was no longer possible to complete the trip in two days. Meanwhile, as we had discovered in our small way on the Kennet, the bread and butter of pleasure tripping lay in private charters. The once-proud service steamers were relegated to the bottom of the earnings league and had to await their turn at locks along with hire cruisers and launches. Only commercial carrying boats, barges and tugs could claim priority, but many lock keepers, myself included, were sympathetic to the needs of the steamer crews and did what they could to pass traffic quickly when the steamers were about.

Only MAJESTIC and CLIVEDEN were left in steam in 1963, CLIVEDEN was based at Windsor and mainly worked downriver, but MAJESTIC was based at Reading (Caversham Bridge) and was a frequent visitor, though the upstream service between Reading and Abingdon only ran, as stated at weekends and high season. She was captained by Jack Spriggs, one of the old timers and engineered by a wizened little Welshman, known universally as 'Taffy'. Taffy's head was normally crowned by an ancient beret, he wore circular-lensed spectacles, one side of which had a normal arm, the other one having a piece of bent wire. My first encounter with this duo was at Goring when MAJESTIC came downstream from Oxford at the beginning of the season. There was a strong stream running, one buck weir was still about half drawn, we were filling the lock with a chamber-full of boats when MAJESTIC came in view from Cleeve. Her name was very apt as she bore down the reach in a stately manner, gracefully nudging against the heavy white piles on the weir side of the lock entrance.

The egregious EMU was in the lock, Henry the assistant pushed the house-side gate, I pushed the other side. As I did so I noticed that the weir current was beginning to swing MAJESTIC'S stern downstream. The corollary of this was that, as she pivoted amidships, the elegant clipper bow was swinging across the lock cut. I heard Jack Spriggs ring down for 'full ahead', saw him put his helm hard over to starboard and saw water begin to boil under his counter. At this stage I observed EMU'S skipper cast off and head out of the lock. The rules distinctly stated that boats should enter and leave a lock under the lock keeper's direction, so I called to him to wait until the steamer was under control. His answer was 'I bloody know what I'm bloody doing, Pommie' with which he accelerated hard out of the lock mouth, heading for the gap between the piles and MAJESTIC'S swinging bow. White steam gushed forth under the awning as the skipper blew a warning whistle. EMU shot through the gap, but the steamer's pointed stem post fouled the collection of stainless steel railings and davits on EMU'S stern. There came a rending crash, followed by a stream of Antipodean invective. Too late the steamer's deck hand lassoed a post and drew the bow straight, but at least I was able to release all the other craft in the lock safely.

Meanwhile EMU, her skipper literally dancing with rage in his wheelhouse, made several angry, buzzing circuits in the wide reach. MAJESTIC slid into the lock and Jack Spriggs immediately came back as I was closing the gate. 'What's going on?' he asked angrily 'don't you know better than to loose that silly bastard before I was ready?' 'Steady on, skipper' I said pacifically 'he ignored my instructions'. By then EMU had managed to tie at the upstream landing stage, trailing a sorry tangle of bent railings and a squashed dinghy. Down the lock came her owner, red faced as a turkey cock. 'You bloody stupid old fool' roared he 'don't you know how to steer that filthy old heap of scrap?'

As Dick Knightley would have said 'That was where he made his mistake'. Jack Spriggs stiffened 'Man and boy, I've been on this river 40 years, and you don't talk to me like that'. 'I'll talk to you anyway I like, you stupid Prat'. Jack's eyes began to glitter dangerously, I moved towards them 'That'll do, otherwise I shall take your name. If you want to make a report. . .'. I trailed off into nothing, for advancing down the lock, wielding a massive Stilson pipe wrench came Taffy, in the best tradition of Men of Harlech out for Saesnegg blood. 'Some bastard asking for a thick year-'ole by yur?' he singsonged. In spite of everything I found it hard not to laugh. The pipe wrench was nearly half as long as he was, but there was no gainsaying his determination to use it.

'Steady on there!' I said, with as much authority as I could muster and turned to the skipper of EMU. He was hastily scrambling into his wheelhouse and casting off. 'All right, mate' said Jack 'forget it'. He turned to me and apologised, but I told him there was no need. Just for the record I filled in a report and got him to sign a statement, which I gave to Peter Harvey in due course, but I never heard any more of the incident. However, I had made two more friends on the river.

The other steamer in steam CLIVEDEN (known as 'the Clivvy' to lock staff) was a much grander vessel of steel construction, broad of beam and with a cruiser stern counter, not unlike a canal motor boat's. She was still in Salters' old black livery and paid rare visits to the Reading area. One feature of note was the brass lamp in a splendidly ornate brass frame, not unlike one in a Wild West saloon, which graced, and lit, the engine room. Steamers of course, had no electrics originally, but as they were dieselised, electric lighting came in. She was powered by a big triple expansion compound engine. 'The Clivvy's' sister vessel, of similar construction and dimensions was MAPLEDURHAM (always shortened by lock staff to 'Maple'). As a small boy I remember her being pointed out as a 'Dunkirk' boat, but in reality she did not go across to that military debacle. She was, however, 'called up' and held in readiness, seeing a certain amount of service on the tideway, along with 'Clivvy'. I was told by several river men that the Salters' steamers had to be fitted with fresh water tanks and condensers when working on salt water, and this limited their range — though an open sea passage would have in any case been a lively experience. What they seem to have been used for was dispersing troops and wounded from ships in the lower river to points upstream of the Pool of London. In this role they would have been excellent being capable of carrying large numbers and of going alongside piers and landing stages even at low water. One tale that was told me by a Salters' skipper may have been apocryphal, but bears repetition.

One day during those fraught June days of 1940, when Dunkirk blazed and Calais endured its last desperate siege, MAPLEDURHAM came plodding up Limehouse Reach freighted low with weary, dispirited and wounded soldiers, who not many hours before had been strafed by Stukas and shelled on the open beaches. Ahead of her was a Norwegian coastal tramp ship, presumably diverted from her normal port of call by the Nazi occupation of her homeland. Off St Katherines she sounded her hooter giving a signal which, doubtless in Oslo, Bergen or Stavanger meant 'I am mooring on the port bank', but which was taken by the operators of Tower Bridge as a request to pass through. The crew of MAPLEDURHAM saw her sheer off to port and overtook her, then, to their amazement, saw the bascules of the bridge start lifting. By the time they reached Tower Bridge it was fully open, buses, lorries, cars and taxis queueing in an orderly fashion either side. The bridge workers goggled down as MAPLEDURHAM, which could pass easily beneath Abingdon Bridge, swept between the piers in solitary majesty with the mate, adding insult to injury by lowering the funnel. Even the dejected soldiery chuckled.

The other boats were, like MAPLEDURHAM, all dieselised by then, and fell into two main classes. There were the beamy steel ones such as HENLEY, OXFORD and GORING. The last one was always confused in my infant mind with the portly synonymous Reichemarschal whose Luftwaffe was currently battering our towns and cities. For years I was prejudiced against poor old, harmless GORING. She could be recognised head-on from afar by two life belts carried athwart ships at her fore end. These resembled enormous eyes, such as the Chinese paint on junks enabling them to see in the dark. A slight oddity in this group was HAMPTON COURT, which had her cabin companion way off set on the starboard side instead of amidships.

The older class of steamer was of iron construction and narrower in the beam. These included SONNING, READING and WARGRAVE. A much smaller craft, which would probably have passed through the Kennet & Avon Canal had she been stripped down was NUNEHAM. She was of the standard layout but painted in the new red and white livery. In the 1962-63 period she worked the Reading-Henley-Marlow local service and was captained by a young ex-merchant navy man, Bob Tanner. I had got to know him when working ENTERPRISE the summer before, and Bill Fisher and myself had made occasional trips aboard her as his guest. As a Conservancy official I was given free passages up and down river for the asking, but the arrangement was strictly unofficial and staff were not encouraged to do this in uniform lest it smack of bribery and corruption. The once-large tripping fleet of the Thames had, apart from Salters, been much reduced by 1963. MAJESTIC was the last wooden steamer in service, it was said that dieselisation would shake her to bits, QUEEN OF THE THAMES had been taken out of service and laid-up in the Oxford area, but one firm still very much in business, and with wooden boats at that, was Jacobs of Windsor. We did not often see them so far upstream, but occasionally they worked up to Reading on charter. They were handsome boats indeed, having hulls of varnished planks, albeit diesel-powered, and with saloons furnished with more luxury than Salters. The crews were smartly turned-out, giving the whole outfit an air of panache. I wished I could have seen them in steam, for the tall funnel somehow set a boat off, quite apart from the wonderful general atmosphere that steam gave, but I was doomed to disappointment, or so I thought.

Nearly a quarter century later I was coming upstream one summer Sunday morning with a pair of narrow boats. Approaching Hurley Lock, I saw that the lock was against me, so crept slowly up the lock cut towards the lay-by. As I did so I caught a sudden whiff of boiling rice, then my ears detected a long-forgotten sighing sound somewhere to my left.

A pool led off the lock cut and there, as I slowly crept by the entrance, lying in this pool was a most beautiful restored Jacobs steamer, complete with spotless varnished hull, raising steam for a trip. It was a heart-stopping moment for me but the lock was opening for us, we had a deadline to meet at Henley that lunchtime and so I could not linger.

The dieselised steamers carried a crew comprising skipper, engineer, deckhand, purser and canteen steward, invariably a motherly lady, and sometimes supernumerary characters who assisted at locks or else ogled eligible females among the passengers. The boats were generally secured amidships when passing a lock, and this was where the heavy rope whose end was secured to the cabin railings came in. The bows were secured by lassoing a post or bollard, a Thames accompliment practised by all professional watermen on large craft. The art was to throw the rope coiled so that the loop opened in mid-flight. It was released with a negligent upward flick, by one of the crew, many of whom bore a passing resemblance to 'gaff lads' at a travelling fair.

There were two other steam craft in the Reading area in the early sixties, neither in public service, but both vessels of character. The smallest of these was a pretty little private steam launch called VICTORIA. This last belonged to, and had been built by, an engineer who kept her in the reach below Caversham. She was strictly speaking a day boat but the family made several longer trips with her. I seem to recall hearing that they went up the Oxford Canal, which was an unusual excursion for any Thames boat in those days. Certainly she went up the Kennet several times and boosted morale on the river. The general layout was the classic Thames one, a long well-deck forrard, the engine and boiler amidships, and a closed cabin astern. In VICTORIA'S case, this was fairly short, no doubt to ease the problem of supporting a lengthy drive shaft. The boiler was a vertical one, wooden lagged with brass bands. She ran like a sewing machine, with a deceptive turn of speed. All these steamers and their descendant motor launches had hulls designed and built by men who knew and respected the river. Consequently they were capable of travelling comparatively fast while making very little swell, just as a canal narrow boat, when properly designed, will amaze every one by hurtling along on a river. This is because the water is fed to the propeller by the underwater 'swim' of the boat while the hull presents little resistance because of its beam in relation to its length, the water can get past the hull with comparative ease, so such craft waste little fuel. The slab-sterned, over-powered and top-heavy looking cruiser was still in the future in 1963, but its harbinger was amongst many of the new designed craft.

Without doubt, DONOLA was the most splendid steam vessel on the river. For eleven months of the year she lay carefully sheeted behind Caversham Lock Island, above the weir. Her boiler was carefully maintained and tested in the yard, and several boatmen worked full time on preparing her. The Chief's boatman, Brian Parker, was in charge of the boat and turned her out most perfectly. She had an iron-built hull of the same general aspect as Salters' steamers but smaller - a gracefully curved bow, sweeping sheer and hull lines, terminating in an elegant counter stern. The hull was glossy black with green boot topping, but whereas the bigger boats had a deck fore and aft at gunwale level, she had none. Instead there were two mahogany or teak cabins, glossy varnished, with plate glass windows, one forrard of the engine, the other astern. The boiler was of locomotive type, unlike the bigger steamers which had 'U' return tubes in them to save space. The funnel was buff with a polished brass rim. Inside the cabins were Pullman-style Victorian plush and mahogany, cigar humidors, bottle racks and similar gentlemanly essentials. White-coated stewards completed the opulent scene.

In this style, the Committee, accompanied by the Secretary and the Chief Navigation Inspector, made their way upstream from Teddington to Lechlade, stopping overnight at suitable hotels with landing places. In the Reading area they stopped at Sonning, then made a brief detour up the Kennet to inspect Blakes Lock next morning before continuing.

A ceremony in the early part of the summer, and one which ushered in a season of riverside ceremonies was the River Board Inspection. This was when the entire Board of Conservators made a stately progress from Reading downstream aboard MAPLEDURHAM, which was spruced up in fine style for the occasion. White napery, silver cutlery and cut flowers graced the saloon tables, brasswork glowed, ropes were scrubbed and carefully coiled, the crew wore clean white deckshoes, blue trousers and jumpers while the skipper cast aside his usual cloth cap and battered reefer for a white-topped cap and glowing brass-buttoned uniform jacket.

I was on duty at Caversham when the Board arrived. Inspectors fussed about nervously – the Chief and his Deputy were both aboard, Dick lurked furtively, even though it was his day off, wearing his best uniform. It was at the height of the Profumo scandal and the name of a certain lordly Conservator had been bandied about in the Press as having been involved in what my mother termed 'hanky panky' with naughty ladies. I was somewhat non-plussed therefore to see, when MAPLEDURHAM swam into the lock, My Lord's unmistakable features, crowned like all the other old buffers aboard, with white-topped yachting cap. I closed the gates and walked down the lockside to assist with landing the party. 'Old Joe' was busily assisting the assembled dignitaries ashore. I irresistibly thought of Kipling's ship's engineer McAndrew. 'That reminds me of our Viscount loon - Sir Kenneth's kin - the chap

Wi' Russian leather tennis shoon',
And spar-decked yachtin'cap.
I showed him round last week. . .'.

The deckhand, a wry grin flickering about his face, slid the amidships railing apart and the old buffers began to come ashore. I was glad that I had meticulously checked the Gents, for a large number straight away began to head in that direction. Several more gazed at the rain gauge in the middle of the lawn and one elderly gentleman went into Dick's garden shed, to Dick's ill-disguised horror, where he fell over the motor mower with a loud clang.

My Lord was coming ashore when he was accosted by bluff, genial old Sir Alan Herbert emerging from the saloon. Sir Alan was the famous 'APH' of pre-war *Punch*, the librettist of several notable musicals; one-time University MP who reformed divorce law; author and, most importantly for me, President of the Inland Waterways Association, besides being a Conservator. 'Hello there, Herbert' said My Lord 'good to see you'. 'And good to see you too' replied Sir Alan 'been dipping your wick, so I hear, eh? What? Ho! Ho!' 'Old Joe' caught my eye and a ghostly twinkle appeared before he said 'Start drawing off, Blagrove please'.

Gradually the Board returned to MAPLEDURHAM, I shut in when the gunwale was level with the lockside, and signalled to upstream boats to wait at the lay-by below. A small private cruiser appeared flying an IWA burgee and heading upstream. With sinking heart I recognised Charlie, a well-known campaigner, a lovely old chap with bright inquiring eyes, but stone deaf. He, unaware of the pomp and circumstance, began to circle round in the weir stream. Dick walked down to the bottom gates having got rid of those Board members who wished to question him on the working of the lock. 'Better get him to hold against the piles till we've got 'Maple' out' he advised. I cupped my hand to my mouth, took a deep breath and called: 'Hold against the piles please'. Charlie, smiling broadly put his hand to his ear. 'Hold against the piles' I shouted. Still the broad smile and hand to ear. Dick joined in with his best CPO's quarter-deck voice, but Charlie continued circling and smiling amiably. The Board were all aboard now, the lock was nearly empty. Together we both roared 'HOLD AGAINST THE PILES!'

Charlie continued, smiling and circling, Dick called across the lock in exasperation. 'Oh Jesus! the silly old bastard's bloody deaf!' The grin left Charlie's face to be replaced by a venomous glare. 'Don't be so bloody rude' he called.

Another ceremony involving steamers and for which the whole river was vigorously preparing took place nearer Midsummer. This was the Lock Garden Inspection and was the most keenly awaited event of the lock keepers' year. Substantial cash prizes were offered for the best-kept lock and garden on the river, then there was a District prize, one for the most improved lock and so forth. Whilst there was little that could be done with locks such as Caversham or Osney, they were nevertheless brought to a high pitch of efficiency and cleanliness, whilst the more favoured locks and gardens underwent rigorous spring-cleaning and intensive cultivation. On my beat, Fred at Whitchurch was a front runner, both for the District and for the whole river. Carefully nurtured bedding plants were brought out of seed boxes and pots. Sam and Fred reduced the neatly-shaven turf to the condition of a billiard table, early morning saw them, clad in TC dungarees scrubbing down the lock walls with stiff brushes and caustic soda.

Harry at Goring declared war on weeds, setting about the pathways with sodium chlorate, hoes and rakes. The lawns on the sloping sides were tended lovingly, dandelions and clovers being systematically eradicated and stern 'Keep off the grass' notices placed everywhere. This caused a notable scene one Sunday, when Goring was invaded by a large excursion aboard NUNEHAM.

Bob Tanner, who had embarked his passengers at Caversham, had confided in Fred that they were a rum lot. Fred rang up and Harry took the call. He came out on the lockside looking puzzled. 'Wot the 'ell's the 'Woodcraft Folk'?' asked he. I told him I thought it was the Left Wing's answer to the Boy Scouts. 'Bloody lot of Commies, eh?' he commented 'Well I ain't havin' no nonsense from 'em'. 'Why should you think they'll make trouble?' I asked. ''Cos they're bloody Commies' he muttered darkly.

Some time later NUNEHAM hove in view, bearing the revolutionary youth, who seemed to me to be as well-behaved as any Scout troop I had seen, but also accompanied by a large party of Czechoslovak 'Youth Pioneers'. This gave rise to trouble when they came into the lock and proceeded to leap ashore intent on taking pictures. Harry became incensed when they tramped over his lawn and edging. 'Hey you! stop that!' he called down the lockside. The Czechs looked puzzled at his angry face, the effect being heightened by the omission of his teeth, which were reclining snugly in the Oxo tin. 'Pliss?'

A bold spirit among the English group leaders told Harry that he was a Capitalist lackey. This set off a yet greater explosion, which even the Czechs recognised as constituting unfriendly feelings. They withdrew, muttering, to the safety of the steamer and Harry, now in his stride, told them that they were lucky to be in a free country where the photographing of naval installations would not end them in prison. 'What d'you mean 'naval installations'?' I asked him when the steamer had gone and calm once more reigned over Goring Lock. He patted the battleship grey balance beam by way of answer, then stalked off.

Harry was not normally so protective of his environment, but the strain of the Lock Garden Competition was beginning to tell. Much rode on the decisions of the Lock Gardens Committee, not just the prizes and cups, but a man's local standing and prestige, not to mention many unofficial side bets.

Mapledurham was carefully nursed by Len, and Dick smartened Caversham. Even though neither were front runners, to have neglected them would let the side down. Excitement rose higher when it was reported that steam was being raised in DONOLA.

I had been tipped-off by the Chief and saw the inspection at Blakes, for I was anxious to see any craft on the Kennet, let alone one so distinguished as this. Great pomp ensued here, because Reading Sea Cadets had the use of part of the island for their huts and craft. In deference to naval tradition this shore installation was known as TS (training ship) JERVIS BAY, and since the Conservators only charged them a peppercorn rent, the Cadets showed their gratitude by putting on a display for the Committee. The lads paraded well in advance of DONOLA's arrival in full RN parade ground fig - white gaiters containing the bell-bottoms, Lee Enfield rifles with white slings for the guard of honour and so forth. The ensign was flown from the mast on the spit below the lock tail and all looked very tiddley, even though the backdrop of Reading gasworks with its pervasive tang of sulphur did not enhance the scene.

DONOLA arrived, the Chief Petty Officer's pipe shrilled, the flag was dipped, one of the stewards dipped DONOLA'S TC flag at the stern in response, the lads sprang smartly to attention and the Guard presented arms. 'Old Joe' solemnly raised his many-ringed sleeve in a naval salute, and DONOLA entered the lock.

Blakes was perhaps the most urbanised of all the Thames locks, being placed amid gasworks and Victorian terraces, and there was something rather touching in this little ceremony. Doubtless, today there would be plenty of sniggers, but the boys, many of whom were recruited from the mean little surrounding streets, took it very seriously. Newtown, as the area was called, may have been mean in aspect, certainly it smelled of gas and biscuit-making, and was overlooked by the railway, but it was not mean of heart. Many an older generation of sea cadet had served in convoys, minesweepers and other thankless tasks given to the RNVR in wartime, many Newtown men had served full time in the Royal or Merchant Navies and this humble little island down by the gasworks still kept that tradition alive. A lesser organisation than the Conservancy would not have been bothered with the boys, but at least the Committee, genial old buffers in yachting caps as they may have been, acknowledged their presence with all the gravity of naval ceremonial.

As I was not on duty on the great day, I missed the spectacle of the more beautiful locks being inspected, but shared the expectant tension after DONOLA had disappeared upstream, and while the Committee considered its verdict.

The results were a close-run thing. First was Bert Batiste down at Bray, second Fred at Whitchurch and third, Vic Dyer at Sonning. Fred of course won the District Prize, Harry was rewarded for having the most improved lock, Len was commended so there were celebrations all along my beat. The locks looked their absolute loveliest; for me knowing nothing of gardening, it was difficult to say which was the most superb. In celebration Fred and Sam decided to give a party and this was destined to continue the profound changes about to occur in my life.

Chapter 6 — SUMMERTIME

It was a glorious July afternoon at Sonning Lock, the gardens with their profusion of blooms were resting on their laurels after the Lock Garden Inspection. I had gone down there to work a day off, for the Conservators gave one an extra day's leave in lieu of overtime if one wished, and this seemed to me to be a good idea. The next relief man downstream to me was Harry Brunek, a brisk, efficient but kindly soul. I had gone as his assistant for the day, and a memorable day it had turned out.

The combination of warm weather and Henley Regatta brought the crowds out in droves. Normally Saturday was quiet, but today private launches and cruisers pressed upon us ceaselessly from 9.00 a.m. There were even a few skiffs and punts, while every steamer was out and packed with passengers.

Sonning was, as I have previously indicated, the most famous of all Thames locks. It was beautifully situated at the base of a wooded hill, whose spreading trees overhung the towpath for half a mile or so on either side. On the Oxfordshire bank a level flood plain spread across to the base of the Chilterns a mile or so distant. Shrouded in magnificent beech trees, surrounded by flowers in pergolas and beds it was a beautiful spot.

As the warm afternoon wore on, women aboard the passing craft became even more scantily dressed presenting the lock staff with a succession of intriguing sights. One well-proportioned young woman clad in the tiniest of bikinis caused Harry to draw my attention to the beautifully cut-in boot-topping of the craft aboard which she was. At one point I had the feeling that I had suddenly entered the time warp, for MAJESTIC came down with a charter party of jolly East Enders aboard; a party of what Victorians would have called ''Arrys and Arriets'. Most of the men were in their shirt sleeves with knotted handkerchiefs on their heads, the women wore cotton print dresses and sun bonnets or straw hats. A cheery red-faced man on the top deck was keeping the party going with a large 120 bass piano accordion, belting out music hall numbers and, inevitably, 'Cruising down the River'.

The Cockneys, waving bottles of light ale and stout, joined lustily in the chorus.

> The old accordion playing,
> A sentimental tune,
> Cruising down the river
> On a Sunday afternoon.

One of the women performed a spirited knees up, displaying a well-rounded rump clad in Union Jack knickers. Jack Spriggs, a glass of ale beside him, sat on his high stool behind the wheel, wearing a broad grin, Taffy's head and shoulders protruded from the engine room hatch clad in a singlet, for the temperature by the boiler was over 100°F. A brimming glass was in his hand as he surveyed the scene.

The accordion squawked, feet stamped and hoots of laughter rose. Some passers-by looked outraged, as did one or two cruiser crews, but in retrospect it seems so innocent and improbable. They were almost stereotypes of the old-fashioned Cockney. Two decades before we had been so proud of them, 'London can take it', and so on. Now their noisy, good-natured, vigorous way of enjoying themselves seemed outdated, their way of life to be patronised by others, yet they gave not a damn. Just for a moment I felt a flavour of an England which I thought was destroyed for ever in 1914.

Assistants were often afforded privileges by regular lock keepers, I did the same myself, so, as I was assistant for the day, Harry sent me home at 7.30, the traffic having slackened appreciably. I was glad of this, because I was not going home just yet. Tonight was the night of Fred's party and the rumour was out that the girls we had met at Pangbourne the night we went to get the dredger might be there. I hoped that I should get another chance with the slim, auburn-haired one.

Arriving at The Swan about an hour later I was greeted by Sam with the news that 'those old gels have turned up' and sure enough, there were two of them being entertained by a crowd of males at the far end of the room. I had managed to make myself reasonably presentable, so strolled over as nonchalantly as possible for an introduction. 'Not much chance with 'auburn-hair'' I mused, noting that she was with the same swain as last time, but in spite of everything I asked her if she would like a drink. She agreed and I have been buying drinks for her ever since, for she was destined to be my wife.

Eventually we all made our way across the weir to Fred's. A great white full moon hung in the sky, bathing the motionless trees and the shingled church spire in silver, the scents of an English midsummer lay heavy on the air and the weir whispered, shining in the moonlight. It was a highly romantic setting for the commencement of a love affair.

The girl's name was Jean, she was swiftly persuaded of the necessity of seeing Whitchurch Lock in the moonlight. As we sat watching the ripples in the weir pool twinkling in the moon she confided that she had not recognised me from our previous meeting. It was not until I had known her some time that I learned the reason for this, it was that this evening my skin was Caucasian in colour, she had thought beforehand that I was Indian or of some similar dusky hue. This was all due to the leaking exhaust manifold on ENTERPRISE which imparted a black patina to everything until Peter and myself replaced it.

Back in the house, Hazel, Fred's wife, had prepared a splendid spread, the happy juice was flowing and all was lively indeed. Whitchurch had two great advantages for parties: it was far enough away from other habitation to cause no disturbance and it was inaccessible to gate-crashers - unless they came by boat, in which case they were welcome. The jollity lasted well into the small hours, couples danced and fell under the spell of moonlight on the summer river, others indulged in more and more rambling conversation as the night went by. The divers had been down to investigate the gate sills that week and Sam appeared wearing the diving helmet which had been left in the lock office. Somebody unscrewed the plate to communicate with Sam, whose lips could be seen moving through the glass, but no words distinguished, then someone else poured a pint of beer in the hole. The liquid rose up the glass in front of him and he supped desperately before he disappeared in the flood.

The girls had to leave, they had booked a taxi to take them home, so I parted from Jean, extracting the promise of another meeting from her. Gradually the party subsided, I vaguely recall spending the night on a 'Put-me-up' settee, prior to helping with the clean-up in the morning.

It was truly the high season on the river now, and the pageant of the river's life continued to unfold. Swan-upping came round. This ancient ceremony dated back to mediaeval times when swans were a royal delicacy. Analogous to the Game Laws, an ancient law reserved all swans to the Crown but the Dyers and Vintners Companies of the City were allowed to bag themselves swans for a few days each year, with a view to providing for their Christmas feast. The operation of catching the swans was called swan-upping, and carried out under the direction of the Royal Swan Master. Of course nobody, other than bargemen and ne'er-do-wells, who called them 'Thames Turkeys', had eaten swans for many years. I was assured by one who had that they were rubbery, greasy and tasted of fish, but doubtless mediaeval palates were more robust than ours. However, as is the way of things in England, nobody had stopped the swan-upping, which had become a hallowed tradition. Stanley Spencer painted them one year at Cookham.

The Swan Master and officers of the two livery companies, all splendidly costumed and attired, made their way upstream in an oared boat, hung with banners, upping the swans. This was done with the aid of three implements; a metal crook mounted on a light pole, a gadget resembling a carpenter's tool bag and a set of clippers. The swans were seized by the neck with the crook, pinioned with the carpenter's bag, and their bills given one or two nicks with the clippers to denote their ownership. In fact there was a serious purpose behind this ceremony, unconnected with feasting. Increasingly the swan population was under threat. Overpowered motor boats were sweeping away their nests, discarded fishing tackle got stuck in their bills, yobs with airguns peppered them with pellets, fishermen's lead weights got in their crops and stomachs to poison them. The upping ceremony had become an exercise in conserving and recording the rapidly dwindling population. The Swan-uppers were adept at dealing with the creatures, who were dealt with in angry, hissing batches. They were cleaned of oil, freed from hooks, nicked, ringed and recorded all in one operation, before being released, still hissing and wagging their rumps crossly as they paddled away. The Swan Uppers had not got beyond Windsor for years, the proximity of pubs to the waterside prevented that, but Fred and Harry, who had both served downstream told great tales of the Uppers' prowess with both pole and bottle.

Without any doubt the high point of the Upper Thames' year was Henley Week, for in this the Conservancy was greatly concerned. The Regatta was but one facet of this great carnival of the river, whose spin-offs were felt far upstream and downstream of the pleasant little Oxfordshire town. For several weeks beforehand, TC craft were in position setting the posts which marked the course, and the booms which segregated river traffic from that of the Regatta. Down that majestic reach from Henley Bridge towards Temple Island, the Engineer's Department knocked in their piles and the Navigation launches hurried back and forth. Meanwhile the Umpire's launches were made ready, notably AMARYLLIS a long, slim vessel with superb lines, capable of keeping up with any rowing eight with effortless ease. She appeared at many rowing functions up and down the river, but Henley was both her home and the yearly apogee of her career.

The Reading District had to police the river traffic for the Regatta, the Chief Inspector was expected to be present, the lock staff had to handle an increased volume of traffic, so the Navigation Department was deeply involved.

The world saw the racing on the day, enormous crowds descended on Henley, the clubhouses on the banks were *en fête,* it was a time of champagne and strawberries, of blazers and flannels, the summeriest of dresses. Indeed Henley was, as always, a wonderful place in which to be young and not short of money, but there was of course another side to it. Pickpockets and bag-snatchers made their harvest and, not infrequently ugly scenes would develop especially later in the evening, when too much drink had been taken, and most especially when the circumstances brought a confrontation between arrogant and aggressive representatives of the bourgeoisie and proletariat.

One such encounter was recounted to John Grace by a Reading lad, a friend of John's and who might be described as 'a rough diamond'. 'I sees this toff in one o' them straw 'ats like. I got me mates wi' me, so I steps up to 'im an' takes 'is 'at, puts me fist straight froo the bleeder. All me mates pisses 'emselves laughin'. The toff turn round to me, puts 'is fists up, an' next minute; duff! duff! duff! gi's me a bloody good dustin' over. 'Course I'd 'ad ter go an' do it to an Oxford boxin' blue 'adn't I? I tell yer what lads, I were glad when e'd finished.'

But besides such unseemly incidents, beside the pomp and ceremony, the fireworks and the celebration, the work of the Conservancy went on unheralded and unsung year after year. The Regatta may have had its sporting and political crises, but every year the course was ready on time, the craft were marshalled, the litter bins along the midstream piles emptied, the hordes of arriving and departing boats were attended to, and all so smoothly that no one noticed.

Occasionally hiccups occurred on the river, such as in the late 1950s when my old employers, Willow Wren Canal Carrying Co., were bringing cattle food up to Wallis, Son & Wells at Marsh Mills, just above Henley Town by narrow boat. This traffic had run for some months with little trouble, one of the regular skippers being my old friend, Alec Purcell. Alec was a man with a fearful reputation as a fighter and as a drinker, but, like many such characters, he was in reality a soft-hearted soul who did many kindnesses. It so happened that one load was sent up river from Brentford during Henley Week and, came the Friday afternoon, there were the two teams in the quarter-finals slogging it out up the Royal Mile; there were the Umpire's launches, the BBC and press launches, and the TC patrol launch all foaming along behind, and there, behind, plodding steadily, were REDSHANK and GREEN-SHANK, deep loaded, abreast, with Alec and Lily smiling to the applauding crowd.

An Umpire's launch came alongside, a megaphone bawled, 'Heave to! skipper!' Alec's grin vanished, he 'took no notice' as boatmen would say. 'Ahoy there! skipper! Heave to!' 'Bollocks!' came the retort.

Obviously the Umpires were going to get nowhere, and the crowd was vastly enjoying this spectacle, so off they zoomed, returning shortly with the Patrol Launch. Alec realised this meant business, so he slowed down and the Inspector drew abreast. Diplomatically it was pointed out that, while commercial craft had a right of passage, it would be appreciated if Alec were to wait until racing had finished, or else go inside the piles. This last was not a practical proposition with loaded craft, so Alec agreed to wait a while. This meant that many large launches tied to the inside of the booms had to be shifted while the pair were brought inside. Eyebrows were lifted, noses looked down and much 'tut-tutting' went on, but Alec and Lily were soon safely moored, sitting placidly in the butty's hatches drinking tea. To be fair, REDSHANK and GREEN-SHANK were beautifully kept, brasses sparkling, ropework and canvas scrubbed and Alec had a way with people. Before long he had made friends with many of the craft on the boom, glasses were being passed back and forth, Alec was 'telling the tale' and a great air of conviviality was abroad. This was shattered by the return of the Umpire's launch. 'All right, skipper, off you go!' 'I ay' a-goin,' came back from Alec. The umpires looked incredulous and went once more for the Patrol. The Inspector was not a happy man this time and demanded to know why Alec wouldn't go. 'I can't' he pointed to his watch 'it's too late. The Mills shut at 'ar pass four. It's quarter past now, so I shan't empt until Monday. I'd a' got there and emptied if you adn't a' stopped me'. 'Well you'll have to move from here'. 'a ay a movin' wi-out demurrage. That's Mester Morton's orders'. "Who the bloody hell's Mr Morton?" It was Alec's turn to look incredulous. 'What? You ain't 'eard o' Mester Morton! You must be bloody iggorant'. After some more argument the Inspector asked how much demurrage was charged. 'Five pound per day, per boat' came the reply. Off went the TC launch to a consultation with the Regatta Committee, returning a few minutes later with an official bearing two fivers. These were pressed into Alec's hot hands. 'Now bugger off' said the Inspector. 'It orter be thirty quid' said Alec winningly. 'No it didn't' said the Inspector 'and you know it'. Alec knew when he was beaten, and started up his engine.

Perhaps the authorities had the last laugh, for after the boats were unloaded on Monday, the cabins were invaded by wee-vils, causing Alec to send for the Henley Medical Officer of Health, who 'stoved' the cabins. I met them, their boats tied up in the park above Henley Bridge, looking exceedingly furtive as they sat on a park bench watching their cabins fumigate. I felt sorry for them because bugs in the cabin were a social disgrace among boat people, although both Alec and Lily were spotlessly clean and one can't help if stowaways come aboard with the load. They were terribly worried lest I blab what I had seen to the canal community. I promised that I would not, but nearly four decades have since passed, and they are both now where malicious gossip cannot harm them.

On the Sunday after the Regatta, the river was thronged with boats making for home mingling with the hire cruisers who traditionally hired out from Saturday to Saturday. Sunset was after 9.15 at that time of the year, it did not get dark until nearly 11.00, so the traffic moved late through the luminous summer dusk. The lock keepers no longer fussed so much about algae on the locksides now that the inspection season was passed, so most turned a blind eye to the boats which left full locks behind them. Dark shapes bearing navigation lights loomed out of the dark along lock cuts the night after Henley. I thought of my exploits earlier on that Spring and chuckled to myself.

Imperceptibly though, the summer was on the turn. Sunset had stuck about the 9.20-9.15 p.m. mark for weeks, but by the end of July we were knocking off at 9.00 p.m. Even so, a 12-hour day, on one's feet, working hard on gates and paddles, left one tired out, though pleasantly so, at the day's end. I ceased to ride my bike out to locks as the work load increased, but I had a reason other than tiredness at the day's end for not doing so.

I had met Jean several times and escorted her home to her digs in Reading. She was not a native of Reading, in fact she came from Devon, and knew nothing of locks or rivers, but she took a liking to the life. Soon she was coming out to the locks by bus after work or at weekends, where she became friendly with the regular keepers and their families, in particular with Fred and Hazel. After a few weeks it began to seem as if she had always been there and this, of course, is a dangerous sign for a bachelor. Meanwhile I was glad of a companion with whom to observe the changing pageant of the river.

By the middle of July the river was thronged. The fine weather of late spring broke down, at least at weekends. As luck would have it, my one Saturday off that summer was glorious weather. I spent it with my parents touring my old haunts on the Grand Union Canal, but, whilst the weekdays were often fine, the weekends perversely were not. Once the charter season finished in July, this had an adverse effect on ENTERPRISE'S tripping, for we were very dependent on good weather at those times. On the Thames though, wet weather in the summer had little effect on the traffic.

Some narrow beam craft began to come through the river, coming down off the Oxford Canal en route for Brentford, or vice versa. One evening at Caversham I was startled by the arrival of a fleet of canal boats, two ex-working boats CASSIOPEIA and TYSELEY and a short tug LION. Midland accents filled the air as I made my first acquaintance with Keith Christie of TYSELEY and Malcolm Braine of LION. Both of these have become noteworthy since, Keith became associated with me in canal carrying ventures in later years, while Malcolm achieved fame as a boat builder and restorer at Norton Canes in Staffordshire. These craft, to my delight, went up the Kennet to Sulhamstead Lock before going on down river. I biked out next afternoon and saw them going through Sheffield Swing Bridge.

One pouring wet afternoon at Mapledurham I saw a motorised camping punt pull into the lay-by above the lock. The skipper, a large shambling man with a curious gait, not unlike Quasimodo as portrayed by Charles Laughton, came down the lockside with an oilskin cape above his head, but with his lower half clad in ancient khaki shorts and sandals. At this moment the heavens opened. I invited him in to the office to shelter. He removed the cape to reveal the features of Jestyn Phillips, Viscount St Davids, a prominent IWA number, and one moreover whom Bill Fisher and myself had assisted up the Kennet the year before, and whose punt MAUDELAYNE we had nearly rammed one winter's morning on the Regent's Canal in Camden Town. The curious gait was a result of an injury received during the Spanish Civil War, when St Davids had got himself involved in that conflict through his instinctive sympathies with the underdog.

We spent a pleasant hour or so exchanging waterway gossip and drinking tea while the rain sheeted down outside, then it began to let up. When a break in the clouds appeared over the Hardwick Hills, he squelched off through the puddles to his boat. I let him through the lock and he vanished downstream continuing his fact-finding journey. It was good to know that such a personage was taking an active interest in the waterways and doing so in an incognito sort of role. Apart from the Old Etonian tie holding up his shorts there was nothing about his boat or his appearance to suggest that an active member of the House of Lords was present. He was thus able to obtain much information denied to more official voyagers. Sir Reginald Kerr of British Transport Waterways used to make lengthy journeys aboard KINGFISHER, the ex-Grand Junction Canal Company's inspection launch, but the whereabouts of the gaffer was always telegraphed well in advance. Consequently KINGFISHER would pass a succession of dredgers, tugs and bank boats at the centre of a hive of industry. MAUDELAYNE on the other hand was unremarkable and unremarked, so the normal card schools in flat cabins, moored in out-of-the-way spots continued undisturbed but not unnoticed.

Lord St Davids was not the only distinguished guest that visited Mapledurham that summer. One afternoon soon afterwards I was surprised to see the figure of Robert Fordyce Aickman, founder of IWA walking by. I asked him in for a cup of tea and a fascinating session developed, lasting until early evening, at which time Aickman had to depart hurriedly for a bus having missed out on his original plan to walk the towpath to Pangbourne. Robert Aickman had many enemies. He was without any doubt a self-centred, egotistical, self-publicist with a rancorous nature and a needle-sharp wit. He was also an idealist and a genius to whom the country is deeply indebted. He it was who channelled the enormous enthusiasm and ability of L.T.C. Rolt into forming IWA in 1946, it was his vision and single mindedness that made IWA a pioneer in conservation, restoration and ultimate development of the waterway system. His was the energy and powers that inspired the campaign which turned round official thinking. Apart from the Thames and Norfolk Broads and a few commercially viable waterways, the system in 1946 was moribund. By 1963 it had been saved from extermination but the counter attack and the creation of a new prosperity based on the leisure potential had not yet begun beyond the establishment of a few pioneering enterprises. Aickman also believed that the waterways could never be an authentic amenity without their commercial integrity. To this end he had encouraged the formation of new carrying enterprises, notably Willow Wren, but also my own Kennet Carrying Company. Against much opposition, this is a belief to which I still adhere. The canals will only be truly authentic, and thus a genuine attraction, if they can still perform their original tasks, albeit modified by circumstances. Wherever and whenever it is commercially viable, the traditional craft of the waterways should still ply. This goes beyond the idea of a 'working museum', to the concept of something doing the job for which it was originally intended, but in a modern context.

Another day I received an excited phone call from Sam, informing me that a pair of Willow Wrens was on its way down to me. This was good news indeed for, apart from occasional visits to Brentford, I had seen little of my one-time mates since I left the firm, although with boating people friendships once made were for a lifetime. Whilst the exigencies of the job often meant that long periods would elapse before friends were re-united, I was not expecting to see many working boats on the river for since the Marsh Mills job had finished there were no loads to be carried.

As it happened four pairs had gone upstream from Brentford the previous autumn in order to get round a stoppage on the Grand Union Canal. These craft had loaded timber in Brentford for Tipton in the Black Country and were the last loaded craft to go up the Oxford Canal. Bill and myself had seen some of them come through Reading just before leaving to rejoin the fleet ourselves. The lock keeper at Cookham had been most impressed by Jack Monk's Seffle engine in AVOCET. He had heard the drum-like beat of the engine far down Cliveden Reach as the boats plugged upstream. A Reading newspaper had got hold of the story and sent a reporter to interview Jack. The article was excellent except for the matter of the cargo, for evidently the reporter was unused to boatmen's speech. The load was, said the paper, 40 or so tons of 'hurricane pipe'. What this obscure commodity was the paper did not vouchsafe. Possibly it was large tubes through which one blew to create meteorological disturbances, or pipework for World War II fighter planes. The truth was somewhat mundane. Jack was carrying 'Oregon Pine'. (Jack once told a friend of mine about the problems of carrying 'liver' (liver!). The cargo turned out to be 'leather'.)

About 20 minutes after Sam had telephoned, the boats came into the lock cut. It was Ray White with CRANE and DABCHICK. He had taken a load of coal to Banbury Dairy from Pooley Hall Colliery on the Coventry Canal and, because it was holiday time in the coalfields, had not received the normal orders 'Empty to Suttons' i.e. Hawkesbury Junction in the heart of the Warwickshire coal fields, but instead it was 'Brentford for orders', possibly timber for Birmingham or the Black Country or wheat for Wellingborough Mills on the River Nene. By running via Braunston the trip would take four days, but via Oxford and the Thames it was three and substantially less hard work. The only snag was the tug tolls on the Thames which were payable on an empty motor narrow boat, but in the case of urgency it was still worth the Company's while paying these.

Ray and his wife Margaret were full of news and took the opportunity to return a book lent by Bill Fisher last winter. Since I had left the Company in spring a radical change had taken place in boating. British Waterways' great fleet had been wound up, a new Willow Wren Company had been formed to take over the surplus boats and existing contracts, boatmen were now sub-contractors instead of paid employees, they leased the boats from the Company and were classed as self-employed. Ray was somewhat dubious about the long-term viability of this new system, although it seemed to be working well enough in the short-term. 'What's going to happen' he asked 'when the boats begin to wear out and need heavy repairs? I can't see many of the captains having that sort of money put by. I doubt if we could afford much heavy work done on these'. Alas, his words were to prove only too prophetic. The dying days of canal carrying were then in the future, but I was to live through them, albeit on the sidelines. That is, however, another story. In the meantime the Willow Wren red, green and cream set off by polished brasses and scrubbed rope work brightened up a somewhat overcast summer's day.

Of the other, more normal, river craft we had full measure. Canoes, or rather kayaks, were the smallest generally and had largely usurped the place of punts, skiffs, randans and the like. Sometimes they caused problems by antics in weir pools when the tackle was drawn. Fred used to get very sniffy at this. 'Anything goes wrong, I'm the muggins supposed to get them out. Why should I risk widowing my wife and orphaning my kids for bloody fools?' he would grumble at them, and of course he was right. Though, when the chips were really down, the lock keepers would always take the risk. Fred had been commended for life saving when he was 'up West' at Rushey Lock. Sam later earned a commendation for saving someone from Caversham Weir.

Kayaks, of course, are relatively cheap and easy to construct and are thus an excellent way of getting afloat for youngsters. Each year saw that most gruelling of sporting events, the Devizes to Westminster Canoe Race. This took place over Easter and involved portaging round every lock. The Reading Branch of the Kennet & Avon Canal Trust used to man a check point at Blakes Lock overnight on Good Friday and into Easter Sunday. The old brick lock office was put at the Branch's disposal, but was not really suitable because the easiest portage was at the top end of the lock, this also avoided upsetting the lock keeper because crews had no need to go crashing along the lockside, but it meant a long, cold vigil for those on duty.

More elegant, but rarer than kayaks were the birch-bark Canadian type canoes, a lovely craft for one or two people to explore the river and its byways. There was even an electric version owned and based at Whitchurch. This made even less noise than a steamer - just a ripple from the screw - and caused no wash, it has often puzzled me that such a craft should be so unfashionable.

The Conservators' regulations charged a fee of 3d for any unpowered vessel passing through, over or by a lock, unless clearly marked as 'Tender to' a vessel. This phrase was a catch-all, because there were some who endeavoured to sneak past a lock portaging light craft, and others who would go to the length of shooting a weir. All such freeloaders were liable to the Conservators' wrath if caught, but one anomaly was never satisfactorily explained in my time on the Thames. This concerned a backwater below Sonning and known as 'St Patrick's Stream', which led off the main river to join the River Loddon below Shiplake lock and weir. There was no weir in this stream, which was fast-running but navigable for small craft, enabling voyagers to travel from the head of Marsh Lock to the tail of Sonning without passing a lock, thus saving 3d. The Conservancy occasionally tried to enforce a toll under the above rule, but it was generally held that a right of navigation existed along the stream. Now the Conservancy was quite entitled to insist that pleasure craft using the river

be registered, for which a fee was charged, and it was entitled
to charge all craft for the use of locks and 'navigation works',
but legally registered navigation rights existed. There was evident scope here for one of Sir Alan Herbert's 'misleading
cases'.

Whilst the hordes of small hand-propelled craft of yesterday had largely gone, rowing still remained the great sport of
the Thames valley. Generally regarded, like Rugby football,
as a middle class sport, in the Thames valley it was more
analogous to Welsh Rugby. Every town from Oxford downstream had at least one rowing club, and several villages had
clubs. There were the lordly organisations connected with
Oxford University and the prestigious Leander Club at
Henley, but there were also Working Men's Rowing Clubs,
University and College Clubs, School Clubs and Firms'
Clubs. Henley Royal Regatta may have been the high point of
the year, but all summer there were smaller, local regattas up
and down the river, all involving buoying the course (cheaper
than the elaborate piling at Henley), controlling navigation
and supervising the courses generally. July and August were
still the peak months for this activity, and teams competed all
up and down the valley. Training had been going on since the
early months, when crews had the steely, swirling surface of
the winter to themselves; now in leafy high summer the river
was glassy smooth, all weirs shut in and lasher boards placed
on some of the overfalls and the crews approached the con-
summation of their efforts.

Pangbourne Rowing Club did particularly well that season,
so their Summer Dance promised to be a lively celebration.
This would do, argued Sam, for my first formal function
squiring Jean, so I obtained tickets for one Saturday evening
in late summer at Pangbourne Village Hall. The bar was provided by the landlord of a nearby pub. He was an ex-Royal
Marine Commander and thus deemed capable of dealing with
any trouble which might arise, so I felt confident that my burgeoning romance would be forwarded by a quiet and pleasant
evening's Terpsichorean activity.

All went well to start with. Jean looked better than any
other woman in the hall in her cocktail dress, the band trolled
away interspersing time-honoured quick steps and waltzes
with rock and roll numbers and even the new 'twist', we were

in a jovial group so I did not notice at first the influx of likely lads from Reading which occurred after closing time at the local pub. The hall had a late licence, so of course it was good for an extra hour's boozing and there was no one on the door to eject the incomers.

I noticed that tension seemed to be growing among the Rowing Club, but was more interested in creating a good impression with Jean. The Last Waltz came and went then, as was the custom in those days, there came a drum roll, the dancers stood to attention and the band played the National Anthem.

It was unfortunate that one of the likely lads could not resist the temptation to shout 'Up wiv Christine Keeler!' in the midst of the Anthem (this lady was currently enjoying notoriety through the Profumo Affair). At the end of the music, one of the Committee, an upright youth and doubtless a pillar of the establishment marched straight up to the culprit, his face white with anger. 'How dare you? you disgusting lout'. The culprit looked genuinely surprised. 'Oo? me? wot are you on about?' 'You know perfectly well, clear out the lot of you if you can't behave!' I groaned inwardly. Trouble was about to begin. The likely lads cast measuring glances at one another, but the Committee man plunged on 'Are you going or do I throw you out?' The lad looked at him coolly, they were about the same size. 'Piss off, you toffee-nosed Prat!' 'I won't be spoken to like that by a yob'. 'Oh won't yer? Wot you goin' to do about it then?' 'Put 'em up you!', so saying, the Committee man took a Queensbury Rules stance, his fists manfully raised, as no doubt, his boxing coach had taught him. At this the likely lad butted him straight in the face. Down he went and the room erupted.

So far the locals had distanced themselves from the rumpus, but now it was no longer class war but civil war, Reading against Pangbourne. Townees against the river men. Making one of the rapidest decisions of my career, I shoved Jean and another girl onto the stage and safety, then went to give assistance. The scene was reminiscent of a good night in the saloon at Deadwood Gulch. Fists and bottles were flying, women shrieking, the band nonchalantly packing up their instruments, the ex-Marine's head and shoulders appearing above a whirling mass of bodies as his huge fists rose and fell like threshing flails. As I walked down the hall, I heard pounding feet behind me, glanced round and beheld a spotty youth with greasy hair bearing down on Sam and a group of Pangbourne people with a chair above his head and undoubted malice aforethought. Accordingly I sidestepped and stuck my foot out. He fell over it and zoomed chin-first across the floor.

While all this was going on, two burly farmworkers, regulars at the Marine's pub were slowly sipping their ale, leaning on the bar and enjoying the legally late drink. Suddenly a group of jeering me-laddoes cannoned into them, spilling their beer. One of them said, in slow, measured Berkshire tones 'Oi 'ates these yooung booggers as caan't 'old their liquor Tom'. Tom said 'Ah, an Oi does an' all Sid'.

At this the two of them went to work, grabbing the nearest youth by the collar with one gigantic hand apiece and by the seat of his tight trousers with the other, and tossing him headlong through the double doors like a truss of hay. They then systematically began clearing the hall of all combatants by the same method. The police had by now arrived and had no more to do than to take names and addresses as the bodies flew out into the car park. In less than five minutes it was all over. Peter, who would by virtue of his great size have been of considerable value, had been in the Gents and missed it all. I recovered the girls, who had had a grandstand view and were laughing hysterically, and we managed to catch the last bus to Reading unmolested.

However, such an undignified incident seemed to have made little adverse effect on my courting activities, for Jean continued to accompany me on the locks and to various venues, and this was causing me to rethink my future plans.

Before I left Willow Wren in March, Leslie Morton the manager had promised a pair of boats for me if I wanted in the Autumn. I had broached the idea to Jim, who was enthusiastic and who would have come as my mate, for I had really only thought of lock keeping as a stop-gap. Now I was beginning to see a reason for staying put and settling down, although the lure of boating was still as strong as ever.

As August drew on, and the hours began to shorten with the lengthening nights, I found myself with more time on my hands in the evenings, when such matters might be discussed with Jean. I had thoughts of taking a pair and running it three-handed with her, but she was quite unused to boats and I dismissed this as an unfair solution. She, on the other hand, had a steady job in Reading and did not like the idea of my vanishing into the unknown without her. Meanwhile Jim was anxious to get down to real boating as soon as ENTERPRISE'S season ended. The dilemma was neatly solved when Leslie Morton told me that he was taking on a new young skipper, one Nicholas Hill, whom I knew well as a keen part-time boater, and that he wanted a mate. Thus it was that Jim had a ready-made place to go to and I informed Jean, to her relief, that I intended staying on the River for the time being.

Meanwhile the traffic continued as heavy as ever. The IWA's National Rally of Boats was held at Paddington that year. It coincided with one of my days off, as I visited it along with Jean and Peter. I had last seen Little Venice, where the Regent's Canal meets the Paddington branch of the Grand Union on a murky winter's day and now it was *en fête*. Fairy lights and bunting were hung from the full-leaved plane trees, the pool at the junction was thronged with boats of all shapes and sizes, including one of the last British Waterways narrow-boat pairs still operating, STAMFORD and BUDE. All day I kept meeting old friends and acquaintances. I found myself invited into assisting in the narrow-boat handling competition, we were invited for tea on WAGON MOUND with the Segals, we watched the fireworks after dark from a tiny Loftus Bennett fibreglass cruiser owned by Teddy Cook, the vet from Stoke Bruerne, along with about 20 others, and finally staggered off to catch the midnight train home. En route to Paddington Station, the mighty Peter slipped off the kerb and twisted his ankle, which resulted in Jean and myself virtually carrying him into the station via the deserted taxi entrance from Bishops Bridge Road. As happens with such sprains, the pain came and went; when it came it was agonising. The train, first stop Reading, second Newport, was packed but we found seats in a compartment full of homeward-bound Welsh nurses. In his pain-free moments, Peter tried to chat them up, which worked for a while then, when the pain returned, he would seize his ankle with a roar of 'Sodding bitch!', which did not help his chances one bit. Like John Grace's friend, I was glad when he'd finished.

Such excursions apart, much of my courting had to take place in the evenings, for my days off followed a seven-eight day pattern and so varied each week. However, as the month of August progressed the daylight hours decreased appreciably. Traffic one found, outside Bank Holiday times and weekends, tended to drop off sharply after 6.00 p.m. leaving the last couple of hours or so very quiet. Since I lived in Reading the fact that my tour of duty ended at Caversham was handy, as knocking-off time became progressively earlier, for I was within walking distance of Jean's flat or similar rendezvous. Alternatively Peter would often appear after work to act as my unofficial assistant, and sometimes, especially at weekends I would have Jean's assistance as well, so the lock would be well-manned.

Of course every hire firm was booked fully for July and August, but these were also the 'gin palace' months. Large, immaculately-kept cruisers would appear daily, their owners often betraying a somewhat querulous, over-protective attitude to their craft and attitudes to other river users akin to motorway drivers. By no means all gin-palace cruisers had such owners, but many did. These people reminded Sam of Enid Blyton's Noddy and his car, and privately they were referred to as 'The Noddy Clodboard Steam Packet Company'. By the end of the season they had become plain 'Noddy', a term spread by Jim and others to the main canal system, where it has stuck. I can thus make a modest claim to having assisted at the birth of a neologism, albeit only current on the waterway system.

Another rich source of amusement to lock keepers, Sam and myself especially, was boat's names. The Conservancy regulations forbade the registration of more than one boat in the same name, so the increasing numbers caused more and more ingenuity. Of course there were 'class' or 'fleet' names in the tradition followed by the Royal Navy and the Merchant Marine, as well as the railways. The bigger hire firms followed this pattern. Salters having pre-empted everyone by appropriating the names of riverside towns and places, but there were some odd omissions - no Abingdon, Wallingford, Maidenhead or Windsor for example. Captain Munk's Maid Line boats had the prefix 'Maid', except for ROBERT AICKMAN, Bushnells of Wargrave favoured names beginning with 'G' - GLORIOUS, GLOWWORM etc. while Bushnells of Maidenhead used the prefix GAY. English usage has changed since then. I doubt whether this would be considered good public relations nowadays. GAY BAHAMA THREE was always known to lock keepers as GAY BANANA TREE.

The Star boats from Chertsey were handsome looking river-type cruisers, built by Bates Yard at Chertsey Bridge. All their names had the suffix STAR, and CANOPUS STAR was most unfairly called CANNABIS, but there was a distressing tendency among hire firms to have one standard name to which numerals were added. It was a typically boring modern answer to the problem.

However, the private owner with only one boat could let his imagination run riot, although the Conservators frowned upon 'dubious' names. There had been a famous case in former times when they had refused to register Steam Yacht PHYLLIS, because the juxtaposition of classification letters and name was considered unmentionable, but some curios slipped through the net. A launch with the name of PENEUS caused much merriment among the more uncouth lock staff and steamer men. The day when it appeared in the launch register at Whitchurch and Mapledurham as accompanying one GOS-SAMER caused near hysteria and droll comments from Peter Harvey, who had grave doubts as to the genuineness of the entry.

The gin palace skippers of course despised the hire boat skippers, the more expensive hirers looked down on their less expensive brethren, who regarded steamer men and commercial boaters with nervous apprehension, all the latter of course despised everything besides other steamers and commercial boats, so there was a neat sociological circle of contempt. There was little of the mateyness of the canal world, and few had words to spare for lock keepers. There were some who distributed largesse in the form of cans of beer or even monetary tips, but the mode of donation often offended the staff. I remember Harry in particular, handing back a half-crown with the comment 'Thank you, but I'm not bribed'. One customer that I particularly recall was a Reading publican. He kept a spotless town-centre establishment with the most splendid bar food in the days when such things were a comparative rarity. His Ploughman's Lunches would have satisfied a genuine ploughman: a quarter of a cottage loaf, crusty and fresh, a massive slab of cheese, fresh butter, two great home-made pickled onions and a pint of Simonds best bitter cost 4s 6d. Great hams were carved on the bar, fine crisp-pastried pork pies stood in ranks and the people came in droves. Yet he seemed a most gloomy and disagreeable man, quite unimpressed by his superb food. He had a young grandson upon whom he doted and who steered an open motor launch of modern design and great power. This youth had a habit of appearing above or below Caversham Lock at the end of a long tiring day and demanding passage. One didn't mind so much if it was a large craft, but a little boat seemed an awful waste of time and energy. However, one gritted one's teeth and let him through.

As the pub was near Jean's flat and not far from where Peter lived, we often met there, so all three of us knew the landlord. One evening in late summer the boy came downstream with his grandfather, we were all three at the lock and I was hoping to get away promptly. I politely informed him of when sunset would be, to which the old man grunted a reply. 'Miserable old pig' I thought, 'typical aquatic motorist'. Ten minutes before sunset he came back upstream, wearily I opened one gate to let him in. As the boat rose the publican got out and came up to where I was standing by the top balance beam. 'Very good of you to wait for us. Here's something to spend in my pub'. He pressed something into my hand and walked away. I was speechless and glanced down. It was a new £1 note, 10% of a week's wages!

The summer was beginning to fade, trees began to fruit in the lock gardens, the bedding plants of earlier gave place to azaleas, hydrangeas, Michaelmas daisies, a hint of red began to appear in the leaves and wasps buzzed aimlessly round ice cream wrappers in litter bins. There were several wasp nests at Mapledurham, one of which was discovered by Len when he drove a motor mower over it. Len could have set an Olympic record by the speed at which he cleared the ground between the lock island where the nest was and the shelter of his outside lavatory, from within which shortly came sounds of energetic swatting.

Mapledurham lock office, with its many windows seemed to have an uncanny attraction for these creatures. On warm, sunny days I would open the casements to let air in, and with it would come wasps, on cooler days they would come in the door, buzzing frantically up and down the glass, ignoring open windows beside them. When swatted, they would fall to the bottom of the window, tails curled and seeming much smaller than when alive and buzzing. Len showed me a useful fisherman's trick, for dead wasps were chubs' favourite delicacy. A handful of defunct 'jaspers', as Berkshire folk call them, dropped in the lock would cause a great eruption of mouths on the surface as the chub rose. If the lock was full and a net handy one could land a sizeable fish.

By the beginning of September the wasps had ceased to be a joke. They zoomed round one in their manic way while one tried to fill in the Launch Register and often sat on the control buttons, ready to sting an unwary finger. Discussing this with Len one day, I compared them unfavourably with bees. At least bees were useful and only stung in self-defence. From this the talk turned to the old country custom of 'telling the bees'. Beekeepers, amongst whom my father and grandfather were numbered, always told their swarms of any deaths or untoward occurrence in the family. Len, laughing said 'Why not tell the wasps? we could tell them to bugger off!' So, jokingly, I suggested he put his head in the next wasps nest that he mowed and tell the occupants to keep out of the office. When he'd finished taking swipes at my head, I found an old Report Form, upon which unusual happenings had to be recorded, and wrote on the back in large capitals 'NO WASPS BEYOND THIS POINT - BY ORDER', got Len to sign it and pinned it to the office door. This caused immense amusement up and down the river, but, amazingly it worked. Our swattings dropped dramatically and our peace of mind improved. One morning, a solitary wasp flew in while Len and myself were drinking coffee. Len sternly pointed to the door 'Oi! you! can't you read?' The wasp performed a 'U' turn and flew out, we collapsed in helpless laughter.

Chapter 7 — INTERLUDE ON THE CUT

Suddenly, the summer was gone. The state schools re-opened in early September, then came the private and Public schools, followed late in the month by colleges and universities. Within three weeks the river was empty. Suddenly I realised that Salters were ending their service trips, ENTERPRISE enjoyed a brief Indian Summer as holidaymakers took one last summer excursion in the late summer warmth. Soon it would be time to shut up for winter, and for Jim to be gone. The Kennet & Avon Trust was hoping to get something done about the Bridge Street girders, so we moved BEECH up into position beneath them so as to provide an inspection platform for engineers, and then there were no more trips. Jim was paid off at the end of September, there was one last trip in early October, which I was able to cope with on my day off, and then the season was done.

The river began to take on an air of tristesse. On still mornings mists would rise off the glassy water, an exhilarating sense would come as the mellow sunlight strengthened, gradually dissolving the vaporous droplets until the full panorama of each lock was displayed bathed in the warmth of a Thames valley autumn. Whether it was the reach up to Cleeve below the mature willows, or the steep beech-clad flanks of Streatley Hill, or the noble poplar-lined Pangbourne Reach, or Hardwick Hill and the ochre roofs of Mapledurham, or the rooflines of Reading Town Hall, St Lawrence's Church and the gaol hiding behind the tall railway embankment beyond Kings Meadow, I never tired of the scenes in which I worked. Still there rose the scents of mown grass and flowers in lockside gardens, but the smoke of bonfires spiralled up into the air and their cheerful crackle brought whiffs of woodsmoke.

With September departed both the summer assistants and the white tops to lock keepers' caps. Sam had temporarily left the river and was working with his father and brothers in the family coal business at Goring. I would meet him sometimes for a lunchtime drink. Since he still lived at Pangbourne and drank in The Swan in the evenings, and now the evenings were decidedly shorter, there was more time for social relaxation. On one such evening, Fred decided to hold another party.

It was mid-October, I was on duty at Mapledurham so the arrangement was that Peter would pick up Jean in the afternoon, together they would bring ENTERPRISE from the Kennet up to Mapledurham in time for sunset, and we would all go up to Whitchurch, I would then commute to work next day at Caversham. This had the advantage of keeping the boat in a safe place, under my eye, as well as providing local accommodation. An idea had been forming in my mind for some time about introducing Jean to the canals and this seemed like a useful curtain-raiser. So, about six o'clock one fresh autumn evening, they came sidling through the weir outfall into Mapledurham Lock, now quite devoid of wasps.

Peter had an interesting tale to recount as we went up Hardwick Reach. Coming up the Warren he had, as instructed, given Jean the tiller. The river was both wide and deserted, an excellent place to start learning. However, by evil mischance, a solitary fisherman had a ledger line well out to a float in midstream, there being virtually no current. Jean, handling the boat with confidence, asked Peter why that man was waving and dancing on the bank. Peter glanced over the counter and saw the tell-tale evidence of float and line entangled about the rudder and, some hundred feet behind, the rippling wash of a fishing rod being towed at speed. He quickly cut it loose and opened the throttle to make good his escape and chivalrously to prevent Jean's ears from being assailed by the irate angler.

We slipped up Whitchurch lock cut in the twilight of a windless October evening, smoke rising vertically from the brass-ringed cabin chimney, the stove glowing costly in the lighted cabin. The white lock cottage showed through the trees, its Gothic windows sending a welcoming shaft of light into the dusk. Inside Fred and Hazel greeted us travellers with a table groaning with cold supper.

The party was the outcome of an enterprise run by Fred and Sam during the fishing season. A notice on the lockside announced the sale of 'Best Oxfordshire Worms'. The worms, retailed from a moss-filled bucket, were obtained by the following method. A steel mooring spike was driven into the lawn and a crocodile clip with a single wire ran from there to a domestic three-pin plug, where it was attached to the positive terminal. The worm hunter passed the wire through a window into the house, the assistant switched on and Presto! for a radius of several feet from the spike worms rose by the hundred. After a few seconds the current was switched off, the plug removed allowing the wormhunter to collect a bucketful of the best and juiciest. The proceeds of this trade formed the foundation of Fred's Autumn Beano.

In the course of the festivities Sam came down into ENTER-PRISE'S warm and glowing cabin. We sat over a glass or three and I could see that ideas were beginning to form in his mind. The next time he was to be aboard was also to be at Whitchurch but in very different circumstances.

I had now been in the employ of the Conservancy for six months and as a result was due six days leave. If this were taken in a period coinciding with days off either end, this could be stretched to ten days. What better way, I suggested to Jean in the cosy ambience, of being introduced to the canal system and my friends there, than a trip next month round Brentford and the Grand Union Canal to Braunston, returning via Oxford? The idea was accepted, and another cast of fate's die was made, although I was not to realise it at the time, indeed the magnetic attraction that the canals had for me was so strong that it doubtless unbalanced my mental compasses.

So the stage was set for another aquatic adventure. The last week-end in October, Peter took ENTERPRISE down river to Brentford where, by arrangement with Leslie Morton, he tied her up on Durham Wharf to await our arrival. The following Friday, Jean was able to finish at lunchtime, while Dick Knightley agreed to keep an eye on the lock and weir at Caversham (traffic by now was virtually non-existent) so we caught the bus to Brentford, arriving at Durham Wharf about three o'clock. Normally my arrival would have passed virtually unnoticed by the assembled Willow Wren personnel, but being in the company of an attractive woman, I caused severe disruption of business. The tractor-driver, Jumbo, found it constantly necessary to be running in and out of the tractor shed, Stan the clerk blinked owlishly behind his dark-rimmed spectacles, Morton goggled, boatmen appeared, as if by magic to assist with loading our small quantity of luggage. Jean went to open a case which, unknown to her, the girls at her office had filled with confetti. The beastly stuff flew in all directions, hurtling forth from the cabin doors in a great cloud, causing lusty whoops from the onlookers.

However, we disdained such frivolity and made haste to be off, for dark fell early and there were ten locks to go to my target for the night, The Malt Shovel at Cowley. There were lock keepers all the way up the flight in those days, including one who had been a regular soldier in the Royal Berkshires, so we made rapid uphill progress, though accompanied by knowing nods and winks. We cleared the flight well before the locking-up time of 6.30 p.m. and soon after 7.30 were pulling abreast of a converted butty boat which Morton had arranged for me to tow up to Cowroast Summit. By now it was pitch-dark, especially beneath the trees which cluster below the lock. I have always had good night vision, so, when we had had supper, I led the way over the butty's stern to the bank, Jean following. Alas, the bank sloped slightly and Jean's night vision was non-existent. She scrabbled wildly, waved her arms and vanished backwards with a resounding splash. She was quite unable to swim, but I grabbed her before she sank. The water was not deep enough to cover her when she stood up, but it was black and murky. I got her out, gave her a mug of tea while she changed and dried herself then took her to The Shovel where I poured gin (which she hated) down her as some sort of disinfectant. Apart from a shaking and queasy stomach for a couple of days she was none the worse. On reflection, she must have been quite keen on my company to have stayed – or perhaps she was not sure how to get home from Cowley!

In those days of commercial traffic one knew where most other boats were, the 'state of the road' being a good indicator. In this instance I had heard that a northbound pair had gone up earlier on that day, but that Arthur was expected down with coal for 'Jam 'ole' (Kearley & Tonge's Preserve Factory at Southall). Since Cowley's bottom gates lay open, with paddles up, I calculated that Arthur must have come through on Friday afternoon, hoping to empty Saturday morning and go back to load in the Coventry coalfields on Tuesday. So next morning I dropped the paddles behind me as we headed north, to give him a bit of a chance. As I was working the butty abreast only one steerer was required and Jean was happy to pull gates to behind me and go and get the next lock ready where they were close to. In fact, we had a 'good road' up as far as Cassiobury Park, a lovely stretch of water which looked magnificent under the autumn tints of the beech leaves, then we must have reached the point where southbound Arthur had met the northbound pair, for from then on the locks were against us.

As Jean prepared to walk up from Ironbridge Lock to Albert's Two, I made a swift calculation. 'You may' I said 'see a big chap in blue overalls and red beret come biking up. If so, let him have the lock'. She looked oddly at me but went off. As I dropped the paddles, I heard a bike come creaking up the towpath and sure enough Arthur's mate Ernie appeared, clad as expected. Jean was by now a speck in the distance. 'Boats a-comin' up' he boomed, then 'Oh, hullo Dave. Didn't know you was about'.

We exchanged pleasantries as the boats went out. 'Loose you by above Albert's' I called, he waved his hand in acknowledgement and began cranking vigorously at the bottom paddles.

While the boats rose in the bottom lock of Albert's Two, Jean made a cup of tea and I rushed up to the next lock to draw it off. Just as we were about to go out of the top gates Ernie clanked into view. Jean looked at me as if I were a soothsayer who had just scored a prognostractory bullseye while Ernie was so amazed at the sight of my female mate that, jaws agape, he rode into a strapping stump. When I loosed them by, as promised, in the longer pound above Jean was minutely inspected by Arthur and Rose, Ernie's mum. The fat was in the fire now, for I had been previously marked down by the women of the boats as an eligible bachelor, but now the news that I had been 'hooked' would fly ahead carried by both Willow Wren and Blue Line boats.

By late afternoon we came up through Apsley Mills, seeing the pair which had gone up before us lying forlornly by the black corrugations of the Mill coal store. The couple aboard were unfamiliar to me, but the young captain called out that they would be 'up The Whip & Collar later'.

I had told Jean much about boat people, of their virtues and way of life but so far she had seen little evidence of my stereotype. A gaping lot they had seemed to her so far, and, alas, the couple who joined us could hardly have been less like my idealised picture. To be fair, the man was, I later discovered, widely regarded as a 'rum un' by the other boaters. With hindsight I can see that he was clearly unbalanced. The young woman with him had joined him from a fairground and, although comely in appearance, had a raucous voice, evidently used to competing with Dodgems and fortissimo rock music, with language which was fit to blister paint. With both of them the copulatory present participle was in regular use both adjectivally and adverbially. I did not know where to put my face. It was before the days of universal pub food, and they were both hungry. 'Get us some f...ing crisps' said she as 'Gi' us some f...ing money then'. 'I ain't f...ing got none'. 'Yes you f...ing 'ave'. Jean offered them both some crisps from her bag. The girl said: 'Ta, luv. Course 'e's fed up 'cos I've 'ad a f...ing stew on the f...ing range for three f...ing days and it ain't f...ing cooked yet'. To which her swain added 'I got off at Ricky and bought a noo loof o' bread. Ate the f...ing lot before lock 80'.

Fortunately, Jean was a broad-minded person and was not offended by the language. They were a good-hearted enough couple; although I later heard some odd tales about the young man, I got on well enough with them. Jean never forgot her introduction to boat people, although, as I have said, the couple were by no means typical.

Next day was Sunday and we started away about nine o'clock, having first obtained Sunday papers. The wherewithal for Sunday lunch had been purchased in Rickmansworth the day before, I was beginning to feel that boating with a female crew had its distinct differences from an all-male one. Several loaded pairs met us as we toiled uphill, not least being my old friends the Whitlocks with IAN and LUCY. Once more Jean was minutely scrutinised, but Bill Whitlock, biking ahead, grinned broadly when he met me, stopped and leaned over the handlebars and said: 'We heard you were a-comin' wi' a new mate' before riding off chuckling.

Jean was feeling somewhat tired when we handed the butty over at Cowroast to her lady owner. Since I guessed that Marsworth locks, leading down from the Summit, would be ready for us, I suggested that she lay down for an hour or so before we set off across Tring Summit. The short autumn afternoon was fading when we plunged into Tring Cutting,

1 The author steers ENTERPRISE at High Bridge Wharf, summer 1962. The swans' roosting place (*see* Chapter 2) is in the background.

2 ENTERPRISE in Burghfield Cut in 1961 en route to Sulhamstead. The natty white tops to the caps were an unsuccessful attempt to create a smart image, but soon became grubby and were dispensed with.

3 The author and Eddie Chappell, BW lengthsman, rowing across flooded meadows at Southcote, Reading, winter 1958.

4 Bill Fisher steering ENTERPRISE round the 'Jammo' turns, River Kennet, summer 1962.

5 ENTERPRISE in Burghfield Old Lock, with passengers landed on the lockside. D.D. Hutchings ('Hutch') is in a small boat by the lower gate.

6 Starting to dismantle Burghfield Old Lock before rebuilding in 1966. Note the ex-GWR broad-gauge rails.

7 Bill Fisher in Shiplake Lock, March 1962, the first Thames lock fitted with the now commonplace hydraulic gear and new style lock office.

8 The author on ENTERPRISE in lock-keeper's uniform.

9 The author at Caversham Lock. Note the Salters' timetable.

10 Going up Hatton, July 1964. Arthur & Ada's cottage is in the distance, Joe Skinner stands on the lockside, and Rose is aboard FRIENDSHIP.

11 Stoke Bruerne Top Lock in the mid-1960s. The Ritchies lived in the first house on the right, and their floating shop and REDCAP are tied up left, beyond the flagpole.

12 Iris Segal

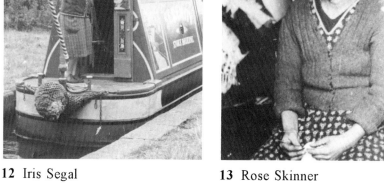

13 Rose Skinner

14 At Stratford-upon-Avon, waiting for the Queen Mother to pass.
L to R: Joe Skinner, Jean, Joan Field (the author's aunt), the author.

15 Rose Skinner looking out of FRIENDSHIP. This boat is now preserved at the Boat Museum at Ellesmere Port.

16 LINDA carrying the Queen Mother, Robert Aickman (behind the sea cadet), Earl Balcarres and David Hutchings.

17 Joe & Rose Skinner, with Pete taking their photograph.

18 Keith Christie and CASSIOPEIA moving the bandstand.

19 Charlie supervising from the bandstand.

and by the third lock of Marsworth, darkness was coming down. I worked down to the bottom on my own (no great problem when the locks are ready for you, and you don't have to shut gates) and tied up outside The White Lion. I put the engine off and went in the cabin to find my crew fast asleep. The fresh air and exercise of two days, not to mention her bath at Cowley, had quite done for her. I made a cup of tea and as I did so, detected the approaching mutter of a boat's engine. A headlight's glow lit up the buildings of the maintenance yard just along from where we were tied, then it came in view, a glowing yellow eye, mirrored among the ripples of the water surface, slowly advancing and joined by the cyclopean glare of a loaded butty trailing behind. I watched, largely blinded, as the motor drew level, then above the noise of the engine I heard Ray White's voice 'It's David with ENTERPRISE'.

I walked round to the lock to help as Ray's loaded pair came gliding in. He decided that he would tie up for the night on the rings above the lock, so later, I sat in the butty's cabin with him and Margaret exchanging news and gossip. They had both met Jean at the Paddington Rally, but she slept on soundly all evening and so was unavailable for social discourse.

Next day was grey and autumnal with occasional gleams of weak sunlight. Ray White had given me a 'good road' (i.e. all the locks were ready) to Fenny Stratford, some dozen miles and seventeen locks northward. Pausing only to replenish stores at the little shop by Red Lion Bridge at Marsworth, we were at Fenny Lock by late lunch time, where we had a 'quickie' in the pub beside the lock. Once below Fenny Lock we were in the Northampton Section, several of whose maintenance men I had come to know following my extended sojourn in Stoke Bruerne during the savage frost of the winter before. I was not surprised therefore when, on approaching Simpson Bank, I was hailed from the cab of a grab dredger. The beaming, cigarette-spiked face of 'Craney' the dredger driver peered out at me. 'Whee oop then, mairt. Where's this ole gel we bin 'earing about?' Jean appeared from the cabin and flashed a great smile. Craney nearly bit his fag in half. ''Ow far tonight? Bottom o' Stoke?' 'Should do' I replied. 'I'll tell old Em' to get 'em in for you' he called as I disappeared round the bend. ('Old Em' was Emily Woodward, landlady of The Boat Inn at Stoke Bruerne.)

Like all other Grand Union flights in those days, Stoke Bruerne was locked up at 6.30 p.m. and the lock went on, top and bottom, at 6.00. This ensured that any boats in the flight were clear by finishing time. In those days the locks all had 'centre' or gate paddles and 30 minutes was not an unreasonable time to clear a flight of seven locks. Today it takes double the time because of a very short-sighted policy of removing gate paddles. As a consequence, I knew we would not get up the locks that night, but was not too worried because I had planned to stop two nights at Stoke. We tied up below the locks soon after 6.30 p.m. in the dark, had supper and then walked up the lane to Top Lock and The Boat.

Time appeared to have stood still for 12 months when I lifted the Norfolk latch on the bar door and stepped inside. There was the same flagged floor and wooden settles, the same old lady with the snow-white curls behind the bar, and the same early-evening locals standing before the flickering fire as there had been the winter before. Teddy Cook, the vet, who had already met Jean, greeted us warmly, I felt more at home here than in any place I had been since I had left the Grand Union the previous spring, even including the Thames-side villages. Old Jack James, once the lock keeper, now the caretaker and doorman at the newly opened Waterways Museum, and years before an owner-boatman based on the Kennet at Reading, came in and greeted us. I was able to give him news of his sister Millie and brother-in-law Jack, who still lived in Reading and whom I saw fairly frequently. We were invited home for coffee by a business man who had befriended me the winter before and who was, I am certain, amazed that I had acquired such a presentable girlfriend and not come to a sticky end. He even insisted on getting his car out and driving us back to Bottom Lock.

Next morning we came up the locks to tie outside The Boat. Colonel Ritchie, a director of Willow Wren, lived in the large brick house by the lock and he and Mollie, his wife, invited us in for baths and sherry. Jean was overwhelmed by our visit, by the welcome given us by so many village people and by the prettiness of the scene. It was not just the old stone and brick buildings clustering on the canal side which gave the impression that the canal was the main street of the village, nor the gentle green hills with their soft autumnal tints in trees and hedgerows, nor the friendliness of the people, but a subtle combination of all those things, and above all the way in which the canal seemed to pull all the ingredients together. As we left on the Wednesday morning, she looked a last time at the scene and said wistfully: 'How I should love to live here'. The web of fate had to have a few more strands spun before her wish was granted, but I suppose it was that moment which made me realise that perhaps this was not just another girlfriend but a potential partner for life.

I had intended going on to Braunston, then up to Hawkesbury Junction ('Suttons Stop' to boaters) for a night before retracing our steps to Braunston and returning to the Thames via Banbury, but on the morning of our departure Jack James had some evil news. A bad breach had occurred in the Oxford Canal between Brinklow and Ansty, thus cutting off Hawkesbury by the direct route. 'Why don't you go to the big dinner at Coventry instead?' he suggested. This was the annual Dinner Dance of the Coventry Canal Society. 'I'll get you tickets' said he, 'and Brian'll give you a lift back'. This last was a reference to Brian Collings, a talented young boat painter, who had acted as mate for us last winter and who lived in nearby Northampton. And so it was all arranged, with, again, far-reaching consequences as we shall see.

Jean was not enthusiastic about the prospect of Blisworth and Braunston tunnels on the next stage, but solved the problem by sitting smoking in the cabin with the lights on until the boat came out into the open. Apart from this we had an uneventful journey, tying up below Bottom Lock at twilight. There were several pairs of boats in, and the men at Willow Wren's repair yard just opposite all made their inspection of my new mate. It was Wednesday, and Wednesday night was the night that the gaffer visited, so we could be sure of company at The Admiral Nelson that evening.

The Nelson was the unofficial headquarters of the narrow-boat industry in those days. An unspoiled rural pub, set down a long lane and beside the third lock of Braunston Flight, it was kept by Hubert and Thirza Clarke, a lovely couple with roots in the boating industry. Once a week, on Wednesday, Leslie Morton visited his outpost of empire in the Midlands and held court in feudal style. Boatmen from all over the Grand Union and its adjoining canals made a point of tying at Braunston on Wednesdays to settle all outstanding matters. Hiring, firing, new boats or engines, were all arranged over pints or (for Morton) whiskies in the cosy little bar.

During the evening I learned that the Ansty burst was a particularly serious one. It meant that the all-important coal trade from the Coventry and North Warwick pits to the London area was in serious jeopardy. The only way round it was for boats to load light and head northwards along the Coventry Canal to Fazeley Junction, south west into Birmingham and then south eastwards back to Braunston via Warwick. This involved heavy lockage, in some cases 40 narrow locks having to be worked twice for each pair and 51 broad locks as against four locks the direct way, and an extra journey of some 70 miles. The boaters were not pleased because their earnings would be drastically affected through less tonnage carried and extra hours taken. Morton was sympathetic but not very helpful. Unless Waterways were prepared to make some sort of financial concession there was little he could do, apart from finding as much traffic north bound for Birmingham as possible. Arthur and Ernie, I heard, had run into the problem the day before and had had to come stern-first for two miles, to Brinklow, where they winded and retraced their steps. Already they were well on their way to Birmingham hoping to load at Baddesley Basin before the weekend. 'Mester Streaks' their boss, was paying them extra, so 'Mester Morton' ought to do the same it was hinted. A fascinating discussion raged back and forth for a long time until the effect of alcohol began to blur the sense of what was said. The subject was dropped temporarily by mutual consent.

Inevitably I was roped in for musical services as the night progressed. Morton's eyes grew more and more glazed and frog-like as the evening progressed. Ever the gentleman, he proferred elephantine gallantries towards Jean, eventually fixing her with a happy smile, his neck and lower parts enveloped in the red velour curtain with which Thirza separated the bar from the rest of the room.

We spent the next day resting and shopping in Braunston. We were expecting Peter next day, for he was going to spend the weekend helping us down the Oxford Canal. Jean was very enamoured of the countryside which, with its deep-set winding lanes and steep hills, reminded her of her home in Devon. John and Anne Crossley had brought their tripping boat LINDA from their base at Foxton for the annual refit, they were full of high hopes for the re-opening of the Stratford-on-Avon Canal, scheduled for next year. The Crossleys had played an active part in the process by which the Inland Waterways Association had persuaded the National Trust to take over this long-derelict canal, and they were hoping to commence tripping on the River Avon and Stratford Canal in the forthcoming season.

There was a retired steam boatman, Tom Walker, who lived in one of the houses by Bottom Lock. I had got to know him when I was a regular visitor to Braunston by virtue of boating. Like many other boaters he was anxious to assure me that rivers like the Thames held no terrors for him. Seeing my reappearance at such an inclement time of the year, he wanted to know where I was bound. I told him that I was about to return to the Upper Thames. 'I ain't afraid o' runnin' water' he said. 'I bin down there wi' water up to the 'oss's belly, down that Oxford River' I pointed out that I had an engine with the power of twenty horses. He looked hard at me: 'One 'oss on the bank's worth twenty in the water. You watch out for them wire 'oles (weirs) on that Oxford River'. Of course, know-all that I was, I did not take his advice too seriously. After all, I worked for the Thames Conservancy. Before I was much older I was to be harshly reminded of his sage advice.

Finally, on Friday afternoon, we made our way by bus and train to Coventry, ready for the Dinner Dance. The centre of Coventry was a harbinger of what was about to happen to our cities as the sixties drew on. Destroyed in the great air-raid of November 1940, its replanning and rebuilding was heralded as a triumph of post-war Britain. Had we realised that it was to be the blueprint for all the other soulless developments foisted upon us by an unholy mixture of insensitive bureaucrats and money-grubbing developers I don't think we would, as a nation, have been at all enthusiastic. Coventry's destruction was at least an act of war, the rape of so many other towns was brought about by the deliberate act of elected councillors and paid officials. To walk about the grandiose, wind-riven, litter-strewn piazzas was to realise the unsuitability of such concepts for the English climate and the English character. Squares, malls and seats are fine in Southern latitudes, or countries where warm, sunny days are usual. They do not suit the evil-tempered English climate, especially that of the Midlands which is so frequently 'sodden and unkind'. Continental town society is gregarious, flat-dwelling and with a strong underlying culture, but English town society tends to be individualistic, aspirant towards one's own 'castle' and its main culture is home-based. Consequently the centre of Coventry already looked tawdry. Allied to these traits, civic pride is not one of England's glories, this was evidenced by the vulgarity of the shop fascias, the awful design of street furniture and the complete subservience of everything to the motor car.

The function was to be at Yates' Wine Lodge, a bogus mediaeval edifice which had escaped both bombs and planners. In the function room I began to meet people I had known on the cut looking somewhat ill-at-ease in their best suits or dresses. Jack James was looking prosperous in a dark suit, Jean had produced a smart cocktail dress. Brian Collings and Janet, his fiancée, were extremely debonair and dapper, some guests were even in evening dress, including the Lord Mayor of Coventry. One couple, however, stood out. This was Joe and Rose Skinner. They were retired boaters whom I had got to know well and who represented the last of the old 'number ones' or owner boatmen. They still had their old horse-drawn boat FRIENDSHIP on which they lived in preference to their cottage at Hawkesbury. They were in their seventies, but hale and hearty. Rose was wearing a twin set of modern style, but Joe was quite resplendent. His feet were encased in solid boots, his suit was of a massive heavy tweed, trousers flaring somewhat below the knees. The jacket had a high-buttoned front and flap pockets, there was a watch-chained waistcoat of the same material, over a pullover, over a heavy striped shirt with a silk scarf at the neck. His clear complexion, a handsome face with bright close-set blue eyes, a cascading white soup-strainer moustache and a good head of hair, his tall, slightly stooping figure, all made a particularly striking impression. A finer example of the Anglo-Saxon would have been hard to find. Many times since have I been struck by his resemblance to that unknown warrior whose likeness is preserved in the Sutton Hoo helmet-mask in the

British Museum.

I shyly professed admiration for his suit. His eyes lit up. 'Ar. That were a good bargain. I 'ad it built by an Oxford man, down St Ebbes. 'Let's see, ar! that were the year of the General Strike'. Certainly it had worn well. I think any self-respecting moth larvae would have retired with aching jaws from a contest with Joe's tweed.

Jack James in his youth had held a bit of a torch for Rose, so he, to Joe's great suspicion, sat next to her when he went to the table. Joe, however, had an eye for a pretty young woman, so Jean was placed between him and myself. By the end of the meal she was aching in the ribs, because Joe, always a perfect gentleman, had nevertheless a trait of emphasising conversational points with a nudge in the ribs from his elbow.

The meal was not a memorable one from the culinary point of view, the soup when it appeared was watery. Silence fell as top table slurped their way into it. Joe, who had wrongfooted our sprig of the table by pinching Jean's bread roll, took an exploratory spoonful and boomed across Rose to Jack James 'Cri-ar Jack mate, this could do wi' a bloody rabbut in it', punctuating the comment with a dig at Jean's rib cage. Somehow the meal ended and the dance began. Joe's dance was an energetic form of polka step, his partner clutched tight and his boots thundering away on the floor, thus ensuring lively footwork on her part. Dances themselves were greatly simplified. They were either a 'fast waltz' or a 'slow waltz'. The steps remained constant though the tempo varied. Jean, worried lest the old boy exert himself too much at his age, suggested, after a particularly energetic number as his partner, that he might like to sit down. 'What? Are you tired my dear?' was his solicitous response.

The Coventry Canal Society, along with the Midlands Branch of IWA had been long concerned with the fate of the Stratford-on-Avon Canal. Now that re-opening was in sight, a National Rally of boats was planned for Stratford next summer. Talking of this with Joe over a pint, I suggested that he and Rose took FRIENDSHIP to Stratford. 'I'll take you with ENTERPRISE if all else fails' said I. Privately I thought Sam would have a boat by then which could do it, but kept my thoughts to myself for the moment. Brian, an old friend of the Skinners, as was Janet, agreed that this would be a good plan.

We were certain that a motor boat could be found to tow them. If necessary, I thought, Leslie Morton and Colonel Ritchie could be persuaded to lend a Willow Wren motor.

Joe and Rose thought it over, then said 'yes, we'll come', so the evening ended with plans being laid for next summer. It was a decision with far-reaching consequences for several lives.

Setting off from Braunston next morning was a weary business, none of us felt like leaping into action, having been returned to the boat by Brian sometime after midnight. Stern duty nonetheless had to be done if we were to make our scheduled stop at Banbury that evening, so by just after eight we were away, crossing Braunston Puddle bank on a gusty grey morning. However, with an extra steerer and Jean keeping us well supplied with hot drinks and food during the day, it was a reasonably pleasant day's boating up Napton and Marston Doles locks and round the twisting Oxford Summit. Across the summit the weather cleared and for a while we had some weak autumnal sun, picking out the rolling landscape, highlighting its russet hedgerows and guardian elms, glinting off far distant roofs and wheeling clouds of starlings. Its westering rays gleamed off the windows of Griffins Farm astride its ridge, which the canal moated on three sides. It was just by the bridge, on the apex of an inside turn, that Joe Skinner's mule, Dolly, had fallen in the cut six years before, an event which brought about the retirement of he and Rose from active carrying.

We came out of Fenny Compton cutting, 'Old Tunnel Straight' as the boaters call it, nearly on sunset. As we drew near to Claydon Top Lock I heard behind me a clanking and rumbling. I glanced back to see, of all things, an ex-Great Western 'Castle' class locomotive speeding along the Stratford & Midland Junction Railway, beneath which had just come. There was a rake of mineral wagons behind her, probably bound for the Great Central at Woodford Halse which was a comedown for an express engine. This was the last train I was ever to see on that railway. Within six months it was closed completely. What was particularly ironic was that the train should have had such unusual motive power, for its usual locomotives were dowdy black ex-LMS or British Railways standard types

In the quiet evening, a practice bell was clanging from the curious little belfry of Claydon Church, welcoming us back to Oxfordshire. Jean and I walked ahead to get the locks ready, while Peter brought ENTERPRISE down. In the twilight it was almost eerily still, the soft silence was broken only by the last gurgles of the filling lock and the distant, muffled popping of ENTERPRISE'S Armstrong-Siddeley. From a farm gate several fields away came the rustic call of a cowman to his herd 'COOM UP YEW BOOGGERS!' Long before Cropredy it was dark, but we headed on, finally tying above Banbury Lock as the town clock chimed eight.

After supper we crossed the lift bridge below the lock and, following the steps of L.T.C. Rolt in *Narrow Boat*, made our way to the curious little street corner pub called The Struggler. In Rolt's day this was a noted boating pub. He describes in one of his books an uproarious night in the company of boaters and Romanies. By 1963 it was much quieter and kept by an engine-driver's widow, whose son still worked on the railway. The landlady's late husband had been on the footplate of the Abingdon 'Bunk' when it had failed to stop on the approach to Abingdon Station, hit some stationary coaches and propelled them over the buffer stops and through the booking office, completely wrecking the old station, which the Great Western rebuilt in handsome style. This exploit was legendary in Abingdon in my youth, for years as a small boy I would never linger behind buffer stops on any station, so it was, for me, a fascinating experience, to hear tales of the railway from those who made that mode of transport so full of life and interest. In any case, it made a change from boats and canals. The Struggler was supposed to have been 'Struggler' Grantham. He was one who would always struggle to get by, and its name epitomised the cheery, down-to-earth philosophy of the cut. It was little more than the ground floor of a terraced cottage. The Gents was in the back yard and ladies had to go upstairs, through the landlady's bedroom, but for all that, it was a friendly, good-natured place. It was a sad day when it lost its licence.

During the night we woke to hear rain drumming on the cabin roof, morning came amid sheets of rain and gales. At least, I thought, we'll have some water below Banbury, and my hunch proved correct. All morning the rain drove at us in stinging gusts, I was very glad that ENTERPRISE still had some ballast in her, but even so it was a continual battle to stay in the channel.

As we dropped through Somerton Deep Lock I saw, across the flat meadows of Cherwell valley, a boat's cabin side moving painfully slowly towards Oxford. I pointed this out to Peter who said 'Rather him than me on a day like this'. Long before reaching the next lock, Heyford Common, we had caught up with it. It was an old wooden Joey boat, with a full length cabin on it, being bowhauled by a group of students. Through the gale I asked where they were going 'Thrupp' came the reply 'we want to get there tonight'.

In those weather conditions it would have taken about a week to cover the ten miles or so. Against my better judgement I offered them a tow, which was gratefully accepted. Peter muttered about not getting to Oxford for a train home that night, but I pointed out that there were plenty of buses from Kidlington, just beyond Thrupp. I made up a pair of cross-straps from some old rope and off we went. Of course it meant double-locking every time and the students seemed disinclined to do much to help. They huddled miserably in the cabin (I don't even think they had the means of making tea) until I pointed out, somewhat tartly, at Allens Lock that if they didn't work their own boat, I would leave them behind.

Dusk fell at Northbrook Lock, it being very dark under the trees. I inadvertently left ENTERPRISE in neutral below the lock instead of in astern with her fenders against the bottom gate. Consequently, when Peter and I drew the bottom paddles off she went down the pound. Jean was cooking supper in the cabin blissfully unaware of our shouts from the bank. It took several minutes to retrieve the situation.

All day I had covertly been glancing at the Cherwell, looking for signs of flood, but so far there were none. It must have been about 6.30 p.m. when we came onto the 'Old River', a section where the Cherwell was incorporated into the canal and which could be nasty in flood, especially with a butty. Although we flew down the length of nearly a mile it was nowhere near as bad as it had been last winter when I had come down it alone. Soon we were through Shipton Weir Lock, where the gate stood open to receive us, to my heartfelt thanks, and plodding down the last stretch to Thrupp. I loosed the Joey off at the drawbridge, the students tied her up without a word of thanks, let alone the offer of a drink but I didn't really care. ENTERPRISE was back within a day's run of home and I knew the road like the back of my hand – or so I thought! We tied up, still in lashing rain, on the wharf just before Longford Lane. Peter squelched off to the Oxford bus stop a few yards away and Jean and I turned in early, lulled to sleep by the incessant rain.

The rain had eased next morning, but the wind was mounting in fury. It was getting on for midday when we arrived at Kings Lock there I had decided to get onto the Thames via Duke's Cut. A Waterways lengthsman told me that the river was rising fast, but confident in my ability to handle ENTERPRISE on the fast-running Kennet, I carried on. 'I ain't afraid o' running water' I said to myself. It was a rash decision. There was a Conservancy stoppage at Benson, just outside the Reading District, until December. I had resolved to go down river this far that day and catch the bus back to Reading from Benson. My leave expired next day, as did Jean's so this was to be our last day afloat. Jean packed up all our things, and busied herself about lunch while I steered up the Wolvercote back water, which was high and running much harder than usual. It is a twisting channel under willow trees – very pretty in summer, with wide grassy expanses of flat meadow beyond. In the several times I had used it, I had never experienced the slightest difficulty, but this time was to be different.

For a start the wind was blowing from the west at almost hurricane force, so that then I came into the part where one has to make a right-angled turn upstream into the weir stream of Kings Lock, it was broadside on, pinning me against the side and, as the fore end came out into the weir stream, it forced it downstream. The second factor was the current in the river which, by evil mischance, was running in the same direction as the wind was blowing and running hard too. One weir gate was drawn, I could see.

Twice I tried cautiously edging out, and twice I was forced round. The only thing to do, I thought, was to rush at it, full speed, aiming for the far bank and try to get my stern out of the mill stream into deep water. So, in desperation I tried once more, backing down the mill stream then giving her full power. Water creamed under the fore end, I cut the corner as much as I dared to get the fore end facing upstream and she nearly came round. Suddenly a huge blast came out of nowhere and forced the fore end out into the fast-running weir stream. I held the tiller hard over, but she would not come round, instead she careered broadside-on down the weir stream towards the yawing brim of Kings Weir.

I threw the gear lever astern and held back for all I was worth. The current slammed the stern against the left bank, but we were still travelling fast. I leapt ashore with the stern line desperately looking for something on which to strap her and check the headlong career. There was nothing save grass. I took the line round my shoulders and tried to become a human anchor. Still she bore down on the weir with Jean, all oblivious, in the cabin. A great white post, with a notice saying 'Danger', loomed up by the fore end and the stem post struck it. It must have been 12 inches square and it broke off with the blow. ENTERPRISE rolled violently and came to rest, her fore end on the jagged stump, her stern on the bank, jammed right across a rising weir stream.

I breathed a sigh of relief and, as a white-faced Jean came out of the cabin doors, tooted 'SOS' in Morse on the hooter. The lock keeper and his grown-up son appeared through the bushes on the lock island. Never was I so relieved to see another human being.

All four of us tugged at the stern line to try and free the boat, but she was stuck fast. The lock keeper eventually released us by closing the gate. Although the water immediately began rising up the meadow bank, the vicious ripping current slackened. At once ENTERPRISE floated free and I was able to back her up to the entrance to the mill stream. With hindsight, perhaps I should have backed up to the lock cut, while the river was shut in, but Jean had been badly frightened. I was somewhat shocked and not thinking straight and the lock keeper was understandably anxious to open his weir gate as soon as possible.

The upshot was that I decided to tie ENTERPRISE up securely at the top of the mill stream and go home, she could not be brought to Reading until Christmas, six weeks away yet, so she might as well stay in a safe, if remote, place until such time as I could move her. After all Oxford was not so very far away from home.

So Jean and I loaded up our bags, I locked up the cabin and, after a farewell cup of tea with the lock keeper in his kitchen, we set off down the towpath to Godstow Bridge and the Wolvercote bus.

Within the hour we were having a wash and brush-up in the palatial City Council lavatories by the Martyr's Memorial in St Giles and then, feeling much more like human beings, we went for tea in the Cadena Café in Cornmarket. The warm, coffee-scented atmosphere, the Kunzle cakes and plush seats made the frantic struggle out at Kings Weir pale into a disturbing memory. But somehow the knowledge of perils jointly faced and survived had forged a deeper than ever bond between us. We both dozed off during the hour-long bus ride back to Reading through the dark early evening, for somehow each other's company gave us a feeling of security.

As a sequel, on my next day off, which happened to be a Saturday, Peter came with me to Oxford. We walked out from Wolvercote and found ENTERPRISE riding quite unharmed where I had left her. The engine started first touch on the starter. We stripped all the awning and cloths off to reduce windage, but there was hardly a breath of wind that day and she pulled out of the Mill Stream into the Weir Stream with no trouble whatsoever. The lock keeper was pleased to see that no damage had occurred. I asked what he'd done about reporting the broken pile. He chuckled. 'Th' ole Inspector come up a couple o' days arter you got stuck. 'E says 'What's 'appened to that there ole danger post?' I tells 'im a bloody girt tree come down in the flood an' bust it orf'. Lock keepers' solidarity was truly a wonderful thing.

Chapter 8 — WINTER WATERS

Although the pleasure craft had largely vanished from the Thames by end-October there was still life on the river. As the boatowners, one by one, laid their craft up, sheeted down, batteries disconnected, engines and stern gear greased and silent, the year-round life of the river came into its own. True there was not much in the way of traffic, but weir work became much more important. A radical change had come over water management since the disastrous floods of 1947, and weirs were either being rebuilt, or scheduled for rebuilding. The change reflected the parallel changes in land use, transport and society in the Thames valley, not all of them, in my view, changes for the better.

From earliest times Thames weirs had been regulatory, the oldest method being paddle and rymer tackle. Unlike the Severn or Trent, the waters of the Thames were impounded from a remote time to serve various interests, chiefly navigation and mills, but also fishing and agriculture. Most of the flash locks, which must have been terrifying installations, were removed before the 19th century, although several survived 'up West' until the 1930s; but with the setting-up of the Thames Conservancy after 1857 it was necessary for the controlling authority to take into account an increasing number of important functions. These came to include water supply, land drainage, pollution control and flood control as well as safeguarding and maintaining existing rights of navigation, milling, fishery and so forth. As the times changed, so did the emphasis of maintenance.

Traffic until the mid 19th century was predominantly horse-drawn. Such pleasure traffic, or more serious passenger traffic as did exist was largely rowed or sailed. Sailing was possible for commercial craft in the lower reaches, whilst the influence of the tide rendered bank haulage impossible below Brentford or Strand-on-the-Green. There was, however, a continuous towpath above this point with bridges over side streams, gates where it passed through field boundaries, and ferries where it changed from one bank to another. In places where the bank was obstructed, as just above Pangbourne

Weir, floats were kept so that lines could be passed to upstream craft. Where the navigation channel passed outside islands, trees and bushes were cut down to prevent snagging of towlines. Nevertheless, horse towing on the Thames had many drawbacks, notably bridges where the navigation arch was in the centre. Going downstream the animals would be whipped up to give steerage, then the line unpegged at the last moment and one shot the archway. One of the last horse drawn contracts was house coal from the Coventry area and Wilfred Townsend of Abingdon told me of shooting Shillingford Bridge in flood with two boats abreast going sideways through the arch and, once through, revolving slowly as they swept on with Uncle Alf on the towpath with the horse swearing fit to bust as he tried to catch up.

Going upstream, the horse hauled from the roadway, often through a specially provided snatch block, until the fore end of the craft was almost directly below. The horse was then unpegged, the horse's end of the towline dropped through the upstream side and retrieved aboard and made fast, then the end which had hitherto been attached to the craft was now attached to the horse and passed through the arch. The horse returned to the towpath and carried on. This was the origin, on older Thames bridges of deep rope grooves on the upstream spandrel of arches and the downstream parapet.

Ferries were another problem. These were flat-bottomed punt-like craft and some horses did not take kindly to boating. They had to be coaxed aboard and once aboard prevented from shying or rearing, then they had to be coaxed ashore. Just in my length there were four ferries at one time: above Goring Lock, Gatehampton, below Mapledurham Lock and Roebuck at Tilehurst. On top of this was the awkward approach to Whitchurch Lock, with an obstructed approach leading to a weir from upstream, and no towpath at all in the downstream lock cut. Upstream boats were poled up from Whitchurch Bridge, downstream ones were flushed down to the cut by drawing the lock paddles behind them.

Yet navigation, awkward and cumbersome as it was, was possible at most states of the river. Many old boaters have told me of boating 'wi' water to the 'oss's belly'. Jack Garner of Reading said his Dad would go 'when the steam tugs was tied up'. Jack James, his brother-in-law, told me that his earliest

memory was drifting down on the water 'up West', his father
having taken the horses round the 'high road to Yarnton', and
mother bringing the boats down abreast with a weight over
the stern. On this occasion the floods were 'out' as Thames
people say and Mrs. James took a short cut through a flooded
farmyard near Eynsham. Tom Walker, he who was 'not afraid
o' runnin' water' had frequently gone up and down river with
horse boats in flood, so had Joe Skinner and many others I
knew. Why therefore was it so nearly disastrous when I tried
it with ENTERPRISE?

The key to change was the device of the paddle and rymer
weir. When floods came in ancient times, the first thing was to
draw the top paddles and rely on overfall weirs. This merely
created a surface current and the river behaved like a reservoir
behind a dam, rising up and flooding the meadows. This
retained a head of water in the mills which were vital to the
local economy, and silt to be deposited over the valley bottom
meadows instead of being carried away downstream. When
things got really desperate another row of paddles and, ultimately, the rymers would be drawn. When the word went
round 'all tackle drawn' there was nothing more to be done.
Lock keepers and ferrymen would retire upstairs to await the
river's return to normal. Riverside towns and villages were
both small and built on bluffs and terraces above the flood
plain. Bridges were few and only occurred where one or both
banks were well above flood level. Not surprisingly the fact
that the Thames virtually bisects southern England east of the
Cotswolds made it a natural barrier. It was the ancient frontier
between Wessex and Mercia. William the Conqueror fortified
its crossings, Stephen fought Matilda up and down the valley,
the Civil War saw battles sieges and skirmishes from Brentford
to New Bridge, even Hitler's invasion plans envisaged seizing
the Thames crossings before dealing with London.

The Great Western Railway started the profound changes.
First it dealt a mortal blow to water traffic either by direct competition or by controlling the Kennet & Avon and (for a while)
the Thames & Severn Canals. This made it increasingly uneconomic to maintain ferries and towpaths although the Thames
Conservancy continued to do this until the Second World War.
Such water traffic as survived on a large scale operated by tug
and barge which rendered towpaths unnecessary.

The less obvious changes were perhaps more profound than the obvious ones. Agriculture changed slowly but inexorably. The Corn Laws were repealed, American and Canadian wheat came in to England with the opening up of the Prairies by railways and the development of trans-Atlantic steamships, so one by one the mills began to fall derelict. Refrigerated steamships brought meat from the other side of the world thus reducing the need for meadow land with its rich hay crops. At the same time fast trains and the first underground line began to make city merchants cast their eyes westward in search of a pleasant place to live within an hour of town. In the late 19th century the broad gauge of Brunel's original line gave place to a quadruple main line into Paddington and commuters began to discover Taplow, Maidenhead, Twyford and, above all, Reading. The pressure on riverside land became acute. It is not to be wondered at that two of the most famous literary works set against the Thames background: *Three Men in a Boat* and *Wind in the Willows* both date from the period between 1880 and 1914 when the railway began to popularise the Thames valley.

Stately mansions and bijou residences sprang up in those pre-planning days all along the banks and backwaters, on what was once meadow land. As towns grew, sewage pollution became a problem, so did water supply, so did flooding.

Buck weirs probably originated as fish traps, then seem to have been adapted to control undershot mill wheels. They rise upwards from the river bed and thus create, as soon as they are opened, a deep, scouring current. They also require lifting gear. For these reasons they were not much used in ancient times, but they do have the advantage of being capable of discharging large quantities of water quickly. The technology of the 19th century meant that large buck weirs could be built in iron and later steel, also mechanical lifting gear could be provided enabling a lock keeper's muscle to raise or lower a much bigger gate. Thus a greater volume of water could be discharged quickly.

The replacement process was slow, hindered by World Wars and financial depression, and was not by any means complete by 1947. In that year a severe winter was followed by heavy flooding. Although water control had improved, not all locks had telephones and there was still a mixture of weir tackle on the river, including much paddle and rymer gear which was not intended to run water off quickly. Very heavy flooding occurred in areas which had been built over meadow ground in the late 19th and early 20th centuries, notably South Oxford (acres of council estates housing car workers were inundated) and the Caversham Road area of Reading.

Since the 1940s ever increasing pressure was coming on riverside land, London's and other towns' demand for water was increasing, so heavy capital works were carried out. The great weir at Caversham with its electrically operated radial gates dated from the mid-1950s. The corollary to this new attitude to water control was that the new weirs created new problems. A faster run-off in flood-time meant more topsoil washed away and no silt deposited on the land. Such fields as survived in agricultural use beside the river now had to be expensively fertilised with artificial substances containing nitrates which often leached into the river water. Faster currents above and below weirs created scouring and silting. Fewer cattle were being kept in the meadows which remained, so the young shoots along the banks were no longer grazed. In many places the towpath became separated from the river by a screen of trees, some of which were of substantial girth. This, apart from anything else, made it increasingly difficult to get ashore from craft in the river. Although in summer the Thames had its benign, placid face, in winter and in flood time it was a much more dangerous river than formerly.

The attention of the lock keepers became concentrated on their weirs as winter drew on. The November rains brought a major rise in water levels and the first significant increase in flood since the spring. From now on I found myself adjusting levels almost daily, and, remembering both Fred's advice, as well as my experience at Kings, took care only to venture onto the remoter weirs with a safety line about me, whilst I never touched a paddle and rymer weir without such a safety precaution. When flood warnings were imminent, men from the Engineer's Department would be sent out as 'weir runners' to assist lock keepers in raising large gates or drawing high rymer weirs.

At other times the Engineers treated the winter as their open season for lock repairs thus foreshadowing the unpopular 'stoppage season' instituted by the British Waterways

Board in the 1970s. The Conservancy did, however, play the game. Really lengthy stoppages were not common and mainly caused by the need to enlarge and rebuild lock chambers to cope with increasing summer traffic. Shorter stoppages of up to two months duration were more often the norm, including those for the mechanisation of locks. With the winter season coming on, Engineer's traffic increased considerably, the Conservancy having an impressive fleet of tugs and barges based at Reading.

The Reading District Engineer had two tugs at his disposal, one being a small river-type vessel called CHERWELL, the other being a very imposing looking craft called CHURN. I recall CHERWELL'S predecessor, which was a very handsome-looking ex-steam tug, KENNET, with a tall funnel and boxy wheelhouse, her replacement was more humdrum. Her skipper was a jolly, stout man called 'Pedlar' Palmer, whose mate Phil Wilkins steered the barges that she towed. Phil was somewhat taciturn until he learned that I knew some of the bargemen who worked in and out of Brentford and Limehouse. Both of them were old river hands and were fascinating to listen to if one could get them yarning while the lock emptied or filled. I tended to see them mostly when I was at Caversham, but they worked all through the Reading district. CHURN'S skipper, David, was a much younger man and took great pride in his charge. The tug had been built at Thorne on the Humber, and had come round the East Coast under her own power. She was like a miniature ocean tug, with high steel bows, a sweeping sheer black hull and elegant counter stern. A squat buff funnel sat behind the wheelhouse giving a further air of puissance. CHURN drew nearly six feet under way, it was said that she could not go above Clifton Hamden, and most certainly she brought up all manner of good things from the bottom when she traversed Caversham Lock Cut.

All the tugs and barges were handled quietly and very professionally by the Engineer's Department men. It was a pleasure to watch them bringing a tow of barges or flats through difficult water. Some of the big dumb barges would carry 70 tons of dredgings or spoil, there would frequently be a mess-flat in tow, or perhaps a sheerlegs for lifting gates or sunken boats, or one of the Reading District's curious narrow boat/barges. These last mystified me, I believe they were built somewhere on the canals, hence their seven foot beam, but they had barge-type fore ends and a stern with a transom like the old Kennet or Wey barges. The Engineer's men were generally a characterful lot. There was one seemingly ancient man, Arthur, whose legs were curiously bent, and who had the habit of making curious vertical gyrations with his index finger as he talked. 'Art', as he was generally called, sometimes acted as lock keeper when the regular man was on leave or sick. He would shamble along the lock side in a sort of walking-sitting-down manner revolving his finger. 'Bwoat a-comin' thur bwoy' he would advise his assistant. Art lived in a badger-like state in a caravan in a field near Moulsford.

There was a cheery general labourer and factotum called Ernie who had a sovereign specific remedy for every known disease, mostly involving severe pain or drastic evacuation of the bowels or both. He was a kindly soul, and anyone feeling the slightest off-colour could be sure of Ernie's ministrations. ''Ead ache bwoy?' he would say to someone suffering from 'hangover vulgaris'. 'You wants ter try a drap o' my missus's rhubarb wine. That'll fix y' up' and so it would, but the patient perforce had to have free and rapid access to the lavatory.

There was a stoppage at Whitchurch involving driving a coffer dam. For some odd reason several locks had no provision for placing stop planks. This was done with a steam piledriver powered by a vertical boiler which also operated a pump to keep the workings dry. Ernie was employed as watchman-cum-boilerman over week-ends and on one occasion, when I was on duty, the Reading office rang wanting to speak to him. It turned out that there was some dispute about his timesheet, so I left him to it and went out of the office to give him some privacy. Ernie, however, was one of those who believed that it was necessary to bellow sufficiently loudly down the telephone to be heard at the other end without benefit of electricity. The fortissimo conversation echoed round Whitchurch. 'ULLO! YES, IT'S ME..... 'COURSE I KNOWS 'OW TER FILL IN A TIMESHEET. WOT? YES, I WORKED TWENTY FOUR HOURS LAST SUNDAY, BLOODY WATCHMAN AIN'T I? O' COURSE I PUT DOWN TWENTY FIVE HOURS .... I KNOW THERE'S ONLY TWENTY FOUR HOURS ON A SUNDAY. I

WORKED ME DINNER HOUR DIDN'T I?'

The expert pile driver, 'Cuff', which was an abbreviation of
Cuthbert, was the proud owner of a telescope. Much was said
of the telescope's power and of the uses to which it was put.
One school of thought claimed that Cuff and the gang had it
mounted on the carpenter's flat for the better observation of
riverside wildlife or planetary conjunctions for, they said,
most of their time was spent bird-watching or star-gazing.
Another, and more widely adhered to, opinion was that it was
used for observing open-air couplings of animals and humans,
and that the gang ran a sort of information-bureau for those
curious of such matters. Probably both these views were
defamatory, for the bank men were always envious of those
with a trade.

Only the Conservancy would have employed a one-armed
bricklayer, but the man in question 'Wingey' was remarkably
fast in spite of his disability. He generally worked with a
Ukranian painter called Sylvester on building maintenance.
The duo were very competent and, in their tea or lunch
breaks, they would sit in the lock office warming themselves
and yarning. I found Sylvester particularly well-informed on
politics and suchlike topics. During the early days of January
he failed to appear at Mapledurham, where he was working. I
asked Wingey if he was ill, and he shook his head 'No mate,
it's 'is religion. It's 'is Christmas now'.

I discovered that not only was he of the Orthodox faith and
thus followed the Gregorian Calendar, but that he was a priest
outside his working hours. Very few of the men swore or
indulged in improper talk in his presence, though he was a
very broad-minded and enlightened man.

At one time during the winter the heavy gates of Goring
finally got to Harry and he took to his bed with a bad back. At
about the same time the gang arrived to decorate the house and
to point up the brickwork. One of the massive chimney pots
was to be taken down and renewed. This was obviously not a
task for Wingey, so he was provided with a mountain of a
labourer who acted as hod-carrier, mortar mixer and crane. The
pot was removed, the labourer took it in his hands and promptly
stepped off the scaffolding onto the roof tiles, which caved in.
He descended, through a jumble of battens, rafters, lath and
plaster, into Harry's bedroom, still bearing a chimney pot.

Harry's convalescence was rudely disturbed when labourer and pot came bursting through the ceiling and threatened to join him in bed.

By way of a contrast were the other navigation staff, the boatmen, who were a breed of men quite unlike their canal namesakes. They were something like aquatic chauffeurs in that they generally steered the inspection launches for the Inspectors and were responsible for maintaining the craft. The job also entailed a good knowledge of the river, its shoals and currents, and considerable tact and diplomacy. It was the first step on the promotional ladder for a man hoping to rise in the Conservancy service. The normal pecking order was assistant lock keeper, relief lock keeper and lock keeper, but assistants and reliefs sometimes became boatmen and thereafter Assistant District Inspector. It was the Conservancy's equivalent of 'coming up through the hawse pipe' in the Royal Navy, for there was still a distinct 'other ranks' feeling about the Navigation Staff as far as Inspectors were concerned. The boatmen were profitable sources of gossip and scandal, for they spent long hours in the Inspector's company patrolling the river. They were out in all weathers and all seasons but winter was the time for major overhauls of boats. At such times the boatmen would be in evidence about the yard on Caversham Lock Island, clad in overalls as they scraped paint or removed cylinder heads. Frequently they would come into the lock office at tea or lunch breaks for a natter. When Phil Harrison and Dick Knightley got together the 'crack', as the Irish would say, was well worth listening to. Both were ex-Chief Petty Officers RN and I would hazard a guess that between them they were aware of every species of villainy known to man. Outrageous tale upon outrageous tale of doings on and about the seven seas would flow, frequently leaving me helpless with laughter. One sample will suffice for this chaste record.

Phil's ship had docked at Portsmouth, so he and other members of the stokers' mess, a class of men not noted for refinement, went ashore to a show. By the time of which I write, the Music Hall tradition had degenerated to strip shows, nudes and blue comedians. Phil and his mates were ensconced in the front row stalls and amused themselves by taking a rise out of the very 'camp' comic, who rose to the bait and became very cross, fluttering his hands and lisping spitefully at his tormentors. After the show they forgot about this affair. Phil went home on leave and took his wife to Bellevue at Manchester. They too sat in the front row stalls. When the comedian came on it was the very same one, he caught sight of Phil in his uniform and evidently recognised him, because he brought the house down and caused Phil much marital strife by saying: 'Ooh! Hello sailor! I say, didn't we have a gay time in Portsmouth last week?'

The most long-running maintenance jobs were on the Chief's launch WINDRUSH and the stately DONOLA. With the latter an elaborate programme was required to keep her in pristine condition. It was said among the boatmen that 'The Don' cost £25 per week just to maintain, without any major repairs. This was more than the wages of two lock keepers. Notwithstanding the fact that 'The Don' spent 50 weeks of each year at Caversham yard, she was regularly repainted, while the boiler was lifted out with the yard's grey derrick crane and given its hydraulic test ashore. It would, I often felt, have been appreciated had the Conservancy let 'The Don' be seen more often, say at Henley or Oxford Eights week, but it was not to be. She lurked coyly in the weir stream until at length being presented to the National Maritime Museum at Greenwich. At least she made the voyage there under power.

At winter week-ends fishermen would be more in evidence than any other river users. Generally they were tolerated by the Navigation staff and many were very good friends with the local Conservancy men. I certainly learned a great deal about the lore of the river from many fishermen at Goring, Mapledurham and Caversham, where they fished from the banks. Only at Goring were they allowed, with a permit, to fish from the weirs. At Caversham fishing was not allowed from the Clappers because a public footpath ran across it and fishing tackle caused a dangerous obstruction. At Mapledurham the fishing rights belonged to the local estate. From the river anglers I heard tales of pike and their rapacious habits, of how they would pull down ducklings and moorhens, but the greatest tales of all came from old Jack 'Wormy' Webb at Whitchurch.

There was no bank or weir fishing allowed at Whitchurch, so old Wormy with his boat had a clear monopoly in the area,

hence his frequent appearances. I learned that he hailed originally from Blisworth in Northamptonshire and thus knew
something of the canals. He had been a professional fisherman all his working life and, like Captain Ahab he had one
enemy left to destroy. This was 'the Gatehampton Monster'.
Somewhere, between the Grotto and Hartslock Islands lived
the greatest, oldest, wickedest pike on the whole River
Thames. I believe that the Thames record for pike then stood
at 44 lb and Wormy reckoned that this one 'were near arf
'undredweight'.

He had had at one time, a patron called Captain Blew-Jones
and Wormy had many a tale of the Captain's prowess with rod
and line, but the Gatehampton Monster saga was in a class of
its own. Wormy had a rather creaky voice which growled and
rumbled as he talked. Sitting over a cup of tea by the roaring
range in Fred's office, he unburdened himself. 'We was a-
fishin' quiet-like in the ole' punt, atween the Grotto and the
railway bridge. Only 'ad a mudweight out upstream to 'old us
steady. Captain Blew-Jones was a-lightin' 'is pipe. 'Webb' 'e
says to me, 'when's this 'ere monster o' yours goin' ter give
us some sport?' 'You wait your time, sir' I says. All of a sudden, bang! e'd took Captain Blew-Jones' bait an' 'e were orf.
Cap'n Blew-Jones struck 'ard an' 'ad im. 'Bring 'im in
steady sir' says I, but bugger me, that pike knew what 'e were
at. 'E go full ahead an' we goes arter 'im punt an' all!' 'Punt
and all Jack?' I laughed. 'Yes mate, punt an' all. Y' see we
was laid on top of a ledge, in shaller water. Th' ole pike gie'd
us such a snatch, the mudweight fell orf the ledge into the
deep water and weren't no good, so orf we goes downstream
bloody near fast as a tug an' barge. I pulls the weight in an
'olds tight. We must 'a' gorn two 'undred yards, right under
the railway arch, an that 'ole pike go right round the pier an'
back through the other arch. Bloody near tips Cap'n Blew-
Jones an' meself in the dannell, but he busts the line on the
brickwork an' we loses 'im'. 'Is he still there then?' I asked.
'Oh ah! 'e's still about. 'E's a big bugger an' all. I've laid for
'im many times since – and I seen 'im take a cygnet – but I
ain't never took a hold on 'im again. One o' these days I'll get
'im, an' that won't arf make them match fishermen sit up'.

Whenever he had the time during the coarse fishing season,
Jack would lurk about in his punt under the bare willows up

by Gatehampton, but I never heard of him landing his quarry.

The rights of bona fide fishermen had to be upheld by lock keepers. I had an official-looking card authorising me as a toll collector under the Railway & Canal Acts, and to act as a water bailiff under the Thames Conservancy Acts. The powers of lock keepers had been curtailed, for at one time they included the power to arrest and detain offenders until such time as they might be brought before a Justice of the Peace. Just where one was supposed to detain the offenders was unclear. The lock office? most were made of wood and fairly flimsy, chain them to a lock gate or a post, like field punishment No.1, I suppose. Only once did it ever come near to violence, and that was at Caversham.

In spite of notices forbidding fishing, many fishermen were tempted to try their luck. If they just brought a rod and keepnet, a blind eye might be turned, but of course there always has to be the one who pushes his luck too far. This type would arrive with umbrella, hamper, maggot tins, camp chair, bags of food, transistor radio and bottles of beer. He would then set up camp across the weir bridge, which was a footpath, and swear at anyone who tried to pass. One such character had several times been asked to move by Dick, and on each occasion had treated him to vigorous abuse and threats. When the lock was busy it was difficult to do much.

Eventually, one autumn Sunday, several members of the public complained, so I set off to investigate. Sure enough, the path was completely blocked, your man sitting in the middle with his radio blaring. I politely pointed out that he was committing an offence and asked him to move. This unleased a tirade of abuse and offers of violent action. I pointed out that I should have to take his name and address and produced my warrant card. That did it. He shouted and bawled, that he was fed up with being shoved about by the likes of fornicating lock keepers. However, I was bigger than he and not terribly impressed by vulgar abuse. I also noticed that he made no effort to put his threats in practice, so, rightly assuming that he was a noisy windbag, I resisted the temptation to drop him and his tackle in the weir and instead rang the police. When the police arrived he promptly abused them heartily, which did him no good whatsoever. Out came the notebooks. I could visualise the scene: 'On approaching the accused, Your

Worship, I informed him that he was committing an offence, to which he replied...'. The word soon got around the fishing fraternity and we had no more trouble. I wished it had been his rod that Jean caught with ENTERPRISE.

Politics tended to rear their head in winter. In summer lock keepers were far too busy to worry overmuch about working conditions, but when things quietened down all the gripes of the season began to be expressed. The long hours of summertime, coupled with the sheer physical hard work of drawing paddles and opening and closing gates perhaps 50 or 60 times in 12 hours, especially at places such as Goring were exhausting enough for strong young men, but productive of much strain and physical illness among the older men. In earlier years when traffic was much lighter and the job less hurried, lock keeping was a steady and less demanding calling, but by the sixties it needed a different type of person. The lock keeper was not merely a menial servant but the Conservancy's shop window dresser, public relations officer, policeman, troubleshooter and diplomat. Men of such calibre were available, and I was privileged to work with them, but they could only be recruited and retained if working conditions were improved. Generally the lock staff were a peaceable and contented lot, who were loyal and conscientious servants of the Conservators, but occasionally discontent came to a head.

There was no union as such. Lock keepers, reliefs and boatmen were probably far too independent and individualistic to put up with closed shops, demarcation disputes and similar manifestations of contemporary unionism. Certainly none of them had any great wish to alter the structure of society. Harry Coley once expressed this view succinctly to me: 'I don't want no 'Itler tellin' me what to do, and I don't want no Commies doin' the same, but I tell you what. Some bloke come round canvassin' me for the elections, I couldn't tell you what 'e were now, Tory or Labour it don't really matter. But 'e tells me all the wonderful things they're goin' to do if they gets in. I turns round an' I says to 'im 'whatever you do, you ain't goin' to stop this ole river runnin'', an' that's the truth. Even if 'Itler 'ad come an done fer us all, this ole lock an' weir 'ud still be 'ere an' someone 'ud 'ave to look arter the ole river'.

But like so many of that sturdy, independent English stock from which they sprang, there came a time when they could

not be pushed further. It was as Kipling's Norman Baron
advised his son:

> 'When he stands, like an ox in the furrow,
> With his sullen set eyes on your own,
> And he grumbles 'This isn't fair dealing'
> My son, leave the Saxon alone'.

So there was an unofficial sort of union called 'the Lock-
keepers Defence Committee' which met from time to time to
present a united front to the Conservators, by which was generally meant 'Old Joe', the Chief Navigation Inspector. In
truth, the Navigation Inspectors were fairly sympathetic to the
lock keepers' problems, but they were also responsible for
discipline. Inevitably a feeling tended to arise of 'them and
us' with the Inspectors, whereas the real villain of the piece
was the Secretariat in London.

The Reading District Committee, to which I was invited to
belong, used to meet on winter nights in the old brick toll
office at Blakes Lock on the Kennet. Eric Schofield, who it
will be recalled had set me on course for a Conservancy
career, was based here. Although the lock was one of the quietest, its lock keeper had other duties and Eric was the Chief's
boatman. He was also an ex-sergeant in the Reading Borough
Police, and like every policeman I have ever known enjoyed
nothing better than a good gossip and scandal. Eric was thus
in the position of a 'double agent'. The Committee kept in
with him because he knew what the Inspectors were up to,
whereas the Inspectors kept in with him because he knew all
the 'buzz' up and down the District. He later became lock
keeper at Sonning and subsequently took over a post office
which would have suited his diplomatic talents admirably.

When the meetings took place there tended to be a somewhat
conspiratorial atmosphere. It was recognised that 'Old Joe'
would know next morning exactly who was there and what was
discussed, so the lock keepers generally took the view 'be hung
for a sheep as well as a lamb' and turned out in force, or sent
their apologies. Thus there was some real solidarity. At the time
of which I write, two burning issues were being debated, one
was the affiliation of the Defence Committee to a established
union, the other was a reduction in hours of duty in summer.

As to the first, there were some, regarded as dangerous rev-
olutionaries, who wanted affiliation with the Transport &

General Workers Union. Others, more moderate, wanted affiliation with the National Association of Local Government Officers, which sounded much grander. A disgruntled T&GWU supporter made the point that NALGO stood for 'Not a lot goes on' which brought laughter. Others again took the view 'a plague on both your houses' and counselled independence. I seem to recall that NALGO won the day, but debate was spirited and well-fought.

The other matter had everyone united, there was even wild talk of taking strike action or go-slows, which would have been a dangerous card to play for men in tied houses. (The Inspectors muttered darkly about short winter hours and free lock houses.) Though a work-to-rule would have caused chaos in Henley Week, it was greatly to the lock keepers credit that they did not, as some collective bargainers have done since, take it out on the public, preferring to be in dispute with their masters. Long after the Thames Conservancy had disappeared, the Defence Committee did in fact take industrial action and an Oxford District man told me of how he was approached by a Union Convenor from Cowley with offers of flying pickets and all the trimmings. The Committee declined this poisoned chalice with thanks and instead worked normally but refused to collect tolls or fill in forms. This tactic was both popular with the public and effective.

In my time it never came to taking action, but within a year the working week was cut, so that the reliefs only covered three locks instead of four and worked a constant six days on and two days off. The Defence Committee could take credit for reaching an amicable settlement which reflected the ways of doing things on the Thames.

Of course another by product of industrial action was the mechanisation of the locks. Not only did this speed up traffic, but it certainly made the lock keeper's life easier. The electrical control from a centralised cabin, such as we had at Mapledurham and Cookham was abandoned in favour of hydraulics with the control gear mounted on pedestals by the head and tail gates. The advantages were that the lock keeper could always see what was going on, as well as approaching craft. From the control room at Mapledurham one could not see the bottom of the chamber when the lock was empty, nor what was happening in the downstream lay-by. The disadvantages were that the lock keeper had to work the hydraulics out in the open, and that when the power failed it was hard and tedious in the extreme when one had to work the lock by hand. This last criticism was, quite justifiably, made by members of the public who needed to work the lock out of hours. I had my share of it one summer afternoon at Mapledurham when a thunderstorm caused a temporary power failure. Luckily I had oilskins with me, but it was both tiring and tedious working the gates by hand.

After the meetings most people adjourned to the nearby Thames Restaurant in Newtown. Despite its name, this was a pub and a lively one at that. Several nights a week there would be a pianist who would thump away in the time-honoured pub tradition, fag adhering to top lip with an ever-lengthening ash quivering uncertainly above the keys but never dropping. On Saturdays the pub was always visited by the Salvation Army distributing *War Cry*. After the Salvationists had made their round of the pub and collected everyone's conscience money, their elderly Captain would be given a brimming tankard of lemonade. Standing upright in the centre of the floor he would square his shoulders, a hush would descend, the pianist would give a great rolling intro and, in a fine baritone the Captain would sing 'The Old Rugged Cross'. Stout-sodden old dears and hard-bitten working men would have tears rolling down their cheeks as the whole pub joined in the chorus. When he had finished, the Captain would drain his glass in one to loud cheers, then bid everyone 'good night and God bless', turn smartly on his heel and march out.

There were a number of river bargemen who patronised this and two other pubs on the towpath, so The Thames was in many ways the nearest thing that Reading had to a true watermen's pub, although few nowadays still practised their calling. During the winter evenings I made it my business to seek out some of these and talk to them about earlier times on the river. I had not the advantage of a portable tape recorder, so my failing memory must be one of the few places where their recollections have been retained. Such men as Dick Freeke, who had worked through to Bristol and had carried loads in and out of every mill on the Kennet and Thames, were a fascinating source of information.

Sam's grandmother, old 'Nan' Ashley, a sprightly old lady whose memories went back to the 1870s, remembered her family's horse-drawn narrow boats which traded down with coal from the Warwickshire pits. Jack Garner gave me a graphic description of how his father was sunk in the 'Brewery Gut' with a load of plaster of Paris which he was taking from Barrow-on-Soar in Leicestershire to Thatcham on the Kennet. Jack Garner, senior, was uninsured, and lost half of his capital in the shape of one boat out of a pair in the disaster. I marvelled at the stoicism and fortitude of such men who would sigh and then buckle again to as if nothing untoward had happened. They seemed to me the very epitome of the sturdy, common people of England.

As Christmas drew near, another topic began to exercise the minds of the Navigation Staff. This was the Annual Lock Keepers' Dinner and Dance, to which the staff flocked from one end of the river to the other. Now I have always been wary of staff functions, they tend to be a gathering of people whose only common link is their job, the bosses are full of false bonhomie, as are the shop stewards. Everyone watches everyone else, wives, girlfriends and concubines are minutely inspected and commented on by other wives, girlfriends and concubines, and knives are surely sharpened for plunging in one anothers' backs. Later the boss goes home, washes his hands and sends his suit to the cleaners, that no trace of the *hoipolloi* sully his being; the foremen and chargehands mark down their men; the union convenors get what they want on who they want; everyone suffers from indigestion and they all say they have had a lovely time. Meanwhile the caterers prepare yet another repast of cotton-wool turkey, soggy sausage, bullet potatoes and soapy-tasting Christmas pudding for the next wave of punters.

I need not have worried about the Lock Keepers' Dinner. A sort of inner cabal of the Defence Committee made the arrangements, but there was also a mysterious subvention to which they had access. It was rumoured that the Dinner was subsidised by one of the big boat clubs as a sort of 'payola'. More charitable people saw it as a 'thank you' for the previous season. Be that as it may, it was a 'good do'. It was, conveniently for me, held in a function suite in Duke Street, Reading, hard by High Bridge Wharf and on the bus route home or, if the hour was too late, opposite a minicab firm, whose controller was none other than Jim, for his Willow Wren career had proved shortlived.

On the appointed night I found myself, accompanied by Jean, in a galaxy of distinguished-looking men and women whom I had difficulty in recognising as my colleagues. There were lock staff and boatmen from far-flung reaches that I had only met occasionally. Of course, the difference between the atmosphere of this and many other staff social gatherings was that the river was not just a nine-to-five job, it was a way of life. The talk everywhere was of river gossip and of the details of shepherding Old Father Thames to the sea. The place of honour on top table was taken by the Secretary of the Thames Conservancy, G.E. Walker LLB himself. Old Joe and his wife were there, and presiding on behalf of the Navigation Staff, a big sunny smile splitting his tanned face, was Len from Mapledurham. Len was in evening dress with a fine bow tie, which amazed the company when, during his after dinner speech, it lit up and revolved rapidly.

Fred reminisced with Sam and myself about previous dinners. At one of them the Boat Club's representative was the famous comedian Max Miller, notorious in his day for the blueness of his jokes. The gales of laughter which he conjured up during his speech were only equalled by those elicited by another Boat Club guest, Colonel Waldron. The Colonel was a member of the Magic Circle and apparently managed to remove the Secretary's braces while he was speaking to the staff and telling them what splendid chaps they were. Waldron, who was sitting beside the Secretary appeared to be addressing a waiter, then surreptitiously waved the braces on high. The poor Secretary was blissfully unaware of what was happening and thought he was giving the wittiest speech of his career, for the audience was rocking with mirth and holding their sides as he spoke. It was only when Waldron administered the coup de grace and the Secretary's immaculate tailored trousers fell to the floor that he realised the awful truth.

The occasion of this Dinner was not, alas, marked by such exuberance, but it was a memorable affair and, again, seemed to underline the essentially family nature of the river and its guardians.

As Christmas drew near, my thoughts turned again towards moving ENTERPRISE nearer home. Since moving her down from Kings Weir, I had left her in Oxford until Peter was able to move her downstream to Benson, where the stoppage was due to finish just before Christmas. Here she lay snugly on the piles above the lock until, on Christmas Eve, Sam and myself went to move her down to Whitchurch.

It was a calm, clear winter's morning, with the pale icy blue of an English winter sky reflecting in the glassy water. Rainfall had been light since November so most of the weirs were shut in and the river was almost summer-like in its stillness. We walked across from the Oxford bus through crisp frost-rimed winter grass, breath condensing in the freezing air. The staccato throbs of ENTERPRISE'S exhaust caused birds to rise from the bare trees clustering round the lock. Sam and the lock keeper filled Benson Lock, temporarily breaking the stillness with the roar and rush of water through the paddles.

The chill of the morning struck through heavy socks and overcoats, so I lit the fire while Sam steered down the reach towards Cleeve. Ahead lay the long, undulating line of the Berkshire Downs, hazy blue but still distinct in detail. A heavy scarf of smoke trailed from the asylum stack near Chorsey, the weeping willows on the opposite bank trailing their ice-glazed leafless fronds into the water shivered as our wash surged along behind us.

North Stoke, Moulsford viaduct, South Stoke swept past, then nearing The Leathern Bottel at Cleeve we ran into ice. It was only thin and did not hold us up, but it splintered right across, making ringing sounds, followed by loud thumps as the propeller blades hurled lumps under the counter.

We stopped at Goring for lunch, then as the short afternoon faded, went on down Gatehampton, Hartslock and Pangbourne reaches to be greeted in the dusk by Fred. I tied her on the piles where I had originally begun the circumnavigation two months before. It seemed a fitting end to a memorable year I thought as the bus groaned back to Reading through the early, but festive, dark.

CHAPTER 9 — ON THE MOVE

Jean had gone back to her parents for Christmas, but was due back the day after Boxing Day. I went to meet her at the station in fine, clear sunshine, just as it had been on the day we brought ENTERPRISE to Whitchurch. I thought ruefully of the difference from a year ago. Then my boats had been locked in the ice at Stoke Bruerne from Boxing Day until March. At least, I mused, the boats on the Grand Union would be getting a fair chance this year. There was still a little steam-worked traffic on the railway at the time and Reading Station was still signalled with imposing-looking semaphores so, although the train was late, there was plenty to amuse me. I got chatting to the Welsh driver of the station pilot engine, which stood simmering in the Up Bay platform, His engine was probably only weeks away from the scrap sidings yet it looked as if it were about to haul the Royal Train. The footplate was spotless, the steel handles of the regulator, brake and reversing gear were glittering bright. The brass and copperwork was polished and the green paintwork of boiler and cab shone. 'Ah!' said the driver 'it all used to be like this man. Look yer, I've always been a good Labour man, but what's killing it is Nationalisation see. I mean it's all right them nationalising the Southern and LMS, that's all they're good for, but they should have blutty well left us alone.'

I could not help grinning to myself, because a few yards away were the extensive yards of the Southern station. The Southern enginemen shared a pub, The Rising Sun, with Conservancy employees, and one would hear similar statements over a pint, the difference being that it was the Great Western which should have been nationalised.

Further discussions on railway politics were halted by the arrival of Jean's train, up from Plymouth and Exeter. I noted sardonically that, although it was 20 minutes late, it was hauled by a modern diesel.

We saw the New Year in with some style at The Swan at Pangbourne, where two memorable things occurred. One was the collapse of a settee on which Jean and I were sitting, which precipitated us helplessly backwards where we remained immobile for some minutes, to the plaudits of the crowd. The other, much more momentous, was when Sam confided to me that he would like to buy a narrow boat. I put this down initially to an attack of insanity brought on by New Year overindulgence, but some days later, stone sober, he broached the subject again.

At that time numerous surplus boats were coming on the market following the demise of the British Transport Waterways fleet and the decision of the newly-created British Waterways Board to cease carrying on their own account. Most of the boats which had been in trade in the spring of 1963, when the Waterways fleet was wound up, had been acquired or leased by Willow Wren, but there were many which had not been in trade or had been used for maintenance work, and these were constantly coming up for tender.

I had an arrangement with British Waterways to receive tender lists, so was able to keep Sam informed of what craft were available. Along with one of the Conservancy's clerical staff, who lived aboard an ex-Barlow's boat SARAH at Burghfield, and his brother who had recently bought the ex-Fellows Morton & Clayton boat OWL, we began visiting boats tied against tips, maintenance yards, derelict wharves and such delightful places, on days off. It was an interesting way of spending a winter, but scarcely fruitful. I duly sent off tenders on Sam's behalf and then, in mid-February, I heard, out of the blue, that the tender for ALCOR had been accepted.

During my Willow Wren career I had seen ALCOR tied up by the maintenance yard at Hatton, near Warwick. She looked somewhat down at heel, and when we visited her in late January she did not look promising. The engine was taken down and not working, the cloths, planks and several floor-boards were missing, the cabin paintwork was worn. But, on closer inspection, the steelwork was in excellent condition, the bottoms were sound, she still had mast, stands and cratches, the cabin was fitted-out and she had a working range.

Sam got in touch with Dennis Clarke at Braunston, once Willow Wren's fitter but now their Yard Manager. Dennis felt that something indeed could be done, and the boat made into a 'runner' for a comparatively small sum. So plans were made for getting ALCOR from Hatton to Braunston and thence to the Thames. Sam was happy to let Kennet Carrying Company work her until such time as he could take her over himself, for he had plans for living aboard. At this point fate took a hand once again.

I found that increasingly I was consulting Jean on matters appertaining to the future and that she figured ever more largely in these plans. Suddenly I began to find myself thinking of marriage. Since it did not appear to be a bad idea, I began making discreet inquiries about future prospects with the Conservancy.

It was not possible for a single man to have a lock. The Conservancy preferred their lock houses and gardens to be in the care of married couples, so if I were to apply for a lock, then marriage seemed to be an essential pre-condition. I was now in the frame of mind to accept such a thing, so began looking for a suitable lock. In those days the accepted place to start was 'up West', but the pay for the locks above Oxford was the lowest on the river. It was considerably less than a relief's pay in the Reading District. The only way one could make ends meet was for the wife to go out to work, or else develop a lockside enterprise, such as a shop. Unfortunately, 'up West' was beautiful but lonely. The nearest job opportunities were several miles away from locks, bus services were non-existent, cars too expensive and bicycles hardly a serious proposition for every day, especially as several locks were then unapproached by road. River traffic was light, which ruled out a shop.

Jean was a country girl and so would not have objected to rural life, but facts had to be faced. Of course it would have been possible for me to have done as many lock keepers did with their wives and employ her from May to October as assistant, but this still left the problem of the winter. Besides, I was restless and wanted to see things and do things, especially on the waterways, without burying myself in deep countryside. Nevertheless, I continued to make my inquiries and learned that a lock might become available in the Spring. Then there came the flood warning.

Since the rains of November the river had been very quiet, but January saw some snow, followed by heavy rains. February lived up to its name of 'fill dyke', but towards its end it excelled itself. Day after day the heavy clouds trooped in on strong westerly winds, drenching the countryside, caus-

ing land drains to back up to form sheets of water which over-
lay quite high fields. The surface of the river changed from its
glass-like state of Christmas to an angry, browny torrent,
swirling bank-high under the bare rods of willow trees, its
face lined with the effects of eddies and underwater snags. All
the main weirs were drawn, the river boomed and thundered
through the raised sluices. All the lock staff walked everywhere in rubber boots and seaboot stockings.

On such a day I went out to Goring on the early bus.
During my two days off, the river had risen to its limit before
overflowing the banks. As the bus rumbled past Pangbourne
Weir, I noticed that Fred was 'fully drawn'. The rymers and
paddles were piled up like wigwams at the end of each of the
weirs. As I walked across Streatley Bridge I could see that the
weir runners had drawn Streatley Mill, a paddle and rymer
weir just downstream of The Swan, causing the normally
placid back stream to race past the pub's camp-shedded lawns
at a fearful rate. Goring Mill weir was, however, still in place,
when a few minutes later I walked across the mill head on the
approach to Goring Lock.

The head water was not far above normal, but the tail water
gauge showed that the river was backing up in the reaches
below, held up presumably by the narrowness of the single
channel through the chalk hills. It already covered the lower
steps of the lay-by.

The Reading District began at Wallingford Bridge and contained no significant tributary streams until Pangbourne,
where the Pang entered. Even this was rarely a problem
because much of its flow was abstracted to supply Reading
with drinking water. The Kennet and Loddon, below
Caversham and Shiplake respectively, were the only significant streams entering the Thames until the lower reaches. The
only major streams between Oxford and Wallingford were the
Ock, draining the Vale of White Horse, and the Thame, draining the Vale of Aylesbury, both of which were what geogra-
phers know as scarp streams. Such streams running in a clay
vale rise and fall quickly, but dip streams, feeding off great
underground aquifers of chalk and limestone rise slowly and
steadily but inexorably. The run-off takes weeks rather than
days to clear. For this reason we had a reasonable time to prepare for the Cotswold water as it came down from Oxford.

I was not surprised therefore, to receive a telephone call from Reading telling me that the river was rising steadily at Osney. 'You'll have to draw everything' said Peter Harvey, 'is there anything left?' 'Only Goring Mill' said I. 'Best get that out ready, and warn any boats in the mill stream'. As it happened there were no boats in the mill stream, they had all been taken out of the water or else were ensconced snugly in boat houses.

I put on my greatcoat and set out for the weir. This was a paddle and rymer affair which had once controlled an undershot mill wheel. Now the wheel was gone and the mill converted into a private house, with a yawning gap in its walls where the wheel had once turned. The weir was rarely touched, indeed it had not been necessary to draw it at the end of the previous winter in spite of all the snow. Consequently the paddles were firmly bedded in silt.

Since the weir was but a shallow one, I did not bother with a weir line. I drew one paddle, with considerable difficulty, wrenching it back and forth to clear away the mud. It came away, releasing a thunderous torrent of green water through the gap. Immediately twigs, old leaves and scum that had settled on the still surface began to drift towards the gap. I drew another, and laid both paddles against the mill wall. The third stuck fast. I tried wrenching from side to side, then pushing the paddle rod away from the weir beam to encourage water to run in behind and free the paddle. As I did so the paddle suddenly moved. I overbalanced and went in, greatcoat, boots and all.

My first reaction was 'this isn't really happening', then, as the cold water began to soak through my clothes, 'Oh yes, it is'. I realised that I was in great danger of being sucked into the hole and struck out for the weir tackle which was still in place. I tried to bottom the back water to wade out, but the bottom was soft mud. After two strokes I reached the weir tackle.

Although it was mid-morning and this drama was being played out beneath a busy road in the centre of a village, nobody was about to help me. I was in danger of being weighed down with boots and coat, for I could not reach up to the weir beam in order to pull myself up. In desperation I seized a rymer post to heave myself out, got half way up when, with a rumbling clatter, the whole lot gave way, rymers, paddles and all.

I was flung head first into the weir and shot through the gap into the old mill race accompanied by a large quantity of grey painted timber. I scrabbled wildly as I shot under the weir bridge, bringing up sharply against the stonework of the mill. Most of my breath was driven out of me but I managed to cling desperately with my finger tips until I had recovered. My feet were on something firm so I was able to wriggle myself clear of the rushing mill race. Water streamed out of my soaking clothes, I just managed to grasp the wooden deck beam of the bridge and dragged myself up until my waist was level with the roadway. After this I rolled sideways to lie panting, like a stranded fish on the deck of the bridge. The rain beat down but I took no notice. Although possibly only three minutes had passed since I first went in, I suddenly realised that I had come within an ace of death, for had I gone right into the mill race I could never have stopped until I reached the centre of the tail pool, by which time my boots and coat would surely have dragged me under.

After a few minutes I got to my feet and squelched deject-edly across to the lock house to see whether Harry would let me dry my clothes by the fire. His jaw dropped when he saw me, then I was instantly brought into the kitchen, made to strip there and then. As soon as I was out of my wet clothes a large tot of rum was placed in my trembling hands, then I was bundled into a hot bath.

Harry had a spare uniform which he pressed upon me, when I had finished my ablutions. I put it on and came into his living room to hear him berating poor Peter Harvey on the telephone for ordering me to draw the weir. In vain did I try to tell him that it was my own clumsiness that caused it, instead he snapped down the phone. 'Here's the bloody relief 'isself to tell yer' and handed me the instrument. Peter Harvey's voice, sounding worried, came over the wire. 'Are you all right old son?' 'Never felt better' I lied 'I've just had my third bath this morning'. Harvey laughed, relieved, and I heard Chris Groves chuckling too. 'Well, look here old son, you've done enough for today. Bugger off home and we'll get someone else out'. Harry was smiling now 'Oh no you won't' he said taking the telephone. 'I'll look after me own bloody lock'.

But before I left to catch the bus, the good old chap insisted on cooking me a hot meal and fitting me out with everything, including a cap. The trouble was that I was a good deal taller than he and my head was larger. I tottered off home wearing trousers that were a good three inches above my ankles, a waistcoat like a lady's bolero Jacket, and a cap resembling a bell boy's.

I think perhaps I was less perturbed by this incident than was Jean. She had had two frights herself and now here was I going swimming in a weir. The prospect of living and working close to a river did not perhaps seem so appealing to her, yet I knew that if we were going to stay together I should have to make some compromise in my chosen life style.

I had vague ideas of writing for a living and, to a certain extent, I thought that lock keeping might provide a useful base for so doing. I certainly needed some sort of intellectual spur, which was the one thing my life on the water failed to do. I had now been earning my living on the water for two years and had had more than my share of pleasure from it. It had not been terribly rewarding financially, but it had so far been full of other rewards. I had worked in the loveliest and the vilest parts of England. I had met companions and made friends whose company I treasured, yet somewhere there was a small canker, a still, small voice that kept whispering 'You need more than this'. The Goring episode made me, for the first time, realise that if I were to be really happy, then I must have responsibilities to someone other than myself.

That very evening, Jean and I went to dinner with a friend of mine from legal days. We had lost touch for some four years so had much to talk about. He was not content with the assistant's job that he had landed and was most envious of my subsequent career, wishing that he could pluck up sufficient courage to do something similar. I pointed out that all jobs have their minus points and that the minus one for me was that it did not tax my brain sufficiently. He smiled and said 'You know, I really don't know why you haven't thought of taking up teaching'. 'Teaching!' I exclaimed horrified, 'that's the last thing I'd be any good at'. Indeed, I had no intention of darkening the door of a school again. My school career had been neither happy nor distinguished. I still sometimes dreamed that I was back at school and woke sweating. I remembered the contempt in which we boys held the long-suffering authority which ruled us, the boredom, the awful food, the petty rules, the beatings, the sheer discomfort. No, schools and academics were nearly as anathema to me as petty officials.

'Um' said my friend, 'I'm not sure. Anyway, think of the conditions in the state system. They get paid more than you do now, it's a safe job, they only work from nine to four, five days a week and think of the holidays!' I pondered this for a moment and laughed 'Well that's one way of looking at it I suppose, at least one's not likely to come home soaking'.

I thought no more of this conversation until I returned to Goring next day. I returned Harry's uniform, which my mother insisted upon pressing until it looked like a parade-ground one, and settled down over a cup of tea to read the scandal printed in the local Reading paper before tidying up the office and similar chores. My attention was caught by a small item on one of the inside pages which stated that applications were invited from persons over 25 years of age to train as mature students at a new teacher training college, to be opened in the autumn. It seemed almost as if fate were nudging me again. I discussed it that night with Jean and next day sent off my application.

From then on things began to move rapidly. Within a few days I went for an interview and was invited to make a formal application. I discovered that the annual grant for a married mature student was somewhat more than my pay from the Conservancy. At this the pattern began to take shape. Provided I could get a place at college in the autumn, I would get married as soon as possible. I would spend one last summer working the canals and rivers and then try another career. If I didn't like teaching, at least I would have a qualification and there were then plenty of teaching jobs available all round the country. Then Sam asked me when could I go and get ALCOR for him.

I consulted the calendar. I had some ten days leave due, which had to be taken before the end of April, so I calculated that if I took some leave to get ALCOR and the balance for myself, we could marry and have a short honeymoon before May. With two boats to work there might be enough cash flow coming in to keep my head above financial deep water until September. I was encouraged by Len who pointed out that there was always a shortage of holiday reliefs, so I could probably fill in time for the Conservancy if things got too tight.

So one evening, when I was round at Jean's flat I broached the matter of the leave that was due to me. 'I've got a few days spare' I said. She looked at me curiously. 'So what if you have?' she asked. 'We-ell' said I, somewhat sheepishly 'If you were agreeable to it, I thought we might get married before my leave runs out'. She threw back her head and laughed. 'I never thought I'd get proposed to like that'. And so, quite suddenly and painlessly, the die was cast. My days of bachelorhood were suddenly numbered.

The next part of the jigsaw was fitted by an unexpected participant. It happened that one evening in the late summer I had been hailed on the lockside at Goring by a friend from the Kennet & Avon, Tony Opperman. We had both been Council members of the old Association as well as of the Trust and our paths had crossed several times. Tony told me that he was renting the disused ferryman's cottage at Gatehampton from the Conservancy, in consequence of which I saw him several times during the ensuing winter. Now he reappeared with the news that he hoped to rent Shipton Weir cottage on the Oxford Canal, which had no road access (nor electricity, mains water or sewerage for that matter). He hoped to move in mid-March and was anxious to secure the services of ENTERPRISE.

In consultation with Sam, I suggested that we move Tony's goods and chattels from Gatehampton to Shipton en route to fetch ALCOR, which seemed a convenient arrangement.

It was even more convenient when the Engineer's Department urgently wished to move some wrecked boats and other junk up from Reading to Gatehampton tip and found that they had no barges available. I agreed to load the wreckage aboard BEECH and pull it all up with ENTERPRISE, but all now hung on whether or not the flood stream would subside.

I was glad of the prospect of change, for the period since New Year had been a dreary one on the river. Apart from the weir work and the occasional Engineer's or Inspection craft, there was no traffic. The steadily lengthening days which normally make some sort of compensation for the dullness of

winter, merely meant that one had to remain longer at one's
post. Although there had been one outing with ENTERPRISE in
early February, before the flood stream became strong, I had
been unable to take part because of duties. On this occasion
she had gone down to Westminster Pier as part of a Reading
University Rag Day stunt. Jim and Peter had crewed, along
with a few students. For this we disguised her as a pirate ship,
with masts and yards of scaffold tube, cardboard fo'csle and
poop decks and dummy cannon. In this incredible guise she
landed a party of students, dressed as pirates, at Westminster
Pier. The 'pirates' held up people in Whitehall and Parliament
Square and demanded money for Rag Day charities. The haul
was quite impressive.

Mid-March eventually came. Jim took the boats up to the
yard at Reading Bridge and struggled manfully against the
stream to Gatehampton. BEECH's load was light, so the journey was uneventful, though slow. Next morning he assisted
Tony in loading his furniture and other possessions including
the cat, then with Tony and cat camped in the cabin with him,
set off against the still-strong stream to Benson. There Sam
and myself joined them next morning.

Almost immediately I realised that aiming, as I had
planned, for Thrupp that night was over-optimistic. In spite of
the worst of the floods having passed, the river was running
extremely hard, we were making a bare three miles per hour
over the ground, although there was a fine feather of water up
ENTERPRISE's stem bar indicating that speed through the water
was much faster. The reach upstream to Days Lock had
always seemed a drag, this time it seemed interminable.
Clifton Hamden Bridge, with its narrow arches, seemed to
take an age to pass, but by lunchtime we had battled our way
up as far as Abingdon.

The old bridge, rebuilt in the 1920s, had an evil name in
flood with horse-boaters, but I was confident that the wider
arch would not be too much of an obstacle. I forgot that apart
from the silted-up side stream under the mediaeval Burford
Bridge, with its narrow arches and the ancient Swift Ditch,
this was the only outlet for the drainage basin of the Cotswold
dip slope. I should have remembered my downstream journey
of the previous March, when I covered the half mile stretch
from Abingdon Lock to the Bridge in three and a half min-

utes, or at a fraction over eight miles an hour. By contrast to this giddy flight, we hung almost motionless in the bridge hole, breasting the brown, swirling stream.

In desperation I sent Jim into the engine room with instructions to hold the governor rack open. Jim climbed down and wedged his foot onto the lever on the side of the engine. The engine shook like a demented thing. Black smoke shot up the exhaust stack, fumes bellied from the silencer jacket nearly choking poor Jim, but inch by inch we began to claw our way under the reverberating stonework of the arch. Suddenly we were through and inching up the narrow gullet by Salter's Café, where we found wider, slower water. Jim, red-eyed and with his ears ringing, climbed gratefully out of the black hole that was once the engine room.

The next reach, up to Sandford, was another long, slow and uninteresting one, once above Nuneham Islands. The chimney stack of Sandford Mill came in sight and drew nearer with agonising slowness, but at last it was in full view, along with the lower gates of the lock. At this point I made another foolish miscalculation.

The weir stream here runs out at right angles to the lock, below a towpath bridge. I was creeping up close under this bank, taking full advantage of the slacker water and reasoned that this was what horse-boats would have done in the old days, but overlooked that the horses would be towing from the same side as the weir outfall and would thus check any broadside drift with the towline. As we came up towards the outfall, I could see the outrush of water at right angles, sweeping towards the usual Conservancy heavy white piles which formed the downstream lay-by. With hindsight I should have been on the other side, turned into the current and out into the slack water at the lock tail, instead of which I attempted to shoot straight across the stream.

Sam and Tony were standing on top of the cargo, on the gangplanks engrossed in conversation as I headed out into the broadside weir current. Instantly the fore-end began to swing, I attempted to check this by holding the tiller hard over to the right which resulted in our going sideways. I saw Sam's eyebrows upraised questioningly. I could not hear their conversation, but heard about it afterwards. Tony said 'I don't think she's going to come around, Sam'. 'Nor me, neither' replied Sam.

At the last moment I saw the downstream white post looming towards my midships, about half way down the hull. Unlike a true working boat there were no cross beams in ENTERPRISE and when we struck the post the iron sides flexed and gunwale bolts groaned. We rolled to the left sufficiently to dislodge the cabin chimney, which fell over the side, dangling from its safety chain. Sam said 'I reckon she's going over, Tony'. Tony said nothing, but with all his worldly good below his feet in imminent risk of being consigned to the river, there was not much to say. Slowly, it seemed, but in reality swiftly, ENTERPRISE regained her equilibrium and headed into quieter water. When we got into the lock I glanced over the port side, the watermark was within three inches of the gunwale. Everyone said 'Phew!'

Another hour saw us at Folly Bridge and Thrupp began, once more, to seem a possibility. I decided that the sooner we were off the river the better, so took the turn into Sheepwash Channel, just above Osney Bridge. This leads to the lower part of the Oxford Canal, avoiding Duke's Weir stream, which I had no desire to tangle with again when in flood. Jim left us at Osney Lock to get the train home, while Tony went overland to the station in order to persuade the railway authorities to swing the bridge which took the one-time LMS Railway into Rewley Road Station. I had no wish to encounter this structure unless it were open to water traffic, because one has to make a short downstream run in the Sheepwash in order to reach the first lock of the Oxford Canal.

We tied below Osney Bridge until Tony returned with the news that the bridge was being made ready, then once more crept upstream, just clearing the low arch of Osney. Down the Sheepwash we shot, through the swing bridge and swung round to the left towards the lower gate of Isis Lock. I breathed a sigh of relief and pulled the reversing lever back. There a loud 'clunk' from below, the engine raced but nothing happened apart from our fore-end striking the bottom gate forcing it open.

Once in the lock I stopped the engine. While Sam filled the lock Tony and I lifted the inspection plate on the gear box. Tony was an expert with such things, being a trained engineer. After a few minutes fishing with spanners he gave me the gloomy news that the reduction gear had sheared a cog and seized itself solid, shearing its drive shaft as it did so.

So here was a pretty state of affairs. It was now 5.30 p.m., close on dark and little chance of finding anywhere in Oxford which would carry spares for a Parsons reduction gear. Tony opined that the only solution would be to obtain one ex-works, but how long that would take was problematic. A very gloomy trio sat down to supper in the cabin, but I began to reflect on the providential nature of the accident. At least we were on still water and safe. Suppose the gear had failed at Abingdon Bridge, or below Sandford, or under Osney, or indeed above or below any of the weirs. It just didn't bear thinking about.

The news next morning was grim to start with. As we had thought. there were no spares to be had anywhere in Oxford. Parsons Works in Southampton said that if they dispatched by parcels that morning (Friday) it would not get to us until Tuesday at the earliest. 'They say canal transport is slow' I commented, 'if we had a canal to Southampton we could have it by Sunday night'. 'Of course,' said Parson's Despatch Manager 'if you came for it, you could have it today.'

That settled it. Tony said that he could fit the replacement if I got it, so leaving him and Sam to strip everything down, I caught the next bus down the Botley Road to the Oxford by-pass and started hitching.

I was in luck, within five minutes I had pulled a lift to Newbury. I walked out of town and up the hill on the A34, where I was picked up by a lorry driver from Oxfordshire bound for Southampton Docks. He told me that he had to drop a load there, then pick up another at Shoreham for Chipping Norton. I bade him goodbye outside Parson's Works, picked up my replacement parts before lunch time and set off back.

The Despatch Manager suggested that I get a train back, but this was not an easy matter since the Didcot, Newbury and Southampton line had been recently 'axed' by Dr Beeching. However, since the purlieus of Southampton straggled out for a long way, making hitch-hiking difficult, I decided to get a train to Basingstoke and try from there.

I made my last ride in a Southern steam train to Basingstoke, arriving there in late afternoon. I struggled down the subway, carrying the heavy box of parts under my arm, found the Newbury road which passed under the west end of

Basingstoke Station, and set off up the steep hill leading out of the town. By an incredible coincidence the first vehicle to come along was my lorry driver of the morning on his way back from Shoreham. I don't know which of us was the more astonished.

By five o'clock I was back at the Botley Road, but the driver, with whom I had set up an exceedingly friendly rapport, insisted on going into the City to drop me at Hythe Bridge, from which it was a few minutes walk to Isis Lock. Lady Luck at last seemed to be smiling on me. Tony had the replacement fitted within half an hour, so we resolved to be away early next morning in order to make up for lost time.

At first light we set off. A chilly, grey March morning it was too, the stark willows barely concealing the crumbling remains of locomotive sheds and rusty sidings in the old LMS yard on our left, and the tall campanile of St Barnabas looming dully over the crouched houses of Jericho on our right. The exhaust echoed off the blank house backs of Juxon Street, with the odd bedroom window glowing bleakly here and there. Streetlamps were still reflected in the water of Walton Street Bridge as we slipped underneath. Long before Wolvercote it was full day-light, but with a viciously cold wind whipping across the levels of Port Meadow at us. Smoke rolled out of the cabin chimney as Tony brewed a kettle on the hob plate of the cabin stove, the scent of frying came in whiffs from the tiny little galley.

It was just after mid-morning that we deposited Tony and his belongings on the side of Shipton Weir Lock. The cat looked distinctly pleased to be landing on *terra firma* again. He stepped gingerly onto the coping stones, yawned, arched his back, stretched and then went round to the back of the weir cottage to investigate some interesting smells, which must have been a distinct improvement upon the oily-smelling bilges which he had inspected thoroughly since leaving Goring.

Setting off again, we ran steadily uphill all the rest of the day. Having Sam with me meant that we could take it in turns to steer. It was a Saturday but I kept on going in an attempt to make up for lost time. I had planned to get to Aynho the previous night, then Fenny Compton, then Warwick for Sunday, but the breakdown had blown this schedule to smithereens.

However, the important thing was to pick ALCOR up on Monday, returning with her to Braunston for Tuesday, and being back at work on Wednesday, so given some late boating and good luck, we might just do it.

The 'roll up' debacle of last summer had cured me of any desire to wager on the turf, but Sam still liked a flutter. It was only after we had left Tony that he made a terrible discovery. There was now no radio on the boat and it was Grand National day. All the way up the Cherwell valley he was on tenterhooks. Not a lengthsman or fisherman did we see all day for him to ask the results.

Night fell near Somerton, but I sternly put the temptation of Aynho Wharf behind me and we continued on our way, the elegant spire of Kings Sutton standing stark black against the darkening sky. Ahead was the glow of Banbury, but it was a long, slow haul to get there. From Nell Bridge to Kings Sutton it is more direct, but still slow going. It was gone 9.30 by the time we rose in the last lock below Banbury. I had serious doubts about reaching The Struggler before closing time, for the stretch up to Banbury was slow travelling indeed.

At length we crept into what L.T.C. Rolt, somewhat unjustly, called 'the sordid outskirts of Banbury'; by the tar distillery, which had just ceased to receive its products from Leamington Gasworks, to the right and the Dairy, which still received its coal by boat to the left. Just beyond the Dairy was a lift bridge and in the street beyond it, a pub. Sam looked at his watch, it was five minutes to closing time. He jumped off the boat in the bridge hole and tore up the street on a mercy mission for beer and cigarettes. He burst into an amazed bar just as 'last orders' was called. 'What won the National?' he gasped as the barmaid assembled his order. 'What ain't you 'eard?' asked someone. 'No. I've been coming up from Oxford all day'. 'Get away! You're trying to take the mickey'. 'No I'm not! Come on, what won the National?' But in spite of his pleading no one would either believe his story or enlighten him. He had to buy a Sunday paper next morning to find out, and I really can't remember now whether he had won or lost.

Next day was reasonably uneventful. We started early again, meeting no traffic whatsoever. Two-handed on a single boat is possibly the ideal way of boating a narrow canal. In

bad weather only one need get soaked, at least on a long
pound, while in good weather one has company at the tiller,
there is someone to get locks ready, or brew hot drinks, or
make sandwiches, or to take over steering for long periods of
time, so that the day passes pleasantly.

The most memorable event was the encounter with the
moaning lock keeper. In days past there was little love lost
between the Oxford Canal Company and the companies that
eventually constituted the Grand Union Canal Company. This
stemmed from 1793, when the building of the Grand Junction
Canal marked the ending of the Oxford Company's monopoly
of the traffic from the Midlands and north to London. Once
the Grand Junction was open to through traffic, the Oxford
south of Napton became of lesser importance. Today we may
be glad of this, it has resulted in the canal having a remote and
timeless atmosphere, its fabric having been largely untouched
by progress. The shareholders and employees did not see it
this way though and cordially detested the upstart Grand
Junction. Noble families took sides in Parliament when the
Grand Junction Bill was debated. The Duke of Marlborough
supported the Oxford, but the Spencer family of Northants
were in favour of the Grand Junction. Worse than this, the
Duke of Grafton, through whose estates the Junction ran, was
Chancellor of Cambridge University!

The dislike extended to company's men and boatmen. Most
of the Oxford's trade latterly was in coal, carried by owner
boatmen ('number ones') like Joe Skinner, or rather more old-
fashioned companies. The Junction and Grand Union traffic
was more varied and complex, the boatmen looked down on
''oss boaters' and 'them as only carries coal; they only knows
the Oxford Cut'. Even in the sixties, long after nationalisation,
there was a little of the old feud remaining. The Oxford lock
keepers were notorious moaners whenever craft off the Grand
Union appeared. I had experienced this with Willow Wren
and, since ENTERPRISE was an ex-Fellows, Morton & Clayton
boat, knew that in some quarters her presence was not welcome.

The top gates of Oxford locks have a very sensible sprung
collar. This facilitated the stopping of horse boats as well as
making for swift lock work. A stump on the mitre post was
used to check the way of the boat, by means of a strap. This

had a dual effect, one the boat was stopped, two the way of the boat brought the top gate to, saving time and effort. The spring meant that any slamming effect was mitigated.

I showed Sam this principle at Napton Locks, which he put to good use as we worked down. I got each lock ready, opened the top gate, shut the paddles, then took station by the bottom gate. As the boat swept in Sam pulled her out of gear and checked her on the top gate. As soon as the gate began to swing I drew a paddle. The gate bumped gently to and immediately the boat started to drop. A quick change to tick over in ahead gear kept the fore-end resting in the vee of the lower gates, then I went forward to the next lock, leaving Sam to open the bottom gates and step back onto ENTERPRISE as she nosed out of the lock.

We worked down the locks in brisk style to the bottom. The lock keeper scowled at me from the door of his cottage by the lock but neither said nor did anything until Sam strapped in and I drew the paddle. At this he shot forth and began berating Sam. 'You bloody Junction Cut boaters ain't got no respect for nothing' he said. 'Hang on', said I 'I thought that was how you were supposed to do it. Why else have the gates got stumps and springs?' 'That ain't got nothing to do with you. Closing gates like that's been the ruination of the cut'. Sam said 'I thought the railways ruined it.' At this comment the lock keeper stopped as if he had been shot. His jaw dropped, he stared at us both open-mouthed, turned on his heel and marched back into his cottage.

Darkness fell soon after we reached the Grand Union main line and turned left under the wide concrete arch of Wigrams Turn. By the time we reached the top lock of Stockton it was pitch-black, but the top eight locks in this flight are close together so it does not take very long to pass through them. Moreover, there was a beckoning display of coloured lights at the bottom to hasten us on. These, it transpired, were at The Blue Lias a pub just below the eighth lock. Here we stopped for the night and later went in for a drink. The pub was kept by a larger-than-life character, one 'Sandy' Powell, an ex-RAF and test pilot, who welcomed us as long-lost brethren even though this was the first time I had set foot in his pub. I had intended introducing Sam to The Cape of Good Hope at Warwick that night, but this was to be an adequate substitute.

Sandy had a Mosquito fighter in his carpark, which caused consternation to some, who thought it had just landed. The bar was quiet that night, conversation and yarns went on until a late hour, what time we felt impelled to leave lest we did no work at all on the morrow.

In terms of distance it is not far from Long Itchington to Hatton, perhaps 14 miles at the most. There are, however, many locks. The canal descends into the Avon Valley at Warwick by means of 12 locks from The Blue Lias, then climbs up 23 in two and a half miles. ALCOR lay at the 'Shop Lock' of Hatton, i.e. four locks down, but since the top ten locks are very close (the 'thick of Hatton' as boaters call it) we decided to take ENTERPRISE as far as the middle lock, wind her round, then walk up to the workshops and pull ALCOR down by hand. This would save working six locks twice.

It was lunch time when we arrived at the workshops. Nobody showed any interest, so we just untied ALCOR and towed her away. The cabin was padlocked but a search of the engine room revealed the key hanging up. I reflected that it would not be too difficult in certain circumstances to steal a boat at night, lay up during each day in a quiet place, and eventually move her to some independent waterway like the Thames where nobody would know. Apart from the lock keeper at Napton we had not seen a single Waterways employee since Oxford.

I had fortunately brought a long cotton line from ENTER-PRISE for there were no ropes apart from frayed bits of line at either end. The blue paint of the cabin sides was peeling, the engine room was damp and rusty and the hold was a mess of broken floorboards. We bowhauled this sorry spectacle back to the Middle Lock, breasted her with ENTERPRISE and set off back the way we had come. Behind us the frowning bulk of Hatton Mental Hospital emphasised what Robert Aickman once called 'the greater lunacy which sits over canals'.

It was another cold, grey day with little colour in the land-scape. Things were worsened by the steady, cold drizzle which set in. Fortunately there was no traffic ahead of us, so all the locks were as we had left them earlier. The prospect of getting back to The Blue Lias spurred us on. An ominous sign in Leamington was the evidently imminent closure of the gas-works, which sent tar by Thomas Clayton's boats to Banbury.

The Clayton pair was crewed by a good friend of mine whom I hoped to have met, but they were away to Oldbury in the Black Country this trip. The works was still intact, but weeds and rust were appearing in places where last year there were none, whilst many more windows seemed broken than formerly.

The short March day was ending as we wound beneath the bare trees below Radford Lock, where the climb back up out of the Avon valley begins. The first six locks are spread well out 'up the Fosse' and, although there was once a pub where the Fosse Way crosses the cut, it had been long closed. We grimly butted on into the lashing cold, dark, rainy night until, just below Bascote Locks ENTERPRISE picked something up in the blades. I tried to clear it with a shaft in the bridge hole, and pulled the head off the shaft. We looked at our watches. It was gone nine. I suppose I could have carried on, but we were both very tired, so we tied up to the hedge there and then, had supper and went to bed.

Next morning the rain had eased. I recovered the shaft-head and refitted it, cleared the blades, then set off after breakfast. This time we had a trouble-free run, even though the weather was still grey and cold. The countryside between Stockton and Braunston is bleak enough on a summer's day, on a blustery cold late winter's day it is doubly so, but soon the spire of Braunston church was visible, poking its way above skeletal trees. As always, I had a sense of home-coming when arriving at Braunston. The place had tended to feel like home ever since I had first taken ENTERPRISE to Barlows Dock over two years before. As we slipped along the straight towards the Junction, under the twin guardian towers of the church and the sailless windmill, I felt a great feeling of contentment. In less than an hour we would be having a pint and a pie in the snug bar of The Admiral Nelson, I would be back among the boat people, whose company I cherished and whose friendship I valued. What was, perhaps mercifully, concealed from me was that I was coming to the end of my last ever voyage as captain of ENTERPRISE and as a bachelor.

Chapter 10 — RINGING THE CHANGES

Since I had to resume duty on the Thames, I left ENTERPRISE at Braunston, but we returned at Easter, this time accompanied by Jean, and Sam's girlfriend, Jenny. There was much to do to both boats, though ENTERPRISE'S need was mainly for cleaning-up ready for next season. ALCOR needed a complete repaint inside and out, the working tackle had to be overhauled and replaced where necessary, a second-hand National Diesel engine had to be installed.

ALCOR, as an unconverted working boat differed in several respects from ENTERPRISE. For a start she was a much newer boat. Whereas ENTERPRISE had been composite built, of iron with a wooden bottom, in 1903, ALCOR was also composite, but of steel construction dating from the 1930s. She had been built for the Grand Union Canal Carrying Co. by Harland & Wolff at their North Woolwich yard, hence was known to boatmen as a 'small Woolwich'. The design owed a great deal to two men, both of whom I knew. One, Leslie Morton, had been the Grand Union's fleet manager at the time. He was a deep sea sailor, trained in sail with a master's ticket and a passionate belief in canals. The other, Charles Hadlow, the Grand Union's engineer, who had a background of Thames barge-building in his native Kent, was then the curator of the Waterways Museum at Stoke Bruerne. In many ways the Grand Union steel boats were the apotheosis of narrow-boat design. They had good carrying capacity, they handled well and swam well, both loaded and empty, they were business-like, elegant-looking and incorporated the best in inland marine technology of the thirties – electric light, mechanical bilge pumps, chemical closets, well laid-out engine rooms, cabins as roomy as space would allow and steel bulkheads partitioning the bilges.

Whereas ENTERPRISE'S engine room was aft of the living cabin, ALCOR'S was ahead of it. The engine was a water-cooled National Diesel controlled by a revolving control wheel. The great advantage of this last over a lever is that with a lever one is constantly ducking in and out of the slide, or groping about beneath the cabin roof, but with a wheel one merely stands in place, twisting the wheel to left or right. This can be done with the cabin doors closed, which is of great benefit in wet or cold weather. A few carrying narrow boats have been built since the Grand Unions but, although they are technically more advanced and with better carrying capacity on a light draught, the Woolwich design has not, in my opinion, been surpassed.

In those days the canals were still regarded as a transport system first and an amenity second, consequently stoppages tended to take place over Bank Holidays. Since the Braunston Flight of locks was stopped over Easter, there was considerable congestion at the Bottom Lock, outside the Willow Wren yard. All three Blue Line pairs had arrived, loaded with coal for the 'Jam 'ole' at Southall. At long last the Ansty breach had been repaired, allowing traffic to take the short route from the coalfields to London. Arthur's pair lay with their fore ends against the stop planks, which blocked off Bottom Lock. From time to time conversations would take place between the boats, conducted fortissimo from the sterns of each pair. Boat people tended to have loud voices which carried well. After all, a lifetime of passing conversations carried out over the racketing of engines or the thunder of lock paddles tended to develop the use of the diaphragm in speech. It was thus impossible not to be party to all sorts of intriguing information vouchsafed by the women, happy for the chance to gossip, on the subject of pregnancies, forthcoming confinements, rupture operations and similar topics.

Several Willow Wren pairs were in for minor repairs, so the women on them provided a sort of antiphonal chorus, which filled in any details the listener may have missed. There was a narrow channel between the boats but from a distance this was invisible. The impression was of a mass of smoking chimneys, swinging tillers inverted in rams heads, dancing washing and the geometric upperworks of stands, masts and uprights. It was a vital organic village, full of cheerful humanity. The bright paintwork and polished brasses bespoke character and pride. The boats were all huddled together, just like houses in a mediaeval village, yet everyone's privacy was respected. I am often struck by this when, years later, I see gatherings of pleasure craft. By contrast, suburban man afloat keeps himself aloof, crowding round his televisions or videos in his centrally heated cabins or playing 'Scrabble', or 'Trivial Pursuit'. The comradeship of the working boats is the thing I miss most on the canals today. Even the roughest and toughest of the working boat people would never dream of playing a ghetto-blaster at full volume on the cabin top, or making an unholy row outside somebody's house. The bright paintwork of most modern craft is a meaningless sham, people look inwards at themselves. Today the roses and castles, once the emblem of a boater's pride and independence have become twee symbols of a golden age that never was and, perhaps unconsciously, mock the spirit of those that I have been proud to call my friends.

Jean had visited the bakers in Braunston High Street. Being Easter she had returned laden with hot cross buns for the workers. Opposite the two boats lay my old friend George, with an empty pair awaiting some work. Knowing the predilections of his oldest son, Colin, I had warned Jean not to let him on the boat whatever she did. However, the sight of his wistful little face was too much for her, he was standing on the towpath looking longingly at my tin of primer and the brushes, sniffing the aroma rising from the galley. Next minute, to my horror, Jean had asked him on board. His mouth crammed with hot cross bun he made a bee line for the paint tin 'I'll do that for you Dave' he mumbled. 'Just watch it then, son' said I grudgingly.

I had been painting ALCOR'S hull in red primer while Sam and Jenny rubbed down and primed the cabin. Once Colin got hold of the paint tin chaos ruled. He slapped paint on everything, the floors, mast, stands, cratch, ENTERPRISE'S hull, my overalls, himself, in fact everywhere but the sides of the hold. Sam had a long streak of oxide down his face and Jenny's hair had a different tint to it. After two minutes I seized the paint pot in exasperation. He shot up to the far end of the boat waving a dripping brush and laughing. 'Clear off Colin!' I called, quietly, not wishing to offend George. I needn't have bothered. The open doors of the butty opposite erupted with a tremendous roar. 'COLIN! Come 'ere! You can see them buggers don't want you. If you wants ter paint a foggin' boat, come and paint this bastard!' The boy shot up and over the gunwales like a startled cat leaving us in peace.

Later that afternoon a Maid Line hire cruiser appeared and

began to thread its way through the throng of boats towards the lock. Sam grinned at me. 'This should be interesting, when he asks Arthur to move' he said. A chorus of advice and shouts rose all along the line. 'The lock's stopped!' 'You got to wait your turn!' 'The planks is in!' 'They ain't a-loosin' us till Toosday'.

The boaters might as well have been speaking Mandarin Chinese for all that they were understood. The hirers stood in a knot in their central cockpit with a 'who are these people?' expression on their faces. It was more than Colin could stand. He vaulted over a cabin top, landed amongst them and began earnestly explaining that the lock was closed.

The hirers were aghast at this awful boy who had appeared from nowhere, but their culture shock was not yet complete. Colin had pulled the gear lever over to astern and stopped them, when his father, a horrified expression on his face, came striding down the Willow Wren wharf unbuckling his belt. 'COLIN! COME 'ERE!'

The boy obediently jumped across to his father, who dealt him a mighty swipe with the belt. The hirers blenched. Never had they seen a child so treated. George rebuckled his belt, beamed, touched his cap and said politely 'That's the only foggin' language the bastard understands madam!' The cruiser reversed out of the mass of boats. The ashen-faced hirers said not a word.

Old Tom Walker was very interested in what was going on on our boats. He pottered down several times to tell Sam and myself about the perils of the 'Oxford River' as boaters called the Upper Thames. He listened to our tale of Abingdon Bridge and Sandford Lock, nodding his head sagely 'I ain't afraid o' runnin' water, darkness or daylight' he assured us. It was a pity that time was against us. We had to leave on the Easter Sunday, for I had once more to return to duty, so there was no time to be lost if ALCOR were to be prepared for Willow Wren's fitters and signwriters before we left, so we had sternly to ignore the old boy, but, now like so many of the grand old men of the canals that I knew, he has gone, I regret that I did not listen more to his tales.

The yard's watchman was an elderly ex-miner, Jim Golby, better known as 'Jinty'. He had, in the course of his career, been a boxer, which accounted for the curious shape of his nose. This went up in steps, rather like the Great Pyramid, as a result of many encounters with gloves and fists. Jinty hailed from Bedworth in North Warwickshire, and had worked down Lord Newdigate's pits in his youth. He spoke with a very broad North Warwickshire accent, which sounded much more like Lancashire than the West Midlands, punctuating his remarks with frequent 'booggers'. He took a great liking to Jean, and, like Joe Skinner left his mark on her in the shape of sore ribs. For when he sat by her during a typical musical session in The Admiral Nelson he would emphasise points by jabbing her with his elbow, saying, approvingly of any songs which appealed to him 'Eh! That were a reet good boogger. Needn't bother abaht that boogger!'

He nearly caused Sam severe internal damage when he came to sing, in a very fine baritone, a song, which must have dated from the 1914-18 period.

'Ho! Hi went hoop in a hairy plane, wi my ole' college choom'. One verse dealt with the delights of the Lord Mayor's banquet: 'There was sparrow grass (asparagus!), tomato stew, and pig's head stuffed wi' jam'.

I had first met Jinty several years before in Reading, when he was mate to Jack Monk and Willow Wren was working up river with timber from the docks, he had gone on to work with Billy Wilson, Greasy Ocker, and ended up living on his old butty SNIPE as the Company's watchman and general labourer. He was a working man of the old sort; a loyal friend, independent and characterful; outspoken and blunt but with a heart of gold. Many people in later years took advantage of him, but he never seemed to bear a grudge. He suffered from a fearsome goitre on his neck, which he normally hid with a white scarf. When at long last he was persuaded to go into hospital to have it removed, he was extremely put out: 'This yooung nurse, she took all me clo'es off, an' bathed me, like a babby' he told me. 'I says, it ain't reet for a yooung gal to do that boogger'.

In spite of his protestations he was duly operated upon and had nothing but praise for the hospital thereafter.

The only thing that made Jinty mad, to my knowledge, was mention of Winston Churchill. Jinty held that older statesman solely responsible for the Dardanelles fiasco, in which he had, as a youngster, been an unwilling participant. 'That boogger sent me aht there. Oop to me bloody ear 'oles in sheet an' bullets. Ah tell tha what mi ole' pigeon. When that boogger dees ah'll get droonk as a sack'.

As it happened, he did not have very long to wait, for the great man died later that year, and Jinty lived up to his promise.

All too soon we had to leave. On Easter Sunday morning we were all taken to Banbury Station, from whence we soon arrived back at our respective homes. The run down the Cherwell valley took perhaps 25 minutes by train as against twelve hours.

The next thing to exercise my mind was impending marriage. We had at last named a trysting day which was to be mid-April, less than a month away. Immediately after Easter I heard that I had been accepted for teacher training in September, so I felt that, much as I loved the lock keeping work, I would have one last fling during the ensuing summer. I agreed with Sam, that if he had ALCOR available in May, I would work the boat for him that summer in whatever jobs I could find.

At the same time a financial crisis arose in the affairs of the Kennet Carrying Co. which stemmed from the damage to cash flow caused by the severe winter of the previous year. Outstanding liabilities needed to be met before the new season could begin, the only way that was open, other than placing the company in the hands of a receiver, was financial reconstruction.

The result of this was that ENTERPRISE was sold to Jim, who agreed to lease her back for operation on the Kennet for another two years, by which time I would be through training college. Jim would henceforth be the full-time skipper employed by the Company to steer his own boat. I decided to put BEECH in the hands of a boat broker at Aylesbury as soon as possible, thus ensuring extra capital.

Had it not been for the impending marriage the next month would have been a glum one indeed, however, the die was cast and, reluctantly but inevitably, I had to turn my back on a boat with which I had been closely associated for six years, and which I had come to know intimately. Still, it does not do to be sentimental over boats, they are in the final analysis, merely chattels. At least I was still going to be earning my living with a boat for the next half year or so.

We were duly married in mid-April, Sam acted as best man and the ceremony was a brief one in the Reading Register Office, for neither of us wanted the fuss or expense of a 'big do'. In view of the many marriages that I have seen which have taken place in a blaze of ceremony and then failed after a short while, I still have no regrets that this was the way we chose. Just a few relatives, our parents and some close friends saw us 'over the top', but as some sort of concession to convention, we sent pieces of cake to absent friends and relatives, including on Jean's insistence, Jinty. The old boy duly received the small box and thought we had sent him a packet of cigarettes. 'Eh!' he exclaimed to the goggling workforce at Braunston 'It were nowt but a bloody bit of ce-ake. Couldn't smo-ake that boogger!'

We spent our honeymoon in North Wales, walking and exploring the Lleyn Peninsula, and in order to do so caught the Cambrian Coast Express. In those days the train ran from Paddington, which meant either joining it en route or going up to London. An aunt of mine who lived in Warwickshire very generously paid for our first night in a Leamington Hotel so that we could get the train next morning. After we left the reception, we caught a train from Reading to Leamington and in due course booked in to the hotel. After dinner it occurred to me that we were only a few miles from Braunston so I took the opportunity of making a local telephone call to Dennis at Willow Wren. In those days most long distance calls had to go through an operator and were very expensive, but a local call was reasonably cheap.

I asked Dennis some questions about ALCOR's progress which he answered, he then said: 'Is that Jean there with you?' 'Yes it is' she called 'Hello Dennis!' 'Where are you phoning from then?' he asked. I told him. 'What on earth are you doing there?' came the next question. 'We're on our honeymoon'.

There came a great explosion of laughter at the other end of the line. 'Well I'm booggered' said Dennis 'I'd have thought you'd have summat better to do on your honeymoon than ring me up about a bloody old National'.

After this Jean put her foot down and, apart from leaping out of my seat as we crossed Wolverhampton Locks, where a Clayton's pair was working down, I managed to get the canal out of my head for a few days. Of course, Portmadoc, where we stayed, was the terminus of the Ffestiniog Railway, but that is another story.

We returned in late April, I received final confirmation of acceptance at Training College plus an assurance of the grant which would be payable, and after one day at Goring I went down to Whitchurch where I strained my back shoving the top gates open. Of all the confounded luck! Goring's gates had done for many a back, but Whitchurch was the lightest and easiest of all. Added to which nobody would, or wanted to, believe that my back trouble had been caused by lock gates when I had just returned from my honeymoon. Many were the arch 'Ho! Ho's!' up and down the river.

Ernie, the engineer's labourer, was more sympathetic. I met him a day or so later when I tottered down to Mapledurham, supporting myself with a stick. 'Ah! That's a bad do bwoy' said he. 'Tell you what, moi ole missus, she got just the cure, you wants to get your missus to do it to yer'. 'What's that?' I groaned. 'When I gets back, she strips me orf, lays me face down on the bed and thrashes me acrorst the back wi' a big bunch o' stinging nettles. Them ole stingers'll soon set ye to rights'. 'But doesn't it hurt, Ernie?' 'Not as long as you keeps yer bollocks out o' the way'.

However, I made swift recovery without Ernie's ministrations, and with very mixed feelings, gave in my notice to the Conservators. I did not really want to leave a secure and pleasant occupation, but time was running out. I had offers of semi-casual work on the Navigation Staff at any time that summer, so with some measure of security in the offing, I quit the Conservator's full time service in early May. There were boats to get and put into service.

At last both of the boats were ready. Sam was already in Braunston with a mate preparing to bring ALCOR and arrangements were being made for ENTERPRISE. I decided to go to meet them on the lower Oxford Canal the day after I finished. Sam was going to take over my Relief's job, so he had two days spare, after which I would be on my own.

On an idyllic morning in early May I got off a train at Oxford and set off up the Thames towpath towards Godstow and Kings Lock. The great open meadows about Medley and Binsey were coming towards their zenith of luxuriance. The

scents of spring overlaid the mellow stone ruins of Godstow
Nunnery and the old low-arched bridge nearby. It was a
warm, cloudless morning when I arrived at Kings Lock, quite
a contrast from that day of howling wind and slashing rain
when we nearly went over the weir.

The lock keeper was pleased to see me, we yarned in his
kitchen for a while until he rowed me across to the upstream
side of the weir. There was no sign as yet of ALCOR, so I
walked up from the canal junction below Dukes Lock towards
Kidlington. Just before Langford Lane I came across a hire
cruiser undergoing minor maintenance. The engineer was
none other than Jack Waldron, an old Kennet friend, then running a hire business based at Aylesbury Canal Basin. Jack was
taking the boat north along the Oxford Canal, so readily
offered me a lift northwards until meeting ALCOR.

It was now midday. There was still no sign of the boat, so I
accepted Jack's offer. We passed Thrupp, Shipton Weir, where
Tony's cat came out and spoke, Bakers Lock and Enslow
Wharf and still no sign. I began to feel a little worried, but as
we came up towards Pigeons Lock I suddenly saw diamond
paintings moving across a spur of land, and knew that my
quarry was in sight. A quick farewell to Jack and I was aboard
ALCOR once more heading south.

The reason for the delay, I learned, was that Sam had not
managed to get away from the Yard at Braunston until late
afternoon, thus only going as far as Napton that night. Next
day they had pushed on to Nell Bridge where John, his mate,
had mutinied for lack of beer. It was late evening when they
stopped and John had forthwith set off in the direction of
some bright lights in search of refreshment only to find that it
was a petrol station. Worse, next morning they had passed
The Great Western at Aynho Wharf only 20 minutes or so
below where they had tied. Both were anxious to get to
Oxford that night and so avoid another dry evening. As a
newly-wed, I was anxious to return to my bride.

I glanced at ALCOR now that work was completed. She had
been blacked all round and the cabin painted in Willow Wren
colours, that is to say, bright, grassy green with scarlet edging,
separated by a cream band. The cabin sides bore the legend
'T.T. Co. Goring on Thames'. The initials stood for 'Taurus
Trading Company' being the name hit upon by Sam to divert

awkward questions which the Chief Inspector might ask were the names of Conservancy employees to appear.

It was now tea time, by the time we had reached the Duke's Cut it was early evening. Golden, mature sun bathed the meadows when we finally came out onto the broad, sparkling waters Of the Thames. Below Kings Lock the river winds sharply and here occurred the first untoward incident with the new motor boat.

ALCOR'S engine, a reconditioned National, had come out of a trip boat recently purchased by Willow Wren. The trip boat had a modern air-cooled Lister fitted but, her original engine being in good condition, Sam had acquired it reasonably cheaply. Nationals, as I have mentioned, when fitted to Grand Union boats, were controlled by two wheels in the door hole of the cabin. One large wheel operated ahead, astern and neutral, the other and smaller one, was connected by worm and nut to the throttle. The throttle in turn was linked to the control rod by forks and cotters secured with split pins. The trouble began when Sam, who was then unfamiliar with her stuck fast on the mud. The only way was to come off sideways. A friendly hire boat tried snatching, but only succeeded in pulling her cleats out, so Sam and John hitched a lift across to the deep water bank, armed with a long line from the fore end. The river was wide, if shallow here, so they began pulling the fore end round and in an upstream direction. So firmly was ALCOR caught, that they had to pull her through 90 degrees before she came loose. Suddenly, with a wallow, she was free again, but facing the wrong way. Sam coiled up the line and threw it onto the fore end, while I called out that I would motor back up to the lock tail, wind in the weir stream and pick them up there. Across the fields it was but a hundred yards or so, but by river nearly a quarter of a mile. I motored up, began winding and then, horrors! The engine began to race wildly and no winding down of the throttle would stop it. I charged flat out at the far bank, in desperation whirled the wheel to the 'Astern' position, then, as the stern tore towards the towpath, wrenched it the other way. From the meadows all that was visible was the exhaust stack. An astonished audience of Sam, John and the lock keeper saw this stack, with a colossal cloud of black smoke, and my head and shoulders tear back and forth amid a deafening racket of racing engine.

As George said of a similar occasion: 'I thought the bloody
rings was a-comin' up the stack'.

After about four mad charges, I got her in slack water in
neutral and dived into the reverberating steel pit of the engine
hole. Swiftly I shut off the oil. Peace descended and I discovered that a split pin had dropped out of the governor-throttle
linkage enabling the governor to run free, being no longer
restrained by the throttle gear. It was a second's work to
reconnect the linkage and to secure it with a bent nail.

This excitement had eaten up another hour. The Godstow
lock keeper was about to close when we got down to him, so
we decided to tie above Osney for the night. I suddenly
realised that whilst my parents were used to my arriving home
at irregular times, doubtless reasoning that the Devil looks
after his own, or as my Father was wont to say 'You don't get
rid of bad kids that easily', my new spouse would doubtless
be worrying about her husband's safety. So when we tied up
just after ten, I had to make a bee line for the nearest telephone box to let her know that all was well and that I should
return late. Doing this, I missed the sensation in the quiet and
unassuming Watermans Arms when John marched in and
ordered 'a quadruple whisky'. Sam said he had never seen
such amazement on a landlord's face. I caught a late train
home and so showed the wife a good husband.

We both went out to Goring next afternoon to meet ALCOR.
Harry was so excited by the whole business that he put his
teeth in, thus transforming his appearance. This time it was
Sam's turn to be taken aback when he came in the lock to be
greeted by a dazzling facial whiteness and radically altered
features. It was indeed an honour, for Harry normally only
donned his teeth for Sunday lunch and the lock garden inspection.

BEECH, still lying at Gatehampton, was terribly full of
water, so when we got her to Reading I had her pumped out
with a motor pump. This did not take long. Her prolonged
immersion – mainly due to six weeks' rain – had swollen her
timbers and tightened her up nicely.

A day or so later ENTERPRISE arrived, skippered by Jim. For
a few days High Bridge Wharf had three boats lying on it, a
sight not seen for many years. However, this state of affairs
was not to last long. BEECH'S days in the fleet were numbered,

we were due to leave with her, to be handed over at Aylesbury in just over a week. Meanwhile I had acquired a new mate.

I had for many years been interested in the traditional music of England, the autumn before I had been approached by some Reading University students to join a new folk club specialising in such music. One of the leading lights was a student of English called Boris. He was a slight, idealistic, gentle person of great depth and considerable ability, who had an encyclopaedic knowledge of English folk music. He played several musical instruments, notably the Anglo Chromatic concertina and the guitar. One morning soon after ALCOR'S arrival, Boris came down to the Wharf, his face the picture of dejection and misery. He had a tall, statuesque blonde girlfriend, called Maggie, and he had been caught *in flagrante* in the girlfriend's rooms, which were in one of the University Halls of Residence. These days it seems anything goes in the groves of Academe but, although it was the sixties, the University authorities were then far from swinging. The result had been rustication for the summer term and expulsion from the Men's Hall, where he lived. Could I, he asked, use a mate? He would be a mate just for the use of the cabin, he pleaded. As it happened his arrival was fortuitous, for I had been thinking of taking someone on on a casual basis. I set him on there and then, with a week to teach him something of the rudiments of boating before we left for down river.

ALCOR lacked gang planks from the mast backwards. This made getting about the boat when under way a tedious business of clambering in and out of the hold. Since Sam was planning to cabin her completely later, there seemed little point in spending money on new planks, so when I heard that one of Sam's friends had been awarded the contract for demolishing the old Corn Exchange in the nearby Market Square, my ears pricked up. The first job for Boris was to help me carry off several lengthy flooring timbers, courtesy of 'Demolition Dave', Sam's pal, and pull out the old nails. They made most sturdy and reliable gang planks and cost a pint of beer!

Through the good offices of a previous business partner, Mike Roberts, I had learned of a houseboat for sale in the Windsor area. The price was easily affordable, if it was any

good we would tow it up to Reading with ALCOR for it might
make a temporary base for Jean and myself. The next few
days passed in the usual feverish rush one experiences before
setting off on a long boat journey, but at length the day of
departure dawned. After an early breakfast I bade a fond
farewell to Jean, mounted the bike and pedalled off to High
Bridge Wharf. It was another 'sweet May morn', clear and
windless. We had winded ALCOR the night before so that she
lay facing downstream. I threw my bag aboard as Boris
emerged, mug in hand, from the cabin. The engine hole doors
clanged back, I clambered down into the white-painted, oily-
smelling engine room. Oil levels were O.K. I checked that the
big drum of heavy duty oil was aboard, fitted the starting handle and turned the engine over several times. Next I took the
priming lever, a small flat piece of metal with a notch in the
end, inserted it at the base of the injector pump and gave each
pump a quick jiggle. This exercise was rewarded by a creaking noise showing that each pump was full of fuel. Taking a
deep breath, I seized the handle, cranked away till the flywheel was spinning well and, at the right moment, flicked the
decompression lever with my left hand. The National
coughed, spat smoke out of the manifold, coughed again, then
again and again in rapid succession. Smoke rings shot up
from the stack. I glanced over the side away from the wharf to
be rewarded with the sight of cooling water spitting out into
mid-river. Heaving myself out, I glanced at the oil pressure
gauge on the cabin top. It was well up, showing over 25 psi.
We were ready to go.

Boris loosed the fore end of BEECH as the Town Hall clock
struck eight. The current plucked at the stern as I loosed off
from the Wharf. Jim's head appeared out of ENTERPRISE'S
cabin slide, blinking owlishly and wishing us a good journey.
We slipped swiftly down the New Cut to Blakes Lock. Eric
was in his shirt sleeves pottering about in the garden before
going on duty at Caversham Yard. He saw us through, closed
up behind us and wound down the paddles. We would, I calculated, make first lock at Sonning and get down below
Staines that night. I aimed to get to Brentford mid-day on the
next day (Wednesday) for Boris had a folk 'gig' that night and
wanted to get a train from somewhere civilised to do it.

All went perfectly to start with. There was little traffic on the river to start with, and we fairly flew downstream. By ten we were through Henley Bridge and forging down the stately Reach, where 'Cuff' and his mates were already starting to drive the white posts for the Regatta course. We were in Cliveden Reach by one o'clock and about two we came abreast of the Willows Boatyard, where the houseboat was lying. I slacked down, winded in the wide reach and slipped alongside. She was an ex-landing craft with a spacious cabin built on. I was somewhat wary of her sides so slacked ALCOR to a crawl as we came abreast. I jerked the gear wheel into 'neutral', then 'astern'. There came a loud 'clunk' from down below, followed by no swirl under the counter. I wound up the throttle; nothing except black smoke. My heart in my mouth I made a desperate lunge for the houseboat, missed, and saw the gentle river current begin to swing the fore end out into midstream. The weight of BEECH abreast, slowly was dragging her round. I went into 'ahead' gear and still nothing happened. Cursing I dropped down into the cabin and lifted the floor boards. The propeller shaft of a working motor boat passes under the floor and is in three parts: the drive shaft proper, which comes from the gearbox through a pillar bearing to a coupling; the tail shaft, which goes out via the stern bush to the propeller; and the intermediate shaft, which connects the two. It was this last which had let me down by shearing just behind the front coupling. Fortunately the engine was all right, but there was no way of transmitting the power.

I stopped the engine in midstream, then Boris and I began the tricky job of coaxing the powerless pair across to the Buckinghamshire bank to where a lane came down to the riverside. This we accomplished with shafts, using them like a lighterman's sweeps. At length we nosed into the reeds and tied up. I found a telephone box nearby, from which I rang Willow Wren's office at Bulls Bridge, Southall. Stan, the clerk, came on the line. Yes they had some spare intermediate shafts for Small Woolwiches in the store, yes, they'd let me have one, but no, they could not get one out to me. Despair welled up for a moment, then I thought of Mike Roberts. He was a marine engineer by trade and lived on a houseboat in Windsor. By now it was tea time and he was at home when I rang. He came straight out, helped me remove the broken shaft and coupling, then ferried me by car to a friend's yard in

Windsor. The friend tut-tutted at the sight and drew breath through his teeth. Well, perhaps a weld might hold it as far as Brentford, as long as there was no emergency reversing. Best, he said, to keep running ahead or in neutral. So saying he got busy with the welder and within the hour I was back aboard and bolting the shaft to its fellow fore and aft. Mike then insisted that, as it was far too late to start, we should go back to his boat, a fine Dutch barge conversion, for supper. This raised morale considerably, so next morning we resolved to move off at sunrise.

Another perfect May morning came, the sun glinting off the glassy surface of the river, the scent of hay sweeping over the meadows of Boveney. ALCOR chugged off down to the gates of Boveney Lock. With my heart in my mouth I crept slowly up to the mooring piles and stopped her with the stern line. There was no problem, so we worked ourselves through, even closing the bottom gates behind us by dint of pulling them up with a strap, Oxford Canal style. No moaning lock keepers here though or at Romney, below Windsor. Indeed so early were we that the first lock keeper we saw was at Penton Hook below Staines. I paid him the tolls for four locks as well as his and he fairly gasped.

The most remarkable event of the morning occurred below Sunbury lock. There was a popular TV series at that time called 'Square World' which featured the comedian Michael Bentine, one time associate of those cult figures of my teens, the Goons. I knew that Bentine had a boat on the river and frequently poked fun at the Conservators in his programme. As we headed down Sunbury Reach I saw a very smart look-ing cruiser coming upstream. I made out the name SQUARE WORLD on her bows and drew Boris' attention to it. As she came nearer I recognised the steersman as Michael Bentine himself. He raised his hand in greeting, Boris and I did the same. Whether or not the sight of Boris' beard set him off I don't know, but Bentine then made elaborate Arabic salaming gestures at us. Boris then went down on his knees on BEECH'S counter and returned a profound salaam. Bentine knelt down beside his steering wheel and lowered his head to the deck, whereupon I could not resist joining in on ALCOR'S counter. Three evident lunatics swept past one another, leaving their boats to steer themselves and making deep obeisances.

Mid-day saw us at Teddington, with the tide just beginning to run out. Half an hour or so would take us into Brentford, so that Boris could get his train and I could breathe again. Down through Richmond we swept and then, with only two miles or so to go, disaster struck. As we bore down through Richmond Bridge a youth in a canoe paddled straight out in front of us. I sounded the horn but he took no notice. I throttled back, went astern and 'clunk', the weld parted, the engine raced noisily and uselessly and we were drifting on a falling tide, with no power and nothing to stop us before the North Sea.

With a certain amount of desperation, I used the slight way left on the boats to sidle alongside a small eyot, Boris leapt off with a line and secured us temporarily, but this was no place to remain for long. An old riverman was pattering about with an open fishing boat, so I persuaded him to tow us across to the Richmond bank, just above the Half Tide Lock. Boris was at least able to get away for his 'gig', but I was now faced with a pretty problem.

I could perhaps get across to Bulls Bridge, pick up a new shaft and get back. This meant a near-impossible journey by public transport or an expensive one by taxi.

Another alternative was to get a tow to Brentford. I knew nobody on this part of the river and professional tug men wanted £30, an astronomical sum in those days, at least three weeks' money for a lock keeper. I rang Leslie Morton at Willow Wren to see if he had any boatmen at Brentford who would pull me down. He was not helpful. 'None of my lads is a licensed waterman, nor in the Union. It'ld be more than their jobs worth to help you out, sorry!' was all his comment.

I decided to go to Brentford by bus and find out for myself, so that evening found me in The Six Bells in Brentford High Street. I had noted, as I crossed Brentford Bridge, that there were a number of Willow Wren boats in the basin waiting to load. It was not long before two very good friends of mine, Mark and Dolly, came in with several other boaters. They listened to my tale and tut-tutted when I told of Morton's attitude. 'It ain't like the Gaffer to carry on like that' said one. 'No, some o' them lighterage lot's bin gettin' at 'im' said another. A few more pints went down, a few more games of darts, then Mark suddenly said, after a whispered conference with Dolly: 'What time's tide?' 'Ten o'clock at Richmond' I replied. 'If they'll let me out, I'll come up for ye' he said firmly.

I went back to the boats in a much happier frame of mind, and next morning began preparing the boats. If Mark didn't appear, I would drift down on the beginning of the ebb, with a weight over the sterns, catch on to the piles at Brentford Railway Dock and then work into Brent Creek. This was how horse boats used to go down to Brentford years ago, but I was somewhat nervous of trying it, although it was the cheapest method. Perhaps, I thought, I'd better ring Morton to see if he would let Mark go. I found a phone box, got through just after nine, and received a rasping earful!. 'Look here Blagrove' exploded Morton – it was evidently the morning after the night before – 'you've got no right to go canvassing my boat-men'. 'But er! I thought er! um! er!' I said lamely. 'No right at all' he roared 'and Mark's got no right to pull your chest-nuts out of the fire. He's not insured, not in the Union, not a waterman and we're not Port Employers, so you can forget it. Go and hire a River Tug and leave my men alone! If Mark comes up for you he'll get his cards!' with which the line went dead. I looked at my watch. It was nine thirty, the tide turned at ten. With a sinking heart I made my way through the streets back to the river. It was going to be me alone against the tideway.

The tide had flooded up behind the Half Tide Lock, the tide barriers were out of the channel, there was nothing to stop me. I watched the waters gradually slacken until the river was smooth. I placed my mudweight on the foredeck of BEECH, loosed off, then shoved out hard with the long shaft. The boats slowly edged out into the channel, fore ends upstream. I walked along the planks to the fore end ready to drop the weight when the ebb began. Faintly I heard the drumming of a twin cylinder diesel and thought this was unusual for a river launch. Then I glanced up and my heart leapt with joy.

Below the arches of the tide barrier was the unmistakable high-riding fore end of an empty narrow boat. Another glance and I saw Willow Wren paintwork. Even then I couldn't believe my luck. 'They must have a job to do on the river above Teddington' I thought, then I heard a klaxon blast, saw Dolly waving to me. Mark crouched impassively over his tiller with a white Park Drive spiked in his mouth and his son

Ted standing on the planks behind the mast grinning from ear to ear. The motor boat QUAIL circled me, then came up abreast of BEECH. Quickly Ted and myself secured her, winded round again and then we were off. 'Am I glad to see you!' I said to Mark. 'I didn't think the gaffer would let you come'. 'I never asked him' said Mark 'I just told 'em at the lock that my mate was in trouble and they let me go'.

Awful realisation began to dawn on me. By ringing Morton and trying to be helpful I had made things worse. If the gaffer found out, we were in real trouble. Bad enough for me, but I could weather the storm, but for Mark and Dolly their job and home was at stake. The joy of a swift run down to Brentford was clouded by this unpleasing thought.

By 10.30 a.m. we were at Town Lock, by 11.00 I had pulled into Brentford Basin to await Boris' return. I asked Mark what I owed him 'You don't owe us nothing, Dave' was his response.

This was so typical of the people of the canals of those days. If you were their friend, that meant everything. Of course it meant that I would be expected to reciprocate, but there were things that were worth more than money.

I had made a cup of tea and cleaned the brasses when Dolly called over to me. 'Are ye goin' to the Public? The gaffer wants to see you'. 'I'll bet he does' I thought as I made my way down the towpath to The Northumberland Arms which was where Morton and his cronies met at lunchtime.

The bar was empty save for Morton, Mark, the manager of the General Steam Tug & Lighterage and the Union Convenor. If ever I saw a hanging judge and jury this was it. With the exception of Mark, who was impassive as usual, all had grim faces. 'Well!' demanded Morton. I was silent. 'You know what you've done. You've upset the Port Employers, that's dangerous; you've risked Mark's job, that's bloody stupid; you've nearly caused a strike, that's worse and you've put two fingers up at me, that's criminal!'

A ghost of a smile flickered round the Union Convenor's eyes. Morton continued 'In short you've tried to cut corners and you've been a bloody nuisance. Now it's going to cost you, right?' I nodded miserably, 'How much?' I ventured, thinking of that £30. 'Four double scotches' said Morton, laughing for the first time. He reached out and shook my hand. 'It's just the sort of thing I'd have done myself once'.

The Union man said 'It's just the sort of thing you bloody well do now!' and the whole company roared with laughter. A convivial session developed. Morton agreed to have the shaft ready for us on arrival at Bulls Bridge and for Jumbo, the Willow Wren tractor driver, to pull us up the locks that afternoon.

If I thought that my troubles were over that trip, I had another thought coming. For although we obtained the shaft and I fitted it that night, we were still dogged with trouble. Partly it seemed to be due to the shaft being slightly out of alignment, for next day, at Winkwell, we sheared a coupling bolt. Luckily a friendly boatowner provided a replacement set of mild steel ones, which enabled us to get away eventually. In the meantime another mishap occurred at Fishery Lock, Boxmoor. For some reason I had left ALCOR in neutral in the lock. Going uphill one should leave a full-length motor boat ticking over with her fore end against the sill. Perhaps I was distracted by the arrival of my father and Jean, for it was a Friday evening, and she had finished work for the week.

Whatever the cause, I was standing on the lockside. Boris whipped up the gate paddles and ALCOR rode back into the bottom gates, jamming the top of the ram's head under the balance beam and twisting it out of shape.

By the time we had refitted the sheared coupling bolts it was afternoon. We eventually slipped into the length near The Grand Junction Arms at Bulbourne too late to go down Marsworth.

A loaded pair of Willow Wrens was lying nearby. I recognised the captain and his wife as a venerable couple who had, at one time, been put in a remote cottage at Curdworth on the Birmingham & Fazeley Canal. They were told by British Transport Waterways that they could like it or lump it. Eventually Colonel Ritchie prevailed upon Morton to find them a pair of boats until more suitable accommodation could be found. Old Sam was in a jovial mood when I talked to him. The conversation turned to kids who throw things 'I don't bother about no kids' said Sam 'nor do Anna'.

The white haired old lady shook her head vigorously causing her earrings to dance. Sam was leaning in the motor's door holes. Anna in the butty's. He rummaged in the ticket drawer and produced an evil-looking catapult. 'See this?' he said, fitting a pebble into the sling. I glanced at Anna, she had produced a similar weapon. 'That number plate, Anna' he said nodding at the bridge. There was a 'whick!' noise, two slings flopped down and two loud 'clangs' came from the bridge, a good 150 feet away. 'No, we don't bother about no kids, mate'.

It should have been a morning's work to Aylesbury, but the National began to develop valve trouble next morning. All down the Arm, down the narrow locks which entailed double working, it got worse. Near the bottom, where the pounds lengthen, it got so bad that we were limping along amid a great cloud of black exhaust smoke. It was afternoon when we staggered sootily into the Basin and delivered BEECH. I winded and started back, but after two locks there was nothing to be done but to summon assistance. The only thing was to take out the valves, regrind them and retime the engine, a simple enough task, but beyond both my skill and tool resources.

Both Boris and myself had commitments in Reading, so ALCOR had to be left for several days while the fitter did his work. We had intended getting back with the boat in six days from leaving Reading, instead we had taken six days just one way.

Eventually, next weekend Jean and I moved ALCOR down to Bulls Bridge where we left her for a few more days, getting the ram's head straightened on a jig while she was there. Then in the first week of June we came back up river, picked up the houseboat and returned without a hitch, except for getting a blade full of rubbish at Blakes Lock and hitting the gates much to Eric's disgust.

But somehow the changes had been rung. I could see the end of my nomadic life, marriage was not an institution to be taken lightly and the trouble-strewn trip to Aylesbury underlined that. It was no longer just my life at risk, no longer just my time or money to spend but another's, and soon it would be a third's for Jean was now pregnant. Although I still loved boating I was not too sorry to accept a job with my old friends the Conservators for a short while.

I found myself back in uniform, with Boris in full command of ALCOR while I took over Mapledurham Lock for three weeks when Len took his annual leave. It was time to take breath, for the preceding 12 weeks had seen radical alterations take place in my life and lifestyle.

CHAPTER 11 — STRATFORD OR BUST

John Grace had also decided to get married. In spite of the earnest endeavours of his friends to dissuade him from such a drastic step, he named the day and he and his fiancée, Sue, began making the usual preparations.

I forget now just how it was that I persuaded him that ALCOR would be ideal for his honeymoon, but the upshot of deliberations was that the happy couple should come with us to Stratford-upon-Avon for the great re-opening by the Queen Mother in early July. Mindful of my promise of last autumn about taking Joe and Rose Skinner with FRIENDSHIP to the Re-opening Rally, I wrote to Brian Collings to see if he could tell me what was happening. He replied that Colonel Ritchie was making arrangements to get the Skinners to Stratford, and that he and his fiancée would probably be doing the towing with a tug that the Colonel had acquired. Consulting the calendar I calculated that, if John and Sue were married as planned on a Saturday, we could leave Reading on the Sunday morning and arrive in Stratford in good time for the ceremony on the following Saturday. Accordingly I wrote back to Brian suggesting that we made for The Two Boats at the bottom of Itchington on the Tuesday night, which would give me three clear days to get ALCOR there from Reading.

Preparations now went ahead for the voyage. The secretary of Reading Branch of the Kennet & Avon Trust wanted to take a punt to the Rally and back, but could only manage time for a one way trip, so a carriage rate was arranged for carrying the punt as deck cargo, in an inverted position. John and Sue were to have the cabin, so Boris had to be dispossessed. This meant that top cloths would be needed, an expense which neither Sam, nor myself, had budgeted for at that stage. Jean provided a solution. She pointed out that in a street near her old flat was a firm of shopfitters who were advertising old shop blinds for sale. For those whose memory does not extend to the forties and fifties, these were large canvas sheets on retractable iron carriers which let down over the pavement from shop fascias, preventing sun from ruining the display or sheltering window shoppers from the wet. I visited the firm and came away with a quantity of bleached canvas of good quality for the princely sum of five shillings. Admittedly they carried the legend, in big letters 'Freeman, Hardy & Willis, Quality Footwear', but, with reproofing in green, they looked quite the part, and the lettering was not too obvious. I made makeshift sidecloths out of ENTERPRISE'S side sheets, complete with window apertures, tacked to the gunwales by means of their brass eyelets. Surprisingly, it all worked quite well and the hold was quite rainwater-tight.

I finished my stint at Mapledurham and a busy week ensued as final preparations were made. ALCOR was tripping and acting as relief boat for ENTERPRISE until the Friday. Boris brought her round to Caversham on Saturday while Jean and myself attended the wedding.

The plan was that the happy pair would stay at the Caversham Bridge Hotel, thus ensuring that at least their first night was a comfortable one, then after breakfast we would pick them up, along with a large family party, and take them upstream as far as Oxford.

All went smoothly and to plan to start with. We embarked the honeymooners and family on a bright July Sunday morning and set off upstream. It was Henley Sunday and the river was at its summer best. All day we forged steadily upstream in pleasant sunshine. At Osney we bade farewell to the family, along with Jean who had to work next morning, but was going to meet us again at Stratford, and with no excitement beyond pulling a hire boat out of difficulties at Osney Bridge, tied up at Thrupp in the late evening. John and Boris celebrated the successful day's run in The Boat with music, which was well-received. Old Mrs Coles, a retired boatwoman who lived in one of the cottages on the canal side, had a son on early turn at Cowley next morning, so he agreed to give us a knock soon after six.

Monday was another perfect day, starting at 6.30 we were through Banbury by mid-afternoon, too late for a quick one at The Struggler, and made for Cropredy. The lock house at Bourton was a riot of colour, sweet peas, roses and country-garden plants swaggering everywhere in a copybook display of an English country garden.

However, the weather was too good to last. When we left Cropredy on Tuesday morning, it was sunny and clear, but clouds began to roll up at Claydon. By the time we had reached Fenny Compton a dull day had developed, with freshening gusts of cold wind threatening rain.

We gradually dropped the Direction Finding mast at Wormleighton behind and Napton Mill drew slowly nearer as the summit level boxed the compass. Eventually we reached the territory of the moaning lock keeper, but for once passed through without incident.

On a clear day, when one stands at the top of Napton Hill by the windmill, the view is breathtaking, for a great sweep of central England, from the Malvern Hills to the Black Country in the west and Leicestershire to the north east is laid at one's feet. It is easy to imagine James Brindley taking station here with his surveying instruments, for virtually the whole course of the Oxford Canal is visible, from the low saddle between Hillmorton and Barby, where Warwickshire marches with Northamptonshire and Leicestershire, to the Fenny Compton gap, where the canal joins the Cherwell valley. Later the surveyors and engineers of the Warwick & Napton Canal must have used the hill, because long stretches of the latter canal are visible where it crosses the upper levels of the Leam valley before plunging down the hillside at Stockton.

When the weather is warm and clear it is a pleasant place to linger, with the rolling green valley of Shakespeare's Avon spread out like a crumpled baize table cloth, with larks calling above buttercup fields and a gentle breeze sighing in the white sails of the mill. More often, however, the strong south westerlies or north easterlies are channelled up this low lying corridor between Severn and Trent and one realises why this hilltop was crowned with a windmill. Although today it is a private house, the sails are once more in position. They strain and creak to the pressure of the wind, and must, in earlier times, have provided an abundance of power.

The afternoon that we came down Marston Doles into the Napton flight was developing into such conditions. A typically English summer depression was bustling its way in from the Atlantic, sending scudding grey clouds low overhead, tossing the towpath hedges and bursting through gaps and bridgeholes in furious, fore end grabbing gusts. Occasionally stinging and drenching showers would be flung down, making lock work tedious and slippery.

Still, we were mob-handed and had a reasonably clear run down. The moaning lock keeper was not in evidence at Bottom Lock so, putting the kettle on for a brew-up, we plodded on, looking forward to the deeper water of the Grand Union which lay ahead.

From Napton Bridge the land flattens out, the hills recede on the south east side, and today the squalls were beating up from the west with a vengeance. As we came into the straight length, in the middle of which lies Napton Junction, or Wigrams Turn as boaties call it, I saw a low-down black fore end approaching, behind which was a green and red cabin, Willow Wren colours. Riding high behind was the fore end and painted deckboard of another boat. Unmistakeably it was a tug with an empty butty on cross straps. Simultaneously I recognised the pair as being Colonel Ritchie's REDCAP and Joe Skinner's FRIENDSHIP. Inexorably we drew nearer. I throttled down, hoping for dear life that we would not be blown out of the channel, but in vain. The junction was full of mud so as all three boats met on the turn, both motors got blown on the puddle, the butty skidded sideways and all was confusion. John and Boris poled off our fore end, I managed to back into the Oxford channel, while REDCAP'S steerer forced himself into the wide junction bridge with his engine. I recognised Brian Collings in the mêlée, hat jammed over his eyes and coat collar turned up, puffing at a pipe as he thrashed brown water up, while Joe Skinner, his ancient trilby lashed to his head with binding string came leaping along FRIENDSHIP'S top planks with a wooden shaft. Rose Skinner, her red beret secured by a giant hatpin, thrust at the tiller to row FRIENDSHIP round. The wash from the two boats drew ALCOR round slowly, so I let her tick over as we drifted towards the Junction Bridge. Over the clamour of the gale Rose called: 'It weren't like this at the Wine Lodge, were it?' I grinned back at her 'How far tonight?' 'We've got to go where our mates take us'.

Joe clumped down beside her as FRIENDSHIP slid under the bridge, white moustache fluttering in the breeze. 'Bottom of Itchington I reckon, if this Tyscophoon will let us', he called back. I waved acknowledgement and John and Boris once more set to with the shafts as the gale attempted to slam ALCOR'S fore end into the towpath coping beneath the bridge.

By the time we had reached the top lock of 'Wigram's

Three', the other pair were in the middle lock, Joe evidently not trusting the little tug's power in this wind, had loosed off and was bowhauling down the short pound. Long before we had got out of the third lock they were out of sight.

Something seemed to be amiss with the great girders of the Southam railway bridge as we came down the long straight below the locks. The wind was broadside on and lashing the tops of wavelets into spray, the only course was to come down the pound crabwise, trying to keep the counter in deep water. Through the gusts I saw that one girder had dropped into the canal, evidently it was being cut up for scrap by a fairly incompetent gang of contractors. With sadness I recalled how only two years before this line, running from Weedon via Daventry and Braunston to Southam and Leamington, had been busy with massive eight-coupled steam locomotives hauling trains of limestone and coal. I recalled how Bill and I used to forage for loco coal behind the advertisement hoardings by Braunston Station which adjoined Barlow's Yard. I recalled the sad tale of the subcontracting paint gang who had been given the job of repainting the bridge a few years before. They were told to paint underneath the decking and for this reason slung painting cradles from the rails by means of ropes through the decking. The foreman had told them the difference between running rails and check rails (the latter prevent wheel flanges from riding off when a train crosses a bridge such as this) but it was 'in one ear and out the other'. They secured their cradles over the shiny metals rather than the rusty ones then set to, some 15 feet above water level. After about an hour they heard a train coming, so rested from their labours and lit fags. The train thundered onto the bridge and chop! chop! neatly sliced the cradle ropes. The gang's fags were still alight as they hit the water, cradle, paint, brushes and all.

Now the railway was silent, its metals lifted, its telephone wires drooping listlessly from their posts and Joe Skinner was having hell's delight in threading FRIENDSHIP under one corner of the tilted girder as the wind threatened constantly to slam her frail old timbers against the unyielding steel. At last Joe was through and we cautiously followed. Catching up with the pair at Stockton Top Lock I suggested that it might be easier were I to put FRIENDSHIP abreast while Brian and his fiancée Janet went down on their own, this was done and we descended in fine style tying up an hour or so later outside The Two Boats below Bottom Lock.

Since both Boris and John were not only accomplished musicians but great entertainers a lively night developed. Rose produced an ancient concertina, given her by Brigadier Fielding of the Salvation Army, which Boris soon mastered, wheezy bellows and all. Some of the locals joined in with gusto, one of them being convinced that my mates were international stars and that Sue Grace was Dusty Springfield (whom she did admittedly resemble somewhat). The old gent was wearing an American-style cap and became a little incensed when John referred to him as 'Casey Jones', but otherwise all was serene when the party finally ended with Joe and Rose performing a spirited 'Knees up Mother Brown' on the towpath on the wrong side of midnight.

Next morning was bright but blustery and the flotilla set forth accompanied by another single boat, SWAN which had come down the locks late the night before, also bound for Stratford. This boat was an iron ex-Cowburn & Cowpar boat from Manchester, fitted with a single-cylinder Gardner engine and an amazing reverse, by means of which the entire propeller shaft slid back and forth. Later one of the crew, John Liley, was to chronicle the adventures of this boat in a series of diverting articles in *Motor Boat & Yachting*.

ALCOR'S ram's head was giving trouble again, so I took the opportunity, while the rest of the boats went ahead, of draining the top chamber of Bascote Staircase and going overside clad in Wellingtons and armed with a sledge hammer. The clout she had received at Fishery Lock had bent the rudder post slightly which made it a very difficult job to locate it in the cup on the skeg, so carefully positioning the rudder post, I gave it several ringing blows, each one nearly paralysing my arms and making my head spin. The effect of these was to straighten out the shaft of the rudder post sufficiently to enable the rudder to drop directly into its cup instead of swinging up and balancing on the edge. Ten minutes or so of this illegal docking, then we were on our way again, the rudder giving little more trouble thereafter. At Radford Bottom Lock there was no sign of REDCAP and FRIENDSHIP, but in the woods beyond the overflow weir we came upon them, tied against the bank. REDCAP'S gear box had been playing up and now was completely out of action. A glum-looking Brian recounted the news, so I suggested that I towed both boats to the next bridge, by Radford Brewery, from whence the Colonel could be informed by telephone. We did this, in fact moving the boats to a point just beyond where the main Southam Road ran parallel.

The Colonel dispatched Dennis Clarke, who arrived at lunch time, inspected the box and shook his head sadly. New parts were needed and the job would take several days. The disappointment on the faces of Brian and Janet was plain. Joe and Rose resignedly accepted that they would be missing the Rally and all the ceremony. After a private word with both Brian and Dennis I suggested that I might snatch them onward, Joe's face brightened. 'That ain't a bad little motor', he said approvingly of ALCOR. So it came that I was destined to be the tug for FRIENDSHIP after all. From then on, Joe and Rose were my mates, and mates they remained for the rest of their lives.

By now it was close on 3.30 p.m. We should have to get moving if we were to clear Hatton that night, so with little more ado, I started up, dropped FRIENDSHIP'S cross straps onto the dollies and set off.

Once more the weather was proving foul, squalls began developing and once more the grey clouds tore across the sky. Leamington, never at its best from the canal, looked even drearier than in March, the doomed gasworks showing a fine collection of broken windows and rusting pipes. Claytons' traffic from here to Banbury and Oldbury was now a thing of the past and Charlie, my old friend of Willow Wren days was working for Banbury Council. Near the railway station a forlorn-looking cruiser lay sheeted-up on the towpath side, as we went by I saw that was none other than Teddy Cook's JULIA II, doubtless moored temporarily en route to Stratford.

Beyond the main road bridge the wind reached a crescendo of fury, finally a gust caught our fore end as we came across the railway aqueduct and shoved it up the towpath. Too late the shafts came into play. ALCOR lurched to a stop with FRIENDSHIP running up between her and the towpath. Ten minutes were lost while we shoved and heaved the motor back into the channel against a broadside wind and it was gone

5.30 before we cleared the two locks by The Cape of Good Hope.

We were rising in the Middle Lock of Hatton, listening to SWAN'S Gardner banging away up 'the thick' when Boris, who was lock wheeling, came back to say that the lock was 'on' at the next lock. The lock keeper, an ex-boatman known to Joe and Rose, had padlocked it so that the flight could be cleared of boats by seven o'clock. In spite of pleadings he refused to let us go through, so we were forced to tie in what Joe called 'the 'sylum Pound' for the night. The name referred to the nearby mental institution which once had a coal wharf at the middle lock. We were consequently compelled to walk nearly half a mile to The New Inn near Top Lock for our evening's refreshment. I telephoned my aunt who lived nearby and gave her news of our whereabouts, which was subsequently relayed home and thence to Jean and Jim, thus maintaining the Company's boat control system.

We went up the rest of the flight in quick time next day, to be greeted at Top Lock by another old acquaintance of mine from Willow Wren days. This boater, a worthy taciturn individual, had a wife who was very kind and good-natured but had a mouth like a fog horn and lungs to match. I had inadvertently give her a nasty surprise at Longford Wharf once, when I had detected slack at the bottom of the loading hopper. We had refused to load this and left a message for the traffic clerk at Suttons Stop control office to this effect. Somehow the message was not passed on to Arthur and Ada, and disaster occurred next day when they went to load. The motor boat lay ready, beneath the shoots, Ada tidying away the children's toys and other things in the boat's bottom, while Arthur idly toyed with the hopper release catch. Suddenly about half a ton of dust and slurry descended on his wife and Longford rang with her protestations. She was of a good mind to have me crucified, but eventually I made my peace. I was not helped by a cruel humorist who used to sing 'Dat Coal Black Mammy' in her presence.

This morning Ada was in full cry about the goings-on on the Stratford 'There's rucks on 'em gone down, and boats all over the cut' was the burden of her tale and, on arriving at Lapworth, I found out she was indeed speaking the truth.

To start with, there was not much to remark on, apart from

our having to wait our turn to enter the top lock of the southern section. The junction is somewhat complex and involves boats bound for Stratford from the Grand Union rising up one (narrow) lock into a large pool, before commencing the long descent to the Avon. This was forced upon the hapless Stratford Canal Company by the Warwick & Birmingham Company as the price of allowing a junction. It is said that the original junction was on a level, but the Warwick Company obtained legal process to make the Stratford yield a lockful of water for every boat which passed. This arrangement was reinstated in 1995.

On one side of the pool was a long line of sunken, rotting Joey boats providing a depressing comment on the state of canal transport, but in other directions things were decidedly brisk. After a sleep of nearly four decades the Southern Stratford was being woken with a vengeance.

The story of the Stratford Canal's resurrection is one of the heroic tales of the waterways movement. The detailed story is long and complex and foreshadowed much of what has happened on the waterway system since. Briefly the story is as follows: when the Stratford-upon-Avon Canal was first built it was seen as a link from Birmingham to the lower part of the Avon and Severn valleys and later as part of a chain of canals, rivers and horse tramways leading to the south and London. This latter aim was never accomplished, its tramway extension petered out at Moreton-in-Marsh, whilst trade to the Avon never came up to expectations. The Warwick & Birmingham Canal came as a useful adjunct, for the impoverished Stratford saw that, since the canals were a few hundred yards apart at Lapworth, it could form a part of a through route. The Warwick & Birmingham were not so keen to pull a rival's chestnuts out of the fire and insisted, as we have seen, that a lock be placed between the two canals as the price of a junction.

Eventually the Stratford Company came into the hands of a somewhat rascally concern, the Oxford, Worcester & Wolverhampton Railway Company, whose shady career ended with absorption by the GWR. So, like the Kennet & Avon, it came into the orbit of that great company, with rather similar results. In the IWA's early days a great campaign was mounted to restore the Lapworth-Kings Norton section to through traffic. This was successful, Willow Wren even managed to push loaded boats through and so secure its future, but the southern part, leading just to Stratford and the defunct Upper Avon Navigation had become completely derelict. I remember seeing the fine, wide, basins at Stratford in 1955, they were being used as municipal lily pools. The river lock had crumbling, weed-grown gates, and was obstructed by a footbridge across the chamber, by the bus station it was a weedy, rubbish-filled ditch. All this in one of the country's leading tourist spots spoke volumes for the lack of foresight and imagination of the responsible authorities. Further up, cows grazed in the bed, lock gates rotted; the cut awaited the fate of the Wilts & Berks or the Thames & Severn, complete abandonment, infilling and oblivion. That this did not happen was due to the efforts of a devoted band of IWA members and the Warwickshire County Council. This last authority, with all the stilted imagination of modern bureaucracy in 1958 applied for a Warrant of Abandonment on the grounds that no traffic had used the canal for 12 months. Since the state of the canal was as I described above, this was not surprising. The purpose of killing the canal was so that a single road bridge could be replaced by a culverted embankment. All seemed lost, until a Jack-the-Giant-Killer appeared in the shape of a canoeist who had, within the time-limit, not only canoed down the length concerned, but had bought a toll-ticket from British Waterways and had kept it as proof. Consternation then ensued, and the ponderous machinery creaked to a halt. The result was that the BTC agreed to hand over the canal from Lapworth to Stratford to the National Trust.

Back in 1959, we of the Reading Branch of the what was the Kennet & Avon Canal Association had received a visit and pep-talk from a young Coventry architect called David Hutchings. At that time he was engaged in a project to re-open the derelict Wyken Arm of the Oxford Canal. Hutchings was convinced that volunteer labour could re-open disused canals and set about doing so. His success at Wyken and elsewhere made him a natural choice to spearhead the Stratford restoration which began in 1960.

By 1964 it was well on the way to completion, the Queen Mother was coming to open it in the fourth centennial year of Shakespeare's birth and here we were, adding our mite to the general celebration.

I am not certain how many craft went down to Stratford that momentous July, but it was several hundred. There were canoes and skiffs, not to mention our deck cargo of a punt, plywood cruisers with outboards, fibreglass cruisers, short-ened ex-working boats, tripping boats, hotel boats, even loaded boats – for Ray White had gone down with COLESHILL and CYGNUS for Willow Wren carrying imported Japanese motor cycles and sugar from Birmingham for Flowers Brewery. The ancient fabric, with its renovated pieces, groaned at the enormous traffic, but it just about held together. David Hutchings had taken a gamble, 'Stratford or bust' and it was up to all of us to back up his faith.

The Stratford re-opening has entered into canal folk-lore in the ensuing years. There were those at the time who grumbled about corners being cut, about the total impossibility of doing what Hutchings did. They may have been right but, thank heavens, no-one listened to them. In the intervening years the politics of the affair, if not its engineering competence, have been amply vindicated. What really mattered was that a canal was being re-opened. It was the first long length to be restored, pointing tantalisingly at a derelict river navigation and poten-tial circular holiday route. It was heavily locked and narrow, running through lovely but unknown countryside. It had the potential to create jobs and revitalise the local economy. It was a precedent in restoration; in the partnership of volunteer labour and prison 'trusties', which foreshadowed many Manpower Services Schemes; in the concept of bringing a working canal into the context of the late twentieth century. It was bold, imaginative and it was destined to affect the entire attitude of officialdom towards the waterway system. As Winston Churchill said, in another context: 'This is not the end, it is not the beginning of the end. It is the end of the beginning'.

Every boat's crew seemed to be aware of the historic importance of what was going on. After years of being derid-ed as 'cranks' and 'starry-eyed idealists', an important goal had been achieved, a new, more hopeful, canal age was dawn-ing. There was, I realised, a symbolic significance in the pres-ence of Joe and Rose and their gallant old FRIENDSHIP. Here were the 'old 'uns', the representative of that hard-working, cheerful, long-suffering community which, against all odds, had clung on and kept the canal system in being, and here were the new generation taking up the fight. Perhaps the cut would not be the same as the one Joe and Rose had known all their lives, but at least it would live and it would be useful. Its essential fabric and integrity would last for further generations to enjoy and cherish.

Such high-flown sentiments were, I must admit, not evident at that precise moment. What mattered immediately was 'getting 'em ahead', down 33 locks and 13 miles to the River Avon. As far as one could see down the Lapworth Flight, was a solid jam of boats.

The approved way of working down a crowded flight of locks closely-spaced is to wait until someone starts filling the lock below you before emptying yours. This ensures that water is not run to waste over the bywashes at each lock. However, people were so impatient and water was so short that boats were being passed down into pounds already occupied by waiting boats. Joe shook his head and muttered, but there was little choice for us. As soon as our turn came I slipped ALCOR into the Top Lock, emptied it, drove out and waited below while we refilled for FRIENDSHIP.

This led to an unfortunate scene a few locks down. The pounds were a little longer but very shallow at the sides, so I crept gently down in the centre to the head of each lock, put the fore end against the copings and then waited my turn with ALCOR'S stern end in deep water. This manoeuvre was well understood by most, but one couple in a 'crunchable' cruiser took exception, thinking we were stealing their road. The man entered into a vigorous shouting match on the lockside with Joe and Boris, in the course of which he told Joe he was 'an old lunatic'.

Joe's moustache bristled and he was all for teaching the cruiser skipper another use for his windlass, when the woman, seeing FRIENDSHIP swinging across the cut in her direction told Rose, sharply, that if she scratched her paint she would have to pay for it

That, as Dick Knightley would say, was where she made her mistake. Rose may have been old and frail-looking but she had the spirit, when roused, of a wild cat. Sue Grace had been sitting in FRIENDSHIP'S hatches chatting quietly when the explosion occurred. Rose told the assembled company that they'd paid for boats more times than they'd had hot dinners and Sue had some difficulty in restraining Rose from going over the side armed with FRIENDSHIP's tiller. Eventually peace was restored, the other boaters calmed all sides down and, to give them their due, the pleasure boat couple apologised handsomely. Joe's face was like the sun coming from behind clouds, when he took the proffered hand. 'Ah! that's all right mate, we all gets cross sometime'.

This contretemps apart, all went well, albeit slowly, as we worked our way down 'on the water' as Joe said, through the lovely Forest of Arden, through Lowsonford and Yarningdale, towards the bottom lock of the flight at Preston Bagot. Beyond the bottom was a long pound down to the aqueduct over the A34 at Wotton Wawen where there was a large basin and a pub. This, I thought, would be a good place to tie for the night.

It was late evening when I put ALCOR through the bottom lock and backed up to the single bottom gate to await FRIEND-SHIP. A bystander looking on from the narrow brick and iron road bridge which spanned the lock tail, warned me that Ray White had had trouble getting his butty out earlier that day.

Sure enough, FRIENDSHIP stuck fast when I tried to pull her out. What had happened was that the long pound had fallen off several inches, and the locksides had 'come in' over the years. This, combined with FRIENDSHIP's middle-age spread, had resulted in her catching fast by the fore end of the cabin - a favourite point at which narrow boats stick in locks. We tried various devices as dusk fell on very frayed tempers. The usual method is to try 'snatching' and 'flushing' at the same time. The motor boat goes hard ahead with a slack rope and the top paddles are simultaneously lifted. After three such tries, FRIENDSHIP's fore end was through the bottom gate, thus preventing any possibility of filling the lock and retreating. The fourth snatch was followed by a snap as FRIENDSHIP's fore end stud pulled straight out and flew over my head, striking the iron girder of the bridge with a loud clang and missing my ear by an inch. Joe muttered, found an iron bar and rigged up a temporary stud. The next snatch, in the pitch dark under the bridge, ended as ALCOR's National stopped dead in full ahead gear. Casting loose the towline, I drifted out of the bridge into the twilight, to find that I had run over a length of thick coir towline in the bridgehole, a relic of Ray's earlier struggle with CYGNUS. This had completely 'blocked the blade'.

Normally the method of dealing with a bladeful of such proportions means raking out from the towpath of lockside with a shaft, but here the bank was high on both sides and there was no towpath under the bridge. It was impossible to get at it with a shaft, the only thing was a breadknife and a swim. Joe shook his head. It was too late at night for such heroics. 'We'll get her out in the mornin', 'specially if the pound makes up' was his verdict. So saying he got aboard FRIENDSHIP, rummaged about beneath the cloths and produced a ladder. This he placed in the hatches enabling Rose and him get on and off. The boats behind all agreed that we should call it a day, one wag suggested that it was the quantity of money Joe kept in the cabin that was the cause of the trouble.

There was a pub, called The Crab Mill a few yards down the road, and someone proposed that we adjourn thither. Unfortunately we had none of us realised that closing-time was upon us, so when we got there all was dark, shuttered and barred. Boris rattled the door handle, for it was not yet half past ten. A quavering old female voice from within called 'Who's there?' We all looked at Joe, who rose to the occasion ''Tis only us poor boatin' chaps as wants a drink'. 'Go away! I'll call the police!' 'Cor, strike!' was Joe's comment.

We returned to the lock to find a lively scene. The pounds above were full of boats many being lit up, somebody was frying up sausages on a camping stove, Teddy Cook appeared, having become caught up with JULIA II in the jam. He was lugging a large case of beer. Boris and John brought out the instruments and an impromptu party developed on the lockside until the small hours.

At some hideously grey moment in the early morning my alarm went off. I clambered out of the hold clad in my briefs, seized a carving knife and plunged over the counter. The water clutched at me, causing me to gasp, then, a mighty handful of coir began to disentangle itself. There must have been 20 feet of it but, at last it was free. Boris helped pull me back up then I saw Joe standing nearby, a monstrous tin mug in his hands. 'Here y' are Davey. Get this down you mate'.

Gratefully I took the proffered mug in trembling fingers

and took a gulp of hot, strong cocoa laced with rum. Suddenly the whole day took on a new, hopeful, aspect.

After a quick change and some breakfast, I backed into the lockmouth to find that Joe had matters well in hand. A block and tackle had been set up from FRIENDSHIP'S mast. Boris, John and others were being marshalled for pulling duty. Two more boaters from behind were standing by the ground paddles at the top of the chamber; a line on either side went forward from the stern stud to yet more people on the lockside; my job was to snatch with the motor. Rose was at the ready in the hatches, so Joe, taking up a directorial position gave the signal to start.

Up came the paddles, in went ALCOR'S forward gear, people pulled and FRIENDSHIP suddenly shot out of the lock like a cork of a bottle. I eased down beyond the bridge and the crew rejoined the pair, Joe coiling up the long mast rope with a grin splitting his face from ear to ear and acknowledging the cheers of the crowd.

Nothing much befell us as we nosed carefully down the long pound. Depth seemed reasonable and the country was beautiful, even if the morning was grey and cloudy. We were, obviously, the first boats of the day to come down, and news of our coming had sped before us. At Wotton Wawen the cut widened into a large basin, and here there were some full-length boats tied up, having given up the struggle. Several people appeared and advised us to do the same, one very vocal lady boomed her tale of woe fortissimo. However, I could not see Ray White's pair. If he could make it with loaded boats, then I was sure that I could. Moreover, Colonel Ritchie's LUPIN had also gone on, so I held on towards the narrow entrance to the A34 aqueduct. The vocal lady became more Cassandra-like than ever. At last I called back 'I've got orders to take Joe to Stratford and that's where I'm going'.

An old gentleman on the towpath gave a ringing cheer and Joe called 'That's the stuff, Davey boy!' Boris and John grinned fit to bust their faces.

We did not have long to wait at Odd Lock, but found the going rather harder once across the Bearley Aqueduct. Speed dropped as ALCOR ploughed through the clay, squirting grey water through the cooling water outlet and occasionally blocking up completely, which meant stopping and clearing the mud box. Gradually we crept into the cutting above Wilmcote Locks to join a queue of deep-draught boats trying to get through the bridge, among these were two pairs of hotel boats from Preston Brook on the Bridgewater Canal.

The problem here was that there was a bad scour underneath Wilmcote Bridge, the one which was to have been replaced by an embankment. The draglines employed to clear the channel could not get at the obstruction and the problem was compounded by the nearness of Wilmcote Locks, which were drawing water off this pound and thus reducing depth.

Gangs of willing hands were pulling each boat over the scour, aided by a Land Rover on the bank. Several trusties were in evidence assisting, so, one by one, the motor boats were eased through the bridge. When our turn came I had pumped ALCOR'S bilge so that she was only drawing about two feet ten inches. We got a rope ashore from the backend rail and I drifted slowly into the bridge with a gang keeping her moving and FRIENDSHIP close up behind. At the first sign of trouble I dropped out of gear and everyone pulled furiously. The stern lifted slightly, stopped, then FRIENDSHIP ran up onto the stern fenders and shoved her over the scour. 'Next problem please!' I called as we drew away from the bridge. I did not have long to wait before my prayer was answered.

The usual boating rumours and tall tales began to circulate, this time concerning the state of Lock 44 in the Wilmcote flight. The queue of boats waiting to go down seemed very slow-moving. Indeed it was lunch time before we began the descent. Down this flight the locks are very closely spaced and a quick reconnaissance showed that Lock 44 was indeed a problem. Like the one at Preston Bagot, its sides had 'come in', which meant that boats were jamming in the bottom and being flushed out. This explained the low water in the pound above.

ALCOR stuck for a few minutes, but I had lifted the cross beams and wound in the cross chains, so a quick flush and heave sent her out fairly quickly. FRIENDSHIP also stuck, but Joe had greased the guard irons in anticipation and had his block and tackle ready. However, the motive power this time was the drawbar of a Land Rover and after a minute or two she floated free.

By now we were more than ever determined to see it

through, and at last the outskirts of Stratford were coming in view. Traffic was beginning to speed up at last as the depth improved – indeed, it had improved too much, because all the water that was coming down could not all escape round the bywashes, consequently the towpath was flooded in places, and at one point the water was all across the locksides as well.

We passed the tripping boat LINDA lying by a wharf in Stratford. She was looking resplendent, but carpets and bunting were still being laid for the arrival of the Queen Mother on the morrow. I heard that the Queen Mother was arriving in the Royal Train, which was on the line which crossed the Oxford Canal between Claydon and Fenny Compton and which was now closed to all traffic, yet some official had ordered the disused station platform at Stratford to be resurfaced in tarmac for the occasion. LINDA'S owners, John and Anne Crossley paused briefly from their frantic preparations to wave, then we had to make preparations for yet another lock.

I noticed that this lock had what boatmen inelegantly call 'pissers' in the side. When full, water runs behind the brickwork into cavities, when it empties it squirts forth in gradually diminishing piddles. ALCOR received one of these through the engine hole doors as she went out. A more severe incident was to occur here next day, when it performed over the Queen Mother. A horrified courtier became a cross between Sir Walter Raleigh and the little Dutch boy by gallantly plugging it with his finger.

The final hazard was the low bridge which gave on to Stratford Basin. Here one was in a Catch 22 situation. Too low a water level and the boats would stick on piled-up rubbish underneath, and there was no towpath, nor any way of getting a line through the bridge, short of rockets. Too high and one would get jammed underneath. All chimneys, including the exhaust stack had to come down so the hole was black indeed.

At last nearly choking with fumes, deafened by the barking of the National in a confined space, cabin top spattered with debris brought down by the exhaust and covered in oily smuts, we crept out into the basin. People stopped and cheered us in. Battered, dirty but unbowed the two boats proudly drew clear and came to rest, breasted up, in the basin

above the lock. It was early Friday evening. We would take up
our mooring on the river, we told the Rally officials, in the
morning, in good time for the opening.

People began arriving. Brian and Janet came over from
Leamington, where REDCAP still lay awaiting the new part for
the gear box. Joe kept a vast dog under the cloths for security
purposes, and he was about to take the great hound for its
evening constitutional. The beast was anxious to get ashore
and shot out from under the cloths like a Polaris rocket being
launched, with Joe clinging grimly to a long chain round its
neck and being pulled along. Brian, Janet and several onlookers scattered as the thunderbolt broke loose. Dog and Joe
dwindled rapidly as they headed for the far side of the park by
Bancroft Basin.

Jean and Peter arrived by train from Reading, along with
several other canal enthusiasts from the Kennet. We were
developing into a jolly party indeed, but accommodation
beneath ALCOR'S rudimentary cloths was somewhat limited.
The makeshift bed had suited me very well, but with Jean on
it as well it was very much 'when Father says 'turn', we all
turn'. Somehow or other we disposed ourselves about the
boat, I seem to remember that most were reasonably well
anaesthetised with alcohol.

Next morning we worked through the Barge Lock into the
Avon. I had often seen the lock as a schoolboy, on educational
visits to Stratford, and found it hard to believe that here I was,
really and truly, going through it with a pair of boats. I also
discovered that it was considerably shorter than a Grand
Union lock. We had to wriggle FRIENDSHIP back onto the sill,
with her ram's head held hard over before we could get the
bottom gates open, and then the swinging arc only just cleared
the fore end by a fraction of an inch. Even then our troubles
were not over, for a bad scour had built up over the years just
below the lock's outfall and it had not yet been cleared away.
We stuck momentarily, but soon got ourselves free when a
passing motor launch sent waves to rock us.

So we came triumphantly past the Shakespeare Memorial
Theatre, under the lee of the public gardens by Holy Trinity
Church, winded round and were directed to moorings close to
the heart of the Rally, amidst a great ruck of full-length boats,
including LADY HATHERTON, once the committee boat of the

Staffordshire & Worcestershire Canal Company, an ex-Waterways tripper called PISCES, then owned by a Birmingham businessman, and Keith Christie's CASSIOPEIA.

Colonel Ritchie appeared, beaming and in expansive mood. He had an armful of bunting and Union flags on dowel poles for us to wave when the Queen Mother passed. He was most apologetic that his tug had failed Joe, but it was not his, nor Brian's fault. It was 'just one of those things'.

Possibly the remark about his affluence had struck home, for Joe celebrated the event by buying Rose a brand new wedding ring, which was prominently displayed all day.

As the day wore on, excitement mounted. My aunt appeared and came aboard, then as the time of opening approached, a hush settled aver the river. Tannoys relayed the Queen Mother's opening speech, and the speeches of the other dignitaries, including Robert Aickman. The tape was cut and the bells of Holy Trinity crashed out joyously. Cheers rose as LINDA nosed cut of the lock, avoiding the scour. Joe was most anxious that our boats presented Her Royal Highness a worthy spectacle and had ensured that all brass was polished, all cotton lines scrubbed, all paintwork mopped off and had rolled up the canvasses protecting FRIENDSHIP'S rich paintwork so that her glory shone forth.

LINDA slowly bore down the lines of decorated boats, crews cheering wildly, horns blaring joyously. It was a triumphal moment. It was IWA's triumph, the justification of everything the Association had argued for so long. I was proud to be a member; not for the last time, but certainly for the first time I realised that the Waterways movement was a truly popular one. It was Robert Aickman's triumph too, the spirit that had masterminded this first great public affirmation of principle had every right to share it. It was the triumph of David Hutchings and his devoted band of volunteers and prisoners, but it was also our triumph. We, the boaters, had come from all parts of the system, we had tackled a waterway that offered a full range of navigational hazards and we had beaten it. We had got down to Stratford in time against all the head-shakings and so we cheered lustily and waved our flags as the seal was put on all our efforts.

Suddenly, as LINDA drew past us, the diminutive Queen Mother waving regally at all of us, and favouring Rose with a dazzling smile, Joe became excited. ''Ere Davey, cor strike! Look at that!''

I felt a sudden rush of adrenalin, his sharp old eyes must have spotted something seriously amiss. 'What is it Joe?' 'Look, there' he cried, pointing to the stern of LINDA, where a dapper John Crossley was flanked by a figure in spotless white overalls. ''Tis ole Dennis, look!' and forgetting the Queen Mother, he gave a grinning Dennis Clarke a truly regal wave.

Chapter 12 — INDIAN SUMMER

The Stratford-upon-Avon gathering was more than just a Rally of Boats, it was a celebration and arts festival as well. There were special performances by the Royal Shakespeare Company, orchestral concerts on a floating stage (including the 1812 Overture with the Royal Artillery in attendance) and a fireworks display, which Joe said was the most beautiful thing he'd ever seen.

On the Sunday morning the huge floating stage needed to be repositioned, which was done by breasting ALCOR and CASSIOPEIA either side of the pontoons. Keith Christie and myself were reduced to the rank of subordinates by Charlie, the ex-Willow Wren captain whom I had unsuccessfully sought in the spring, but who had arrived on site full of enthusiasm early on Sunday morning. Charlie was in his element, springing about from fore ends to pontoon and back with an agility belying his 17-stone bulk.

The magnificent procession bore slowly up river to the Memorial Theatre at which point we had to swing the whole massive structure through 180 degrees. The Theatre Company were taking the air on the theatre terrace, raising glasses and doubtless indulging in theatrical gossip and chat, when they suddenly became aware of the floating stage in all its majesty bearing down on them. A remarkably hasty retreat was beaten by the party, much to the ribald amusement of Charlie. It was, I thought, an incident which would have appealed to the slapstick side of the Bard's nature.

Jean, John and Sue and several Reading people left on Sunday in order to return to work, leaving Boris and myself to bring ALCOR home. The problem of what to do with FRIENDSHIP then arose.

ALCOR'S National had a voracious appetite for 'green oil', as boatmen call heavy lubricating oil, so we needed to obtain a five-gallon drum to see us safely home. We just had enough aboard to get to Braunston, but not if we had to pull a butty. Moreover, FRIENDSHIP needed to go further, to Hawkesbury in fact. On top of all this, we were nearly broke after several somewhat expensive days' celebrations. Topping up with the extra oil required to take FRIENDSHIP home would reduce us to absolutely penury.

Talking it over with Boris we decided that we would take a chance on going via Birmingham, provided that we could oil up before leaving Stratford. Boris was confident that we could live off the land, or at least pubs, by providing live music and entertainment.

The matter was finally resolved on Monday afternoon when we locked up into the Basin, preparatory to an early start on Tuesday. Colonel Ritchie stood on the lockside, deep in thought and Park Drive cigarette smoke as we rose.

We tied up above the lock and the Colonel came, rather hesitantly I thought, along the basin side to us. 'David' said he abruptly. 'How's Joe getting home?' 'I'm going to snatch him back to the Stop on our way back' I said. His face cleared. 'Very good of you. I feel I ought to get him back home, but with REDCAP out of action it's a bit difficult'.

I was about to tell him that, whilst buttying Joe was a pleasure, we were virtually broke and desperately needed oil when he said 'Of course, you must have something for your trouble' and produced two new fivers. I said 'Well, that's very kind of you, because I needed to buy some green oil'. 'Nonsense, you're doing me a favour. Anyway I've got a spare drum of oil that you can have on LUPIN.

He insisted that I took both the oil and the money, which was extremely cheering news to Boris who, as catering officer, had been out foraging for supplies in Stratford on a very restricted budget.

Boris had managed to acquire a pig's head for the magnificent sum of 6d. I did not fancy this revolting-looking object, but Joe and Rose's eyes lit up when they saw it. 'Parts you 'as to boil and parts you 'as to bake' said Rose. I felt that it would be as well to let Rose deal with it on a four-way sharing basis, and she leaped at the chance. The pig's head vanished into FRIENDSHIP'S cabin for preparation.

And so began another memorable journey. It only lasted three days, but in that time I learned much that was to stand me in good stead in later years. Although I had worked with a butty for Willow Wren, most of the work had been on the Grand Union amongst wide locks. Furthermore I had had to guess much of the technique of working a butty through a narrow canal. Now I was the pupil of an expert, and one, more-over, who had always worked with animals rather than mechanical power. Joe taught me all sorts of little wrinkles such as holding the butty forward in a lock by means of a hitch round the top paddle post which enabled one to draw the paddle as well as control the towline. Like all boat people Joe and Rose demonstrated the utmost economy in movement, especially when locking. With no apparent effort they would appear at exactly the right place as the boat slid into a lock, so that the bottom gate would be swinging to, the boat secured and one top paddle raised all in one movement, and with no fuss the boat was rising in the lock in half the time taken to bring in a cabin cruiser under power.

Although Rose had only been down the Stratford Canal once, as a girl, and Joe never, they knew, on the return journey exactly where each lock was, and what its idiosyncrasies might be. Without apparently taking any notice, they absorbed the landmarks and characteristics of 'the road' on their first journey. This is a skill that I have attempted to develop over the subsequent years, but have never completely mastered. There are still some flights of locks or lengths of canal where I am still not too sure about, even after several journeys. Not so Joe, who was able to recommend exactly which pounds we should pull him up with the motor and which he should bow haul.

We left the Basin at 6.30 in the morning and were up to the top of Wilmcote by 11.30. Then commenced the long drag up the Wilmcote pound, where our progress was constantly checked by boats following us and drawing off water as they rose in the locks. We were two hours up this section, during which Rose produced platefuls of the pig's head, accompanied by vegetables foraged by Boris in a derelict cottage garden. I must admit that the boiled parts were not much to my taste, though the baked bits were not unpleasant. Still, a nourishing and filling meal for four for 6d was not to be despised.

FRIENDSHIP slid into the lock at Preston Bagot with no protest, so we pressed on. Traffic was now heavy in front of us, so each lock took nearly half an hour to pass the two boats. We tied up at dusk above Lowsonford having cracked the hardest part of the Stratford Canal.

Soon after ten next morning we worked round the junction

onto the Grand Union level. Joe prospected among the rotting Joey boats in the basin, returning triumphantly with a replacement for FRIENDSHIP'S fore stud, then we set forth for Birmingham and the Bottom Road. Little had changed in the two years or so since last I had passed that way. We swept into Knowle in fine style, up the magnificent broad flight, such a contrast from the cramped, intimate Stratford locks, and soon began to enter the purlieus of Birmingham.

Now, alas, there were no Joey boats running, no horses or their dung on the towpath, or bright rope marks in the ironwork of bridges. Nor were there any boats loading or discharging at Olton timber yard, nor Tyseley depot, nor Sampson Road. Diesels roared on the railway in place of the steam locomotives of two years back, sidings which had once echoed with the clangorous sound of shunting wagons were silent. The smells remained the same though – cellulose and acetate here, hot oil and molten metal there, so did the sounds of humming motors, whirring fans, stampings and rattlings, tuneless whistling, gasping of steam traps and mysterious sighings and gurglings in pipes.

Camp Hill and Saltley were as evilly smelly as ever, the water still foul and oily, the lock-sides coated with black greasy slime. I chuckled to myself at the thought of what the Thames Conservancy would say to such a state of affairs. It would have taken many a pot of caustic soda to have burned that lot off!

There was then no Spaghetti Junction at Gravelly Hill, the main feature of which was T & S Element's wharf, right on the turn where four canals meet which lead to the Thames, Severn, Trent and Mersey. Decaying Joey boats indicated that the Birmingham Canals were still losing their once heavy traffic, as industry turned away from coal, the canal's staple commodity. Wharf after wharf showed this breakdown of the old system. Corrugated iron sheets bulged with the weight of coal behind them, shot in from tipper lorries, sorrel and elder drooped over corroding tying rings. Other wharves were stacked high with broken and twisted motor vehicles, some of which had lurched into the water and now thrust pathetic wings or suspension units above the surface. It was clear that I was not the only one oppressed by the desolate scene, for Joe came clumping along the top planks with the suggestion that I pull him on a long line, so as to speed up. Personally I don't believe towing an empty boat in this manner gains anything. When the towed boat is on cross straps, its fore end tends to prevent the motor's stern from digging in too far and also damps down the wash. In shallow water this is a great advantage. On the other hand, towing on a long line means that the butty has to be steered independently of the motor while the motor pulls well down. This is fine on a deep canal, but no advantage on a shallow one. Also there is the continual problem of the butty overrunning the motor when shallow bridge holes appear. However, I thought I had better humour the old boy so I found a long cotton line, dropped it over his fore stud then went ahead paying it out round the motor's dollies.

I should have known it. Joe had worked in and out of Birmingham for years and, of course, was well aware of where the deep bits were. Water began to bubble under FRIENDSHIP'S fore end, away at her stern I could see Joe's white moustache framing a broad grin as he swung his tiller over to bring the butty round the turns.

Soon we were at Minworth where we began to leave the town behind. Evening was drawing on as we came down to the bottom of the three locks to see the grey triangle of a British Waterways deck board rising in the lock. It was, moreover, a loaded boat.

I slacked right down, noticing that the motor boat evidently had a butty, for it came out of the lock then stopped, while figures cranked away at the bottom paddle.

As we glided nearer, I saw it was the motorboat CARNABY, one of the few working boats retained by British Waterways for the carriage of concrete piles. The Board had inherited several concrete pile factories, at Marsworth, Hillmorton and elsewhere. These had pairs of boats on the strength which took loads to many remote parts of the system. It was cheering to see them, for if they could get along, then so surely could we. The captain, Billy and his mate Dolly, were equally surprised to see us. Blue smoke jetted from CARNABY'S exhaust cutter as the butty was slowly drawn out of the lock. We decided to tie up at a pub just beyond the lock, whilst Billy and Dolly tied up above. Despite its nearness to town, The Boat was a quiet little pub, more like a country one. We boaters almost outnumbered the locals to start with, then

Boris got the music going, and we had a very successful evening.

I wondered why Joe had chosen to stop here, rather than an hour or so further on at Curdworth, where there was another cheerful pub. Next morning I learned. Leaving Boris steering the motor, I was sitting at the stern of FRIENDSHIP as we came into Curdworth cutting. As we came up to the bridge before Curdworth Tunnel, Joe nodded towards the stables at the back of the pub. 'That's where I shot my poor old mule' he said. I looked round and noticed that Rose was nowhere to be seen. Joe's eyes were bright as he told me the sad tale.

They had bought Dolly, the mule, off the US Army at the end of the First World War. For forty years they worked with her. The towpath and maintenance of the canals got steadily worse after the Second World War. Rose wrote complaining letters but these were ignored by the authorities, eventually, as I have told, Dolly fell in at Griffins Bridge on the way back from Banbury. They got her out, and she pulled them to Napton, where she was so ill that Joe had to send her to Coventry in a horsebox.

When she recovered, they went to Pooley Hall Colliery on the Coventry Canal and loaded for the New World Gas Cooker factory in Birmingham. This was only a short run, but the canal was in such bad condition that they were 'blocking' into every lock and through every bridge (i.e. using a block and tackle with Dolly's harness). The effort was appalling. They got to Birmingham, unloaded and set off back. Down Minworth it was obvious that Dolly was very ill, in fact pneumonia had developed. So Joe put her in the stable at Curdworth and, in the small hours, mercifully despatched her with a humane killer. After forty years' work, her carcass was hauled off to the knacker's yard. To Joe and Rose it was like losing a limb. They worked as butty to a motor for a few trips, but, as Joe said 'it weren't the same without Dolly'. They retired soon after. They never again tied at Curdworth. We set about the long, slow descent of the Curdworth flight. Apart from the ranked coolers of Hams Hall power station across the fields, there was nothing to remind one of nearby Birmingham. Open fields and hedgerows ran to the horizon, where, distantly, crouched outliers of Cannock Chase.

The last part of the Birmingham & Fazeley Canal was dreary

indeed. It ran straight for several miles through a flattish landscape. This in itself was bearable, but the canal was abom-
inably shallow. No wonder it killed poor Dolly. We wallowed
slowly forward, sending up black gobbets from the bottom.
'Ar, you knows what that is' said Joe, seeing me gazing at our
wake. 'Peas, beans an' DS. Them ole open boats used to run
up here from Pooley into Brummagen. When they couldn't
get along, they used to shovel the coal into the cut. You stick
your shaft in and see. That's like gravel down there'.

Long years after this time, British Waterways gave the
Birmingham & Fazeley a thorough dredging. I went up the
pound with a pair of boats in fine style and noticed that the
dredgings had been piled on the offside bank. Had Joe lived,
he would have been gratified to see that the mud was well
sprinkled with peas, beans and DS nuts.

By the curious swing bridge approaching Fazeley, a large
sign on the adjacent main road announced a 'Pleasure Park'.
This greatly amused Boris, who proceeded to compose an
updated version of Coleridge's *Kubla Khan*

>'In Staffordshire did Modern Man
>A stately Pleasure Park decree.
>By where the Brum & Fazeley ran
>Through bridgeholes, meaningless to Man
>Out on a funless spree'.

Midday saw us round Fazeley Turn onto the Coventry
Canal. We climbed up Glascote Two and headed off into the
coalfields. Joe pointed out all the important land marks: SE
Barlow's old depot, Amington Colliery basin, Alvescote
Colliery (pronounced 'Awcutt') and a nearby pub called The
Pretty Pigs. Pooley Hall Colliery was still in business, though
it had less than twelve months to go had I known it. When it
closed it took with it the last regular trade on the Southern
Oxford Canal as well as John Dickinson's mill traffic to
Croxley on the Grand Union. There was one surprise in store
for us just beyond Polesworth. Two years before there had
been an enormous opencast pit in the fields between the canal
and the railway. It was possible to see at one point where the
pit had cut through some ancient colliery shafts and galleries.
Then there had been a continuous roar of diesels as coal and
waste was extracted, with a corresponding spoil mountain on
the other side of the canal. Now they were filling it all in and

one no longer crept precariously along the lip of a huge chasm. Three years later when John Grace and myself came the other way, I was unable to recognise the landscape, for reclamation was complete.

We locked out of Atherstone Top Lock just as the town clock was striking six. Eleven miles to go and no more locks for FRIENDSHIP, so we decided to press on so that the old couple could have a drink at The Greyhound that night.

Joe began to get agitated as time passed. At Hartshill he came down onto the motor's counter. 'You'd best give 'er to me' he said 'else we shan't get to Suttons tonight'. Boris looked at me with raised eyebrows but was too polite to say anything. Of course the old chap knew the road well enough, but he could never get on with motors. After several stemmings of the bank, Joe relinquished the tiller with a disgusted snort. It was left to me to drag our way through the silted turns to Nuneaton.

Dusk was not far away at Bedworth. Joe addressed the Gilbert brothers at Charity Dock at long range as we approached, with comments from Rose interspersed. Virtually every bridge hole saw some friend or acquaintance of the Skinners, so our last two miles, through the twilight were something of a triumphal procession. The pumphouse chimney at Hawkesbury rose against the afterglow. I slacked off in the stop lock, loosed off the cross straps and pulled in against the towpath just short of the junction bridge. FRIENDSHIP glided silently past, down the Coventry Canal to her home mooring just beyond. Joe deftly caught the stern, Rose stepped ashore to hold it, while her mate walked forward to secure the other end. They had come home at last.

The 'Stop' was crowded with boats, for it was the time of colliery holidays. I half hoped to get a load of coal for the south, for there were still several coal contracts in existence, notably for Dickinsons at Croxley Mills, Watford, but when I spoke to Miss Edwards, the agent, next morning she was not hopeful. We should have to wait at least seven days for our turn because of the holidays, so saying our farewells to the Skinners, we set off for Braunston, edging ALCOR through the throng of waiting boats, tied two abreast above the Stop Lock. I gazed contentedly at the waiting boats, such a normal, everyday scene at Sutton's Stop, as it had been for 170 years or even generations. Mercifully the future is hidden from us; had I but known it, narrow boating had but six short years to live.

The run home was swift and uneventful. Boris excelled himself at The Admiral Nelson, The Struggler and The Boat at Thrupp, and our cash balance in consequence was fairly healthy on arrival at Reading. For the rest of the summer we were to settle down to rather more mundane tripping on the Thames and Kennet, though two more distant workings were planned for late August and early September.

Just below Caversham Bridge there is a free wharf. These useful amenities have become steadily rarer on the Thames in recent years, indeed some towns go so far as to try and prohibit mooring in any place other than the official place, where a fee is payable. I can understand local councils wishing to prevent abuse of mooring space, but the attitude of some authorities who merely provide a length of unprotected bank, with no bollards or rings and access only via a muddy towpath, seems poor enough. When they have the nerve to ask a mooring fee, it seems well-nigh incredible. At least these charges could not be levelled at Reading Corporation. On the wharf which we used as a base for our Thames operations they even provided a magnificent cast iron public convenience. Since ALCOR was not a regular licensed tripper, we limited passengers to 12. Salter Bros. Limited, who were our next-door neighbours, regarded this activity with tolerant amusement. Their Reading manager was a very distant cousin of mine, so this helped to prevent rivalries. In fact, we were no threat to their operations, rather we complemented one another. Salters often sent enquirers to High Bridge Wharf for ENTERPRISE, and Jim did likewise. Short, hourly trips were in demand and this we did for the next four weeks at the height of the holiday season.

The run we developed was up to Roebuck Ferry and back. It took just an hour and on a good day we got five trips in. With catering receipts we could make sufficient to keep the business turning over nicely. Most weeks we cleared over £30, which was good money for those days, while in 90 minutes or less we could have ALCOR at High Bridge acting as relief boat for ENTERPRISE if things got too busy there.

The only trouble was boredom. Although the Thames is a

broad and lovely river, even the broadest and loveliest pall after a while. I was never bored on the Kennet or on the canals for, no matter how often one did a trip, there was always something different. Five trips a day, past the Warren, up Norcot Scours, through the islands by Kentwood Deeps, and wind flat-out in mid-river; tiller hard over, foot braced against cabin side as the water boiled up under the counter; then back to Caversham Bridge was somewhat tame after the excitements of longer trips. On Saturdays and Sundays, when MAJESTIC was on the up-river service, we varied things with a little fun.

The first Saturday that it happened, we were slipping up towards the Roebuck when I heard a distant 'Hoo-oo-oot'. Looking at my watch, I saw that it was close on 5.30. It could only be MAJESTIC blowing as she threaded the islands upstream of Dodge City. I had Jean as crew, so as I slacked down to await the steamer, I showed her how to sit on the gunwale by the engine room doors and push the governor rack with her foot. I winded sedately and drifted downstream on tick over. Glancing over my shoulder I saw MAJESTIC'S graceful bow slide into view round the bend by the railway bank. Soon she had drawn abreast, a fine bone in her teeth, steam breathing gently from her funnel, and Jack Spriggs looking down disdainfully from his wheel box. Taffy's head and shoulders, beretted and spectacled, leaned out of the engine room casing as MAJESTIC'S compound ticked away contentedly below him. 'Shift that bloody ole coal barge out of the way, boyo' called Taffy. 'I don't want to show up your old tea-kettle' I replied. 'Right you, last one in The Moderation gets pints' came the challenge as Taffy's upperworks disappeared from view. The sound of clanging fire doors and shovelling of coal came from below. MAJESTIC began to draw ahead. Jack Spriggs grinned down at me. Taffy re-appeared. 'Made me shovel like buggery you 'ave'.

The bone in MAJESTIC'S teeth rose and her stern settled. Several passengers waved dismissively at us as the steamer drew a length ahead. I wound up the National causing ALCOR to draw level again, then Jack went down the navigation channel through the Kentwood islands and I followed the towpath. We came out the other side neck and neck, both sets of passengers cheering and waving. Past the Scours MAJESTIC drew

ahead again, until by the start of Caversham Warren she was
again a length in front. But I knew that Taffy would not arrive
at Caversham Wharf with a full head of steam or a blazing
fire. He would only have put sufficient coal on to get ahead. I
played my trump card by sending Jean along the gunwale to
do her bit with the governor.

Black smoke rose from ALCOR'S stack, the stern dug right
down until the fenders were awash and we steadily overhauled the steamer, shooting under Caversham Bridge a few
yards ahead. There was sufficient time to tie up, disembark
the passengers and snug the engine down before reaching the
bar of The Moderation several steps ahead of our rivals.

Perhaps fortunately, the upstream service did not run every
day, but we had one or two more contests before the season
ended; the results were always the same. The steamer was
faster on a full head of steam, but ALCOR'S National ran more
constantly when steam pressure, perforce, dropped.

ALCOR had some more work to do in mid-August, being a
towing job on the Grand Union, followed by a camping trip to
Stratford and back, after which I was due to enter college. It
happened that Bill Fisher was taking some holiday at the time,
so he agreed to take ALCOR off to the Grand Union, while I did
a final stint for the Conservators, this time at Cleeve Lock, the
last in the Reading district. Meanwhile Boris moved on, the
summer vacation was well advanced and he hoped to return to
university next term, so we closed down the Caversham operation. Bill promised to be back on the last Friday in August,
so that we could make ready for leaving next day.

To get to Cleeve meant staying aboard the bus for one stop
beyond Streatley. The bus stop was amid cornfields, by some
outlying barns, whence I picked my way down a track to the
towpath. The scents of high summer lay heavy in the morning
air. The barley was golden, within days it would be cut. Across
the river, the Chilterns stretched into the blue distance, golden
with wheat and barley on the gentle chalk scarp slope, behind
me the Berkshire Downs ran, similarly golden, towards the
West. Here was true wealth I thought, acres of foodstuffs
glowing and swelling in the early sunshine. A lark rose from
the corn, trilling its notes in welcome, while distantly a kestrel
hovered above some luckless small prey. Everywhere rose the
dry, dusty smell of ripening cereal, the orchards towards

Streatley were groaning with fruit, asters and azaleas bloomed in the lock garden. The summer was at its mature peak of fecundity.

Cleeve had, like Whitchurch, but a small rise. Cyril French, the lock keeper, was waiting to go away when I arrived. I spent about 15 minutes with him learning the lock and then he was off, for a few days holiday. I settled down to the familiar task of lockwork, interrupted mid-morning by the telephone. 'Harry here' said the receiver. 'Hullo Harry, what's the problem?' I said. 'Ha! Ha! I might a' known you'd drop in fer Frenchy's relief' he chortled. 'Just fort I let you know, Harvey's on 'is way up'. 'Right ho Harry. No tackle drawn today'. 'I should bloody-well fink not. If this wevver goes on, we'll be havin' to use the short lock to save water'.

He rang off, leaving me to deal with Cleeve's speciality, the fresh water hose. Unlike the canals, which were well-supplied with drinking water taps, the Thames suffered a great lack of such facilities. Cleeve was one of the few places where the Conservancy supplied a tap and hose. Holidaymakers found this facility useful, for boatyards charged heavily for watering-up. I discovered that there was a 'cover charge' which was the lock keeper's perks. No wonder Harry waxed sarcastic about my getting Cleeve Lock!

The lock dinghy was fitted with an outboard motor, which was a great temptation. When lunchtime came, I duly started this up and headed upstream to The Leathern Bottel at North Stoke for a lunchtime pint. The Bottel was a gem amongst Thames-side pubs. In some ways it could well have remained unchanged since Jerome K. Jerome's day. In the cool, stone-flagged bar with its mounted fish on the walls, there was a neat little notice to the effect that on a certain day in March 1947, Old Father Thames reached that height. It gave a list of names saying that those devoted drinkers stood up to their middles in water in the bar and drank the Old Father's health.

In the 15 months which had passed since I first entered the Conservators' service, I had now taken charge of all the locks from Cleeve to Shiplake, I had acquired an intimate knowledge of their weirs, cuts and other idiosyncrasies. They were all, even urban Blakes and suburban Caversham, pleasant places. It seemed somehow appropriate that my association with the Conservators should end at this idyllic spot, nestling under the Oxfordshire hills, looking up towards the great sweep of what the Anglo-Saxons called 'Aescendun'. Somewhere along those hills Alfred of Wessex had struck his first successful blow at the pagan invaders and had begun to roll back what had seemed to be an inexorable tide. Perhaps, in my small way, I could do my bit to roll back a similar tide which threatened to overpower those beloved waterways.

From this idyllic scene, I was abruptly pitchforked back into the realities of narrow-boating. Bill rang up to report engine trouble at Brentford on his way back, on Thursday. As luck would have it. our old friend Charlie was there, holidaying on a boat, and helped him fix it, but the delay cost him the tide up to Teddington. He promised to push ahead next day, but it could mean embarking our passengers further downstream than Reading.

My father and Peter came to the rescue. We loaded all the camping gear onto father's Morris, piling up the roof rack, on Saturday morning and set off towards Windsor hoping to meet ALCOR somewhere. Crossing Windsor Great Park, the roof rack lifted off, fortunately causing little damage.

Meanwhile disaster had struck Bill. He made a very early start on Friday hoping to get at least up to Marlow or Henley, but as he slogged up through Staines the engine began to fire on one cylinder, white smoke poured out of the stack and ALCOR slowed to a crawl. A minute flaw in one of the valve rockers had chosen that moment to declare itself, after 25 years or so. The rocker had sheared in two.

By the most extraordinary good luck, he found a workshop in the town, which was able to weld it, but he was unable to move until Saturday midday, by when the river was at its busiest. Jean managed to round up our hirers and they agreed to come out to join the boat at Boulters Lock rather than Caversham or High Bridge. Bill arrived in the afternoon, we came panting up in the Morris, unloaded and rigged the cloths, the hirers, a party of schoolboys and their master joined us in the evening, father took Bill back to Reading and we all said 'Phew!'

I made a very early start next day, which meant working Cookham Lock by hand (it was electrified in similar fashion to Mapledurham), but at least I had plenty of help in the shape of boys. The first lock keeper I saw was at Marlow and I arrived below Caversham Lock at 1.30 on Sunday, some 24 hours late. Jean met me there with stores, for she was going to come as crew this time, then it was time to be off. Mr. Mearing, the schoolmaster, had arranged to take his boys over Cowley Works at Oxford on Monday morning, so we had to get well upstream that night.

It was another golden summer day. Our progress was triumphal through the Reading District, with Len, Fred and Harry ushering us swiftly through their locks, but even so it was six by the time we cleared Cleeve. Sunset was just before eight, giving us about enough tine to clear Benson, but I knew I should have to tie below Days; for one thing, I had no navigation lights. The Sinodun Hills stood black against the afterglow as I picked my way up past the mouth of the Thame. We slipped under the footbridge below Days Lock in the dusk. Lights glowed dully behind the curtains in the lock house, bats wheeled, crying thinly, overhead. Jean shuddered in the chill of the evening and went below into the lamplit cabin while I put the engine to bed.

Sunrise next morning was about five. I was up and about, Jean groaned. 'No need for you to get up" I said brightly "I can manage on my own'.

I walked up to the lock, opened one gate, then started the engine and drove in. I made fast with a line off the back-end, closed the gate and drew the top paddles. Another perfect morning, dew lying on the meadows, a slight mist clinging to the river and trees thrusting through the vapour. Away across the fields, early sun was striking the ochreous tiles of Dorchester Abbey.

I eased ALCOR out of the lock, caught her on a pile temporarily while I ran back to empty the chamber. When I got back Jean was sitting on the side bed brushing her hair. 'You don't need to get up yet' I said. She snorted 'You try sleeping-in next to that engine'.

As we slipped up the long curving reach to Clifton Hamden, the boys began to appear one by one. One of the lads, Michael, had shown interest in the boat the day before, so I had let him try steering. He had brought a canoe with him, in the (somewhat sanguine, I felt) hope that he would be able to paddle about in the evenings. He was one of the first up, although it was not yet six, and a good job too, as it hap-

pened. The mist was patchy on the river, but approaching
Clifton Bridge it came down thick. I shot up through the navigation arch, to be enveloped in a thick, white blanket immediately beyond. The riverbed is shoal here, I went to knock the
speed off, but too late. In the fog we had got too near the
Oxfordshire bank, and came to a grinding halt, ALCOR tilting
over somewhat to port.

Usually when a boat gets 'farmed up' it is a simple matter
to get free. One can generally get off by reversing, or by poling the fore end sideways away from the point of grounding
(which with an empty motor is generally just below the
engine room). On this occasion we had come to rest with the
stern sitting on a ledge of rock and the fore end in water too
deep to bottom with the shaft. It was at this point that
Michael's canoe came in handy. To the evident delight of its
owner, we launched the lifeboat. Taking a long cotton line, the
lad paddled off towards the Berkshire bank. I could see the
tops of willows above the mist bank and so he tied the free
end to these. There was just enough line to pull on from the
foredeck. Slowly ALCOR swung broadside across the stream as
I hauled the line in, but did not immediately come free. I had
to let the current swing her more than 90° before she gave a
wallow and rode clear. Then I had to pull the fore end nearly
into the willows so that the current would swing the stern
downstream.

In spite of this hold up, we cleared Clifton, Culham and
Abingdon Locks before the lock staff came on duty at nine,
and tied above Osney Lock soon after 10.30. Mr Mearing and
his boys were only a hour late at Cowley Works, which was
quite an achievement considering that we had started a full
day behind schedule.

That afternoon we went up to Thrupp where Jean and I
went off to tea with relatives of mine who lived in nearby
Kidlington. We were promised eggs by my uncle, who had a
chicken farm near Enslow Wharf. This seemed to Mr Mearing
an excellent and economical way of stocking up for his raven-
ing horde, so next morning I slipped up through Shipton Weir
and Bakers Locks to Enslow. It was a short walk up the road
to the battery farm where my uncle was waiting for us. He
was very deaf and normal communications were carried out
by hearing aid. We went into what I can only describe as a

Belsen for chickens. The noise and small was horrific but, as we walked along the lines of wire cages picking up the eggs, my uncle stood watching with a beatific smile on his face. He had unplugged the hearing aid.

The day after, at Marston Doles, we had yet another experience with eggs. At the top lock we were accosted by a jovial red-faced Company's man. 'Like to earn yerselves a few eggs?' he asked. It turned out that he was doing some small maintenance work down the locks and had a wheelbarrow full of materials to take down to the lock at the end of the 'mile pound'. It was a long way to shove a barrow loaded with sand and cement, so we wheeled it aboard, along with several bags of cement and some bricks when the gunwales were level with the lockside. I dropped this load off at the right lock, the Company's man reappeared a few locks down with a box of brown-shelled eggs, which he beamingly presented to Jean. Every egg was a 'double yolker'.

The weather continued warm and sunny all the way to Stratford, once more we were locked in at the Middle Lock of Hatton, once more we heaved and struggled down the Stratford Canal, although this time there were fewer boats to hold us up. A 'trusty' driving a dragline near Wotton Wawen helped us over a shallow bit with his jib chained to ALCOR'S fore end. Somewhere north of Wilmcote we passed LINDA stuck on the bottom waiting for the National Trust to raise the pound. John looked gloomy. Anne grinned and rolled her eyes heavenward. Somehow the promise of the Stratford was fading for them. At Wilmcote I formed the boys in a long line on the towpath with a line off the back end rail, and we slipped through the bridge with little trouble.

Mr Mearing and his boys did the sights in Stratford. Jean and I were whisked off to my aunt's home for baths and supper, and then it was time to set off home. Deep down I knew that this was to be my last journey as a self-employed captain, and I suppose it is this knowledge which caused so much of that journey to be deeply imprinted upon my memory.

By now it was September. The 'season of mists and mellow fruitfulness' was upon us, and the early morning climb out of Stratford was full of the scents of late summer. I had agreed to pull a butty up to Wootton Wawen for an IWA member (it was an ex-FMC boat EMSCOTE) and he had arranged 'trusty' assistance. One of these was the cheery cove who had pulled us with the dragline on the way down. He roared with laughter on seeing me: 'You must be bloody mad coming down this ditch again' he chortled. Nevertheless, Joe Skinner's tuition and plenty of assistance saw us up Wilmcote Locks in style. Then the trouble began. The long pound, far from making up, had actually lost water since we had come down. Every few yards we were sticking, with Mearing and the boys rocking ALCOR from side to side like an ice breaker to keep us moving. Jean's condition now began to tell, so she was put ashore for ante-natal exercises in the form of a walk. She ended up walking nearly to Lapworth!

We came upon LINDA still fast. Getting past her was a problem, so when we stuck abreast of her I turned the engine off, for it was next to useless, and choking up its water intake with mud.

We were invited aboard for tea. The Crossleys explained that they had been on their way to Wootton Wawen to pick up a party when they stuck. I offered to snatch them if I could get past, but they declined, saying that it would make little difference to them and very much to me. Better to wait until water came down, in any case if I was going up hill, I could at least send one lockful behind me. John poured us a very large gin apiece. Jean, never a lover of spirits, looked dubious. Rolling the boat caused nausea, such a drink might have all sorts of results. Mearing and myself surreptitiously relieved her of so fearful a burden.

Meanwhile the boys, who had been desultorily pulling from the bank and shafting, found that ALCOR was just about floating. They wriggled her about and I noticed that she was moving slowly forward. We clambered out of LINDA's fore end as the stern end drew level, and I helped shove her clear.

It was a glorious, warm September afternoon when we dropped the butty at Wootton. The owner insisted on treating us in the pub; the two 'trusties' presented us with two gallons of lubricating oil, from where I dare not ask, and Jean gave them ten cigarettes each. One would have thought they had been presented with the Crown Jewels, they were so pleased.

Next day, we flogged on up to Lapworth, getting clear finally at about 4.30. Now I began to worry. If we missed Hatton that night, we should throw our schedule out of gear. I really needed to be at Warwick that night. Accordingly I set forth onto the 'eight mile' pound of the Grand Union, with some speed, for the lock went on at the Middle Lock at 6.30 and I had no wish to be caught there again. Entering Shrewley Tunnel, I was not gratified to see a wide-beamed boat dawdling along in front of me. If it had been a narrow-beamed one I would not have minded, for we could have shared a lock, but as it was he would merely hold me up.

I drew up close behind him after the tunnel, but the steerer ignored me. He kept on right down the middle at about two miles per hour. I have often noticed that such navigators drive cars in a similar way, this one would doubtless have occupied the fast lane of a motorway with a milk float if he could have done so. I looked at my watch. Ten minutes to go before the lock went on at the Top, so I politely tooted the horn, just in case he hadn't heard me, for at no time had he looked round. I tried again, and was ignored, so I wound on the National a turn. ALCOR'S fore end began to loom over the cruiser's stern then I saw him turn his throttle up. That was where he made his mistake. I wound fully on and sent Jean to do her steamer-racing routine. Down past Hatton Station we swept, fenders awash, black smoke rising. The other steerer began to shout angrily as we overhauled him. The boys chattered like magpies and made the sort of vulgar signs that schoolboys do. Our friend's face was puce with rage. He swore at the boys, then at Jean as she passed, though the racket from the engine drowned his words. Jean smiled sweetly at him. Then it was my turn. 'You bloody lunatic! You filthy bargee! You rotten gippos! I'll have you for this! I knows the Section Inspector! I'll have you off the cut! I'll ....' and so on as he faded astern. I stared stolidly ahead, nearly bursting with suppressed laughter, but out of the corner of my eye I saw my wash take him unawares and fling him hard against the concrete coping. He stopped dead as the water ran away leaving him high and dry. As we turned into the cutting leading to Top Lock, I saw him poling away in the distance. We shot into Top Lock as the lock keeper came up the towpath jingling his padlock. I felt rather sorry for our victim, so I said 'There's a wide boat coming through the bridge. Let him down could you?' 'What name?' asked the lock keeper. I told him. Any sympathy for him vanished when I learned that he normally tied above Top

Lock and was only out for the afternoon.

So we made The Cape of Good Hope that night. Billy and Dolly were tied there with the pile boats, so we had company once again. Later that evening, we all walked down to the pub. Dolly was very obviously pregnant, Jean was less so. We stood by the stern ends chatting. 'What uns that?' asked Dolly, nodding at Jean's middle. 'My first' she replied. Dolly smote her hands on her ample midriff. It boomed like a bass drum. 'This uns Number Ten' she said contentedly. Billy grinned 'And don't it feel good, when you feels the babby move' he said. Jean nodded. Her baby was an active kicker. 'It sometimes kicks me' I said. 'When we're on the cross bed, I often get a kick in the backside'. 'If 'e kicks you in the arse' said Billy 'You ain't the man I thought you was'.

Mr Mearing and the boys held a Council of War next morning. It was now Wednesday, he wanted them home for Saturday afternoon and there was no way, short of working all night that they could be in Reading for then. However, he was quite content to be unloaded at Banbury on Saturday instead, and this was quite within the bounds of possibilities. So we took life easily next day, they spent a morning in Warwick, then we went up to Itchington, with a view to spending the last night at Fenny Compton.

It was after dark when we tied up at Fenny Compton Wharf next night. As we came under the main road bridge I saw that another narrow boat lay on the wharf. Next moment my headlight picked up Jim looking out of ENTERPRISE'S hatches. He had decided that Kennet tripping was virtually at an end and had come looking for us with his girl friend. He had winded at Fenny Compton that evening, for he had to be back in Reading on the following Tuesday.

I draw a veil over the proceedings in The George & Dragon that night. The boys went to bed early, thoroughly tired, and Jim, his girl friend, Mearing, Jean and myself celebrated the end of a hard, though satisfying, trip. There was a long way to go home, we still had to spend Saturday night at The Struggler but even so, it was a bleary-eyed crew that assembled after breakfast next morning.

There is really little more to tell. The weather was hotter, or so it seemed, than at any time that summer. I stripped down ALCOR'S cloths, so once more she was a proper working boat and thus only paid tug tolls on the Thames. Mearing and the boys bade us farewell at Banbury. I never saw him again, but Michael, with the canoe, became a confirmed canal enthusiast. We have met several times over the years.

Down the Cherwell valley, dozing in the heaviness of late summer, we slipped. It was not completely idyllic. ENTERPRISE'S stern gland needed repacking and the replacement packing was in Reading. Several times I had to lend Jim ALCOR'S heavy iron hand pump in order to pump the stern out because she was getting too deep and dragging the bottom; once we became enveloped in acrid smoke when a stubble field was fired all round us near Somerton, but my over-riding memory is of days of warm sun, of glowing evenings when the sun set in a fiery ball turning our chimneys and porthole brasses into a lustrous golden metal, when the still shapes of full-leaved elms towered over the waterside.

On a golden Monday evening we slipped down the glassy, smooth waters of Pangbourne Reach. All our things were packed, we should be going home from here and ALCOR would be handed over to Sam. Tomorrow I was starting a new career. Nearly three years of life on the water lay behind me, unknown and different life-styles lay before us. Probably before Christmas we would be parents. I wondered what world the child would grow to. Would there still be narrow boats or canals when he or she was my age? God willing I would try to keep it so, but all was in an unknown future.

I wound down the throttle as Fred came strolling out on the lock-side to greet us.

EPILOGUE

Three days later I was back at Whitchurch. The newly-opened Training College ran an 'orientation course' for students, on the first day of it we visited Brakspear's Brewery at Henley, on the second we visited the Thames. This was to help me get to know the area. It nearly persuaded Sam and Fred to become student teachers.

Jean gave birth in the autumn to a girl, Sarah. Sam went on from relief lock keeper, via boatman and inspector, to a senior post in the National Rivers Authority. Fred and Dick eventually retired, while Len moved down to Caversham before he retired, then moved away from the river. Harry sadly died and did not enjoy his well-earned retirement, as did Peter Harvey. Chris Groves went to the Norfolk Broads before returning to run a tripper 'up West'. The Thames Conservancy was swallowed up in the Thames Water Authority, and the navigation became a mere division. At the time of writing a new Rivers Authority was about to take over. It has now become part of the Environment Agency.

Jim eventually sold ENTERPRISE after our contract ended. She reverted to the name KIMBERLEY but continued to carry passengers as a camping boat, based at Braunston until 1995. Her last regular skipper was Alec Purcell.

One night in the late summer of 1984, following the reopening of Blisworth Tunnel after five years, I heard a familiar engine in Top Lock, Stoke Bruerne. It was KIMBERLEY with a professional steerer set on for one special trip. The steerer, a tall, handsome man in his thirties was none other than George's son Colin.

Sam and Jenny never lived aboard ALCOR, instead they sold her on half-converted. I never saw her again until the spring of 1983, when I came across her, beautifully kept and converted, at a boat rally at Ellesmere Port. Currently she belongs to the boat painter, Tony Lewery.

Jim had a picaresque career round the system, eventually he went abroad and boated the Continental waterways. Peter stayed in Reading looking after his mum. As for Jean and me, I duly qualified and, through Colonel Ritchie's good offices, we found the house we wanted at Stoke Bruerne. Eventually I managed to combine teaching and commercial boating, but that is another story.

INDEX